ARGUS DEVELOPER IN PRACTICE

REAL ESTATE DEVELOPMENT MODELING IN THE REAL WORLD

Dr. Tim M. Havard

Apress·

Argus Developer in Practice: Real Estate Development Modeling in the Real World

ISBN-13 (pbk): 978-1-4302-6262-6

ISBN-13 (electronic): 978-1-4302-6263-3

Trademarked names, logos, and images may appear in this book. Rather than use a trademark symbol with every occurrence of a trademarked name, logo, or image we use the names, logos, and images only in an editorial fashion and to the benefit of the trademark owner, with no intention of infringement of the trademark.

The use in this publication of trade names, trademarks, service marks, and similar terms, even if they are not identified as such, is not to be taken as an expression of opinion as to whether or not they are subject to proprietary rights.

While the advice and information in this book are believed to be true and accurate at the date of publication, neither the authors nor the editors nor the publisher can accept any legal responsibility for any errors or omissions that may be made. The publisher makes no warranty, express or implied, with respect to the material contained herein.

President and Publisher: Paul Manning
Acquisitions Editor: Jeff Olson
Editorial Board: Steve Anglin, Mark Beckner, Ewan Buckingham, Gary Cornell,
    Louise Corrigan, James DeWolf, Jonathan Gennick, Jonathan Hassell,
    Robert Hutchinson, Michelle Lowman, James Markham, Matthew Moodie,
    Jeff Olson, Jeffrey Pepper, Douglas Pundick, Ben Renow-Clarke, Dominic Shakeshaft,
    Gwenan Spearing, Matt Wade, Steve Weiss
Coordinating Editor: Rita Fernando
Copy Editor: Ann Dickson
Compositor: SPi Global
Indexer: SPi Global
Cover Designer: Anna Ishchenko

Distributed to the book trade worldwide by Springer Science+Business Media New York, 233 Spring Street, 6th Floor, New York, NY 10013. Phone 1-800-SPRINGER, fax (201) 348-4505, e-mail orders-ny@springer-sbm.com, or visit www.springeronline.com. Apress Media, LLC is a California LLC and the sole member (owner) is Springer Science + Business Media Finance Inc (SSBM Finance Inc). SSBM Finance Inc is a Delaware corporation.

For information on translations, please e-mail rights@apress.com, or visit www.apress.com.

Apress and friends of ED books may be purchased in bulk for academic, corporate, or promotional use. eBook versions and licenses are also available for most titles. For more information, reference our Special Bulk Sales–eBook Licensing web page at www.apress.com/bulk-sales.

Any source code or other supplementary materials referenced by the author in this text is available to readers at www.apress.com. For detailed information about how to locate your book's source code, go to www.apress.com/source-code/.

Apress Business: The Unbiased Source of Business Information

Apress business books provide essential information and practical advice, each written for practitioners by recognized experts. Busy managers and professionals in all areas of the business world—and at all levels of technical sophistication—look to our books for the actionable ideas and tools they need to solve problems, update and enhance their professional skills, make their work lives easier, and capitalize on opportunity.

Whatever the topic on the business spectrum—entrepreneurship, finance, sales, marketing, management, regulation, information technology, among others—Apress has been praised for providing the objective information and unbiased advice you need to excel in your daily work life. Our authors have no axes to grind; they understand they have one job only—to deliver up-to-date, accurate information simply, concisely, and with deep insight that addresses the real needs of our readers.

It is increasingly hard to find information—whether in the news media, on the Internet, and now all too often in books—that is even-handed and has your best interests at heart. We therefore hope that you enjoy this book, which has been carefully crafted to meet our standards of quality and unbiased coverage.

We are always interested in your feedback or ideas for new titles. Perhaps you'd even like to write a book yourself. Whatever the case, reach out to us at editorial@apress.com and an editor will respond swiftly. Incidentally, at the back of this book, you will find a list of useful related titles. Please visit us at www.apress.com to sign up for newsletters and discounts on future purchases.

The Apress Business Team

For Matt and Em

Contents

About the Author

Dr. Tim M. Havard has over 30 years of experience in real estate development, investment, and appraisal gained from both practice and academia. He has worked in the UK, Australia, and the Middle East. He has taught at UTS, Sydney, Australia; and UMIST and Oxford Brooks University in the UK. He spent several years with Argus Software and its predecessor training clients on the company's software suite before returning to his own practice. He is the author of *Investment Property Valuation* (2002); *Contemporary Property Development*, 2nd Edition (2008); and *Financial Feasibility Studies for Property Development: Theory and Practice* (2013).

Acknowledgments

Thanks to Argus Software, especially Paul Broadley, and CREModels for their help, support, and product excellence.

Preface

I have written this book with the intention of filling a gap in the market. This book concentrates on the software package Argus Developer.

Argus Developer and its predecessor Circle Developer have long had a dominant position as the primary real estate development appraisal tool. Developer is used all over the world—in North America, the UK, Europe, the Middle East, Asia, and Australasia—on a variety of projects from simple residential schemes to huge and complex master-planned, mixed-use commercial, residential, and leisure projects.

However, there has never been a companion book that concentrates on the practical application and use of the program.

The software does come with a comprehensive user manual that is either bundled with the program or available online—accessed via the Help button—but this manual does not take you through the process of the appraisal step-by-step.

The company does offer training on the software—at a cost. The training is limited, however, and only a certain amount of ground can be covered in a three-hour session, which is the standard package the company offers. Argus delivers two levels of training:

- Standard, which focuses on the basics of the program, and

- Intermediate, which looks at a few more advanced features

There is not time in either session to delve deeply into case studies, to really explore the capabilities—as well as the limitations and pitfalls—of the software.

That is what this book sets out to do. It covers the basics, as is included in a company training session, but then it builds on it by exploring more varied and complex situations.

I feel I am uniquely qualified to write this book. I have 25 years of experience carrying out development appraisals both in practice and in teaching it at the postgraduate level at universities in the UK and Australia. I started using the DOS version of Circle Developer in 1990. I worked for Circle and then Argus and trained clients on the software in the UK, continental Europe, and the Middle East. I also worked with US colleagues at Argus's corporate headquarters in Houston, Texas. Although I no longer work for the company,

I still use—and like—the software, and I know it rather well! In addition, I continue to work with clients in the US, primarily through CREModels, a skills out-sourcing company based in St. Petersburg, Florida.

This book is, however, an independent effort. Argus has had no input into its writing, giving me total independence in the content and the criticism—where necessary—of the software. It is based on training material that I have prepared over the last four to five years but, I believe, goes into much more depth than you ever get at a training course.

Whether you are developing residential housing, commercial office space, mixed-use developments, or "operated assets" such as hotels or golf courses, this book, along with Argus Developer, will provide the knowledge you need to undertake and succeed in modeling and developing profitable real estate projects. Let's get started.

Appraisals: An Overview

Development Appraisals and Financial Feasibility Studies in the Development Process

Before we get into the ins and outs of Argus Developer and how to use it effectively, let's take a step back and understand the goals it is meant to help us achieve.

Why Do Appraisals?

Although this is not meant as a development textbook but one that concentrates on modeling using the industry's main software tool, it is useful to set the context and establish the roles development appraisal, sometimes known as financial feasibility studies, have in the development process.

Financial feasibility studies are also known as development appraisals. They involve the gathering together of all the information on costs and values of a project. This information is incorporated into a framework and used to determine the answer to some key questions. Development appraisal is one of the key aspects of assessing the viability of a development project. It is, however, used throughout the development process to fulfill a number of key tasks.

▪ **Note** Development appraisals, also known as financial feasibility studies, are used in part to determine the value of a piece of property based on what you want to do with it.

Primarily, appraisals are used to determine the bidding price for a piece of land. This can be difficult because a piece of development land has no intrinsic or set value; it only has a value derived from the use it can be put to. The value is determined by the market and restrained by the planning and/or building restrictions on the site.

Every scheme proposed for a site—residential housing, hotel, retail, and so on—will generate different values. If a piece of development land has been fully exposed to the market, then a range of appraisals based on different schemes will be made on the site by different prospective developers. The landowner will generally sell to the developer who submits the highest viable bid. Thus, the financial appraisal is a key component in determining the highest bid a potential developer can make while still meeting the target return for the project.

The second major use of appraisal in the development process is to determine the profit or loss the scheme will make. This is vitally important because it shows the developer whether the plan is viable or not. Appraisals can also be used to explore the impact of different variations in the project. These variations might concern design, the use or use mix that the site can support, or the different timing of elements in the project. They can also be used to determine peak profitability—that is, when it might be advantageous to sell.

The financial feasibility study will also be used by commercial lenders to determine whether they will lend you money to carry out your plans.

Commercial lenders will look at the financial appraisal very carefully before advancing any funds. In essence they look at two things:

1. **Assumptions.** Lenders check to see whether the assumptions relating to the development values are sound. Lenders will carefully examine all of the components of the completed project. They will look at the rental values and the yields that have been projected by the developer for realism. They will also scrutinize the selling or leasing program to determine whether goals can be achieved. Then they will examine the construction costs and all the other elements of the project. The appraisal lays these factors completely open to scrutiny. In short, the developer and lenders will use the development appraisal to prove whether the assumptions in the development project are based on sound projections.

2. **Profit margin.** If the financiers are satisfied with these factors, they will then look closely at the profit margin on the project by the appraisal. The financiers want to be satisfied that the developer will achieve a sufficient profit margin. It may surprise some that the financiers are interested in the developer's profit, but the lenders are primarily concerned about the developer's financial stability. The profit margin reflects the risk margin on development. Basically, the larger the profit margin is, the less risk the lender will assume by advancing funds on the scheme.

There are no set margins as to what lenders will look for in terms of returns. The normal rules of thumb call for a 20% profit margin on costs for speculative commercial schemes, 10% to 20% returns on cost for commercial projects with leasing precommitments, and 10% to 15% on residential projects.

Note Lenders do not look for set profit margins on real estate development projects. Typical returns range from 10% to 20% based on the type of development.

These are the primary initial uses of development feasibility. There are other uses as well. As noted above, developers will explore the effects of altering, reworking, and changing the timings in the scheme. Projects often require rethinking during the project lifetime. This may involve changing the mix of property that will be developed to suit market requirements. The appraisal will be used to see what the effect of these changes is on developer profitability. Above all, the baseline appraisal allows you to explore all the options and assess the greatest possible profit on the development you are considering.

Common Appraisal Elements

The process of development analysis involves many disciplines of knowledge, including structural and services engineering, architecture, project planning and management, marketing, and urban economics. The feasibility report should communicate the facts, assumptions, figures, and recommendations gained during the analysis process. The person preparing this report does not need to have direct knowledge of all details required, but he or she should at least understand the impact of each critical factor and how and where this information can be accurately determined. This process of information management requires investigative skills, mathematical application of data, and intuitive thought.

In short, anyone setting out to do a development appraisal in today's world will not be able to use traditional approaches using a simplified manual calculation. You will need a sophisticated spreadsheet (and the skills to go with it) or a proprietary software system such as Argus Developer.

The process of carrying out the full feasibility study is beyond the scope of this book. But before we look at models in Argus Developer in detail, it is important to reflect on the basics of development appraisal.

The basic equations for a development appraisal are simple. To calculate development land value (or rather a land bid), the following equation is used:

Value of the buildings on completion

Minus:

The development costs (construction, all fees, all ancillary costs, and all the costs of finance)

Less: An allowance for developer's profit

Equals

Land Value (maximum sum available to buy land)

An alternative equation is used when developers know their likely input costs for land and construction and want to discover whether the scheme is viable—in other words, whether it produces sufficient profit for them to proceed:

Value of the buildings on completion

Less:

The development costs (construction, all fees, all ancillary costs, and all the costs of finance)

Less:

Land cost (including fees)

Equals

Development Profitability

Note that the appraisal is always looking to solve for the unknown element in the equation, either land value or profitability. All of the elements mentioned in the formula will have to be established or estimated.

This is breaking feasibility studies down to their very basic components. If things were as simple as this in practice, we wouldn't need expensive software models! The complexity in appraisal comes from the sheer number of components involved—ensuring that everything has been accounted for, calculating the all the components' correct values, and allowing for when these items will take place, which in itself will have an impact on their values. This process is further complicated by the fact that everything occurs in the future with the developer/appraiser often dealing with a scheme that exists only in outline.

> ▨ **Note** Keep in mind that a development appraisal is always no more than a forecast of a series of future, uncertain events.

Appraisal Challenges

I used to run a master's program in real estate development at one of the top universities in the UK. We had a weekly guest lecture spot for people from industry, and one of my favorite speakers was a grizzled 30-year veteran of commercial real estate. He frequently used the same phrase over and over again: "Development is not rocket science."

He was, of course, absolutely right. The fundamentals of real estate development, as we saw in the last section, are very simple: Build something that you can sell for more than it costs you and bank the profit. The components of building are themselves simple; we have been doing it for thousands upon thousands of years. Bring a Roman surveyor or craftsman back from the past and put him on a modern construction site and, after a little acclimatization, he would soon be very much at home. We have some sophisticated tools now that make our lives easier but, fundamentally, things have not changed that much.

The developer was also slightly wrong. Although fundamentally simple, the process of modeling is complex. As noted above, not only do you need to account for everything required to complete a project, but you also have to put the components into the correct time framework. Although some time elements are predictable, key components, including the critical ones of when something will sell or lease, are very uncertain. The models have to incorporate often-sophisticated assumptions about financing, how money flows in and out of the scheme from a variety of sources, and how to apply differing cost, drawdown, and repayment possibilities. To complicate things further, these timing assumptions may need to change either prior to the project starting or, often, during it, as circumstances change.

An appraisal model has to take these things and many more into account.

An obvious question that must be asked at this point is the following: Why use a proprietary software system such as Developer and not a self-constructed Excel spreadsheet? Excel is, after all, a wonderfully flexible and powerful tool that can and is used globally for complex tasks—and, in fact, *is* used in rocket science! So, why not use it here?

I used to be a strong proponent of Excel spreadsheets, frequently using and creating them, and applying them widely in both practice and in the classroom. I am now more wary of them, even though they are still probably the most widely used tool in the industry. In early 2012, I found myself embroiled in a debate on an Internet real estate discussion site about the merits of proprietary software vs. Excel.

I came across the site accidentally while checking a reference. I was interested in the debate that had clearly been going backward and forward for some weeks and, always enjoying an argument, decided I would join in. Having been heavily involved in this area for a dozen years or so and having originally been a great advocate of Excel, I found it odd to be on the other side of the fence arguing with the site owner. He did make some excellent points, some of which I quote here:

> I have a good friend who is an engineer for a leading aerospace-component design and manufacturing facility here in southern California. They produce nacelles mostly, but that's beside the point. Their parts are used by both Boeing and Airbus. Their work requires modeling the physics acting on their parts, and extensive and sophisticated testing is required by regulators and for simply quality control purposes. What do they use? Microsoft Excel with Visual Basic. The planes you and I ride in were in part designed and tested with Excel.

> I have a colleague who works on Wall Street creating and trading financial derivatives for a leading investment bank. His whole firm (and industry) use Excel. Why? Because of its power and breadth and because they—like every other MBA from a top university—used Excel for their finance and statistics classes. All the leading texts (particularly Bodie/Kane/Marcus) in finance go through examples in Excel. And this isn't simple discounting we're talking about but CAPM, linear regression, options pricing, and so on. Excel is the standard.

> As much as I like to think that real estate analysis and valuation demands brilliance and a firm grasp of complicated and arcane mathematics/statistics (and good looks to boot!), it simply doesn't. Beyond logic (if this, then this . . .) and high school math (but not even as advanced as calculus), commercial real estate analysis requires only an understanding of Present Value (mathematically speaking). The modeling we do for real estate is child's play compared to the capabilities of Excel, as evidenced by its much more rigorous applications.[1]

---

[1]Landon M. Scott http://incomepropertyanalytics.com/alternative-to-argus/ #comment-896. Accessed 7th May 2012, reprinted with permission.

These are very good and valid points. It is natural, then, to apply Excel to property development. It looks like the ideal tool for the job and, indeed, many practitioners pride themselves on their Excel abilities and the sophistication of the models they use.

But I no longer would use it and the reason simply comes down to the risks of error involved and the high stakes involved. Real estate development is a high-stakes poker game; you can win a lot, but you can also lose huge amounts. That is a huge part of the appeal. However, there are enough risks involved with the sector in general without adding to it elements of risk that come from using self-constructed models.

These errors can arise from a whole host of sources:

1. *Errors due to time pressure.* Many workplaces are high-pressure environments, with appraisers having to do complex work within a short time frame.

2. *Failure to properly audit the spreadsheet.* Auditing can eliminate errors from the spreadsheet, but each time you create a spreadsheet item or make a change to a spreadsheet model requires you to follow an audit trail. That costs you time. Standardized models such as Argus Developer do not need the same audit and, therefore, save you considerable time in checking the mechanics of the calculations.

3. *Incorrect modification of an existing spreadsheet model (and a presumed failure to audit).* This is a common set of circumstances. Development projects are not static; there are always many changes from the initial appraisal, where many assumptions have to be made, up to the final appraisal immediately prior to commencing work on-site.

4. *Application of an existing model to new development projects.* It is a natural thing when considerable time effort has been invested in the creation of a spreadsheet model to spread the cost (and save time) by applying and adapting the model for different projects. This not only opens up the possibility of modification errors as in number 3 above, but also in the perpetuation of errors from earlier projects. That's because people will assume that the applied model will have been audited and is error-free on the earlier projects.

So, in summary, the challenges of doing a development feasibility study is producing a reasonable and logical forecast of expenditure (money out) and receipts (money in) within an uncertain time structure. This is hard enough in itself, but adding in the additional uncertainty of a self-produced cash flow model with the extra time needed to create and continuously audit it is an unnecessary complication. That's why a program like Argus Developer will make your life much easier.

Appraisals vs. Feasibility Studies

You will notice that I have already used the terms *appraisal* and *feasibility studies* in this chapter. Using both terms reflects what happens in practice; the terms are used interchangeably throughout the industry, particularly now that cross-border, international development has become more common.

Strictly speaking, however, the terms are different. An appraisal in real estate is a formal statement of value produced by a professionally qualified person. A development feasibility study, strictly, is just what the name implies—an exploration of "what-ifs" to see if a development project is viable. Language, however, is not static; it changes. People can be doing what they term a development appraisal while others are performing a development feasibility study and yet others are producing a development financial model, but, in fact, they are all doing the same thing.

This partly relates to the fact that these development models are used for such a range of tasks. The outcome can be used to value a site or parcel of land, either to determine a bid price or as part of a formal appraisal. The same set of calculations can be used in a slightly different way to determine whether a project should go ahead at all or to explore different layouts, designs, or production schedules. They are the same thing, they are constructed in the same way, and they are based on the same assumptions.

"A rose by any other name is still a rose," to paraphrase a far better writer than I!

Note   In this book, the terms *appraisal* and *feasibility study* are used interchangeably.

Development in the 21st Century

Property development as an activity has seen considerable changes over the last 25–30 years, and these changes have had an impact on appraisal practice and techniques. Although this book is going to concentrate primarily on the techniques and tools available to the appraiser, I feel it is important to understand the context in which they are used.

Development has become broader both in its scope and in the type of people who are involved with it. With the encouragement of TV lifestyle and make-over shows, the easier availability of finance (up until the credit crunch of 2008 at least), more and more people have been carrying out forms of development. A common model is the purchase of a run-down house or flat, spending a few weeks remodeling, refitting, and redecorating it, and then either holding onto it and renting it or selling it. As a result, people of very different backgrounds have been brought into the development and investment industry, which has been, until now, dominated by builders and professionals.

Many of these new "developers" do not carry out detailed appraisals even though they perhaps should. The earliest such developers were protected in many respects by the almost continuous rise in house prices that was only arrested by the credit crunch and severe economic downturn of 2008. Until this time, it was actually quite hard not to make money out of developing property. The new, more difficult market may require these developers to take more care in assessing development projects. It seems increasingly likely that they will turn to more professional approaches, which will include the use of proprietary software.

What has made the issue more complex has been the urban regeneration movement and the increase in fashion of urban living.

Having spent most of the 20th century seeing wealth and population migrat-ing to the suburbs and fringes of the urban areas, the last decade of the 20th century and the early ones of the 21st have seen a sharp reversal of this trend. Partly this is due to investment in the urban environment, thus improv-ing it greatly. Other factors include fashion, the development of late-night/early-morning entertainment in city centers, increased wealth, and an increas-ing interest in buy-to-let investment opportunities from private investors. In addition, the rise in energy and transportation costs has made living closer to work more attractive. This latter trend seems likely to strengthen in the com-ing decades; the days of cheap energy and transportation seem to have gone.

Whatever the case may be, this trend means that development models have had to be able to deal with the special requirements of residential develop-ment in established city areas. These include staggered starts and completions, deposits, buying off plans,[2] and complex disposal patterns as well as technical issues involved in the refurbishment of older structures often with restric-tions on space and working time, all of which have to be modeled. These components are uncommon in commercial projects and this has had quite

---

[2]"Buying off plan" refers to customers agreeing to buy real estate at the design/planning stage before it is actually physically built. People do it to get in at a lower price on a project that is forecast to be extremely popular. It's a high-risk strategy—it was done a lot in countries like Dubai, where many of the developers subsequently went bust and the projects were never built.

major implication for practitioners in the field. Most development appraisal books (and sections in books dealing with development appraisal) from earlier times have concentrated on commercial development, for this was where the bulk of the work was for professionals. Now the picture is very different and advisers must be able to model all types of projects.

Development and development appraisal has also shifted from being a local concern to an international activity. Of course, development has always taken place in every country in the world, but generally development used to be a primarily local activity carried out by local contractors and developers. Now, increasingly, with cross-border investment and the rise of international advisers and professionals, many developers, surveyors, and development specialists are working across borders in many different countries. The methods and models used must, therefore, have applicability in many countries.

Development projects have also seemed to get much more complex. I say "have seemed to" because this may be an illusion; developments have always involved complexity—it is just that our ability to model them has become much greater in the last 20–30 years with the advent of computers, spreadsheets, and development appraisal software. One area, though, has become ever more sophisticated and complex: financing.

In the 1970s and 1980s, the years when the majority of development appraisal texts were written, the vast majority of appraisals would have been undertaken using valuation tables, perhaps aided by pocket calculators. To carry out the appraisals in a reasonable time frame, the calculations had to be simplified (and also, therefore, made less accurate). This is why the residual appraisal technique (described more fully below) came to be so entrenched in the profession; it is nothing more than a simplified cash flow used to ease the burden of calculation. Once established, it has been hard to shift. Today, however, we are in an era where the tools that are available to us have become infinitely more powerful and our understanding of the modeling process has been greatly increased.

I think is important to appreciate all of these trends and the impact they have had on the appraisal calculation process. The market has become wider, more complex, more international, and less parochial. The days of doing manual calculations using valuation tables are gone. The trends have pushed us toward cash flow models that are constructed on computers. This implies that most appraisals today should be conducted using cash flow models generated on self-constructed templates using a spreadsheet such as Excel or Open Office Calc, or else using one of the commercial development appraisal packages such as Argus Developer or Estate Master DF, which use the cash flow as the primary calculation tool.

New Tools, Old Methods

You will note I say *cash flow models* and not *automated residual calculations*, something which, of course, is an easy approach to computerizing appraisals and producing quick calculations. The reason I say this is that, as noted above, residuals are just simplified cash flows and the simplification has the effect of reducing accuracy.

I feel that this point requires stressing further. It used to be the thinking that each approach—the residual and the cash flow—had a role in the development process.

The residual allowed a quick appraisal to be made, and it allowed the viability of a scheme to be checked in a relatively short time. It was felt that cash flows were only worth the effort when the details of the schemes were known. Cash flows were, therefore, to be used for the final, detailed appraisal and as a project management tool. I believe this rule, with the modern tools available to the development professional, is now obsolete. We can produce cash flow analyses much more easily; reasonable general assumptions can be made about any details of the scheme that are not known at the time of the appraisal, and the results will always be more accurate than taking a residual approach.

This does not mean that residual/pro forma models and layout should never be used. In fact, they have distinct advantages in summarizing the project—the data is presented in a way that is much easier for people to interpret than in a cash flow. It is no coincidence that most proprietary software, including Argus Developer, has an output that is laid out in the traditional residual format. The primary calculation tool is, however, the cash flow.

It is perhaps slightly archaic that the layout should be used even when the underlying calculation is done differently than the residual/pro forma method. Humans like things that are familiar, the qwerty keyboard being a case in point. We all use the layout on our electronic devices and would feel lost if we were presented with something different, yet the qwerty keyboard arose in the days of mechanical typewriters as a solution to allow rapid typing while minimizing the risk of the typewriter's arms bearing the letters to the ribbon clashing with one another! There are no mechanical parts anymore, there is no ribbon, and the typewriter is virtually extinct, yet the qwerty layout survives because it is familiar, and we understand it laid out in that way. Exactly the same is true of the pro forma; it may not be how we calculate things, but everything we need and expect to see about the development project is there in the usual places.

New Tools, New Methods

What we have covered to this point shows that, although fundamentally simple, real estate development projects have become complex. The combination of the need to set out uncertain future events in a logical framework, the cash flow, with the need to model often sophisticated financing arrangements—added to the fact that these models are often dynamic, requiring changing and restructuring at regular intervals—means that the tools used to appraise these projects must also be powerful, sophisticated, and flexible.

This then rules out the old-fashioned static pro forma model and pushes the appraiser towards a dynamic cash flow model. These can (and are) constructed in Excel or other spreadsheet applications, but there are inherent drawbacks and risks involved with their use related to the nature of real estate development.

First, although all development projects share common features, each project tends to be distinct, a one-off. This means that either a new Excel model has to be constructed from scratch for each new practice, or an existing one has to be adapted. The former is very time-consuming; the latter risks introducing errors.

Second, most development projects take place over several years. Elements will change; this will require both alteration of the model and maintenance of existing models as benchmarks. Again this will necessitate changes to be made to the existing model, which may be time-consuming and may risk error.

Finally, these activities take place in a time-pressured environment. Development is a multifaceted activity—developers during the course of one day can be financial experts, construction managers, designers, and salespersons among many other types of professions. They are not necessarily software experts nor do they have the time to devote to learning the necessary programing skills or to continuously audit spreadsheets. What they need is a powerful, flexible, and reliable tool that will meet their technical needs, provide the information they need, and maximize their efficiency.

Consequently, professionally produced proprietary software is essential in the development industry. The market leader is Argus Developer for reasons that will become apparent in the course of this book.

An Overview of Argus Developer

The Basics

In this section, we will start to look at the Argus Developer program itself. The first section is a basic orientation; those who have been through an Argus training session should be familiar with its contents. However, even if you think you are up to speed on the basics, take a close look. It is worth ensuring that we are all starting from the same point when we advance into more complex uses of the program.

Let's start with a word or two on the history of Argus Developer.

History and Development of the Program

Argus Developer started its life as Circle Developer.

Circle was a company founded by Adrian Katz in London in 1990, initially with Developer as its sole product, although this program was soon followed by Circle Investor valuation and investment appraisal software. The original DOS version of Developer sold well into what was then a fairly competitive and crowded market place. In the mid- to late 1990s, the launch of the heavily revised windows version of Developer—initially called Visual Developer—established the company as the dominate player in the marketplace, first in the UK and then globally. From this initial success, the program has continued to be developed though the principle structure, and layout remains largely unchanged.

In 2006, there were a number of key events. First, Circle was bought by its larger American rival, the Houston-based Realm Business Solutions. Subsequently, the whole group was rebranded under the Argus Software banner and Circle Developer became Argus Developer. That same year, a major upgrade of the program was launched, Developer 3, which featured improved functionality of the main program and the addition of a new and very powerful Structured Finance module. There have subsequently been three more version changes that introduced additional functionality in regard to residential development appraisal along with what are called "operated assets"—golf courses, hotels, marinas, and so forth. Throughout, the core way the program works and calculations run have remained constant. Someone familiar with Circle Visual Developer would quickly feel comfortable with Argus Developer Version 5 or 6.

In April 2011, the Toronto-based Altus Group Limited announced that it acquired Realm Solutions Inc., the owner of Argus Software, for US$130 million. This acquisition was completed in June 2011.

While Argus Developer remains the best appraisal software, there are competitors. These include products produced by Estate Master (Estate Master DF), ProDev, KEL, and Caldes. All are considerably cheaper than Argus Developer, and all have their good and bad points. Argus Developer is, however, the clear market leader both in terms of the number of individual licenses, its global coverage, and its capabilities.

Program Outline: The User Dashboard

Argus Developer is primarily a cash flow calculation tool used for constructing development feasibility models. The program can be used to calculate land value (or the maximum bid that a developer can pay for land and still meet profitability targets) or to calculate the level of profitability that the project will make based upon the developer's assumptions.

Data entered into the program is placed within either a preset or user-defined time frame, and calculation is made using discounting based on the interest rate assumptions entered. One of the principle outputs is a pro forma laid out in a traditional fashion. It simply presents the data in a familiar layout to the user and any third parties. No calculation is undertaken using the pro forma sheet, nor is it possible to make data entries into it.[1]

Note You cannot enter or change figures on the pro forma or summary report in Developer. It is fed by all the variables you enter in other parts of the program.

---

[1] It is, of course, possible to amend or alter the figures in the pro forma when it is exported to a word processing application such as MS Word.

Argus Developer traditionally had four main screens or tabs in which data was entered and where the output/results of the calculation was displayed. This has changed slightly for the first time in Version 6, where a "dashboard" type approach has been taken. However, the same basic input and result areas exist, at least when the simple finance assumption has been made (see Figure 2-1). These tabs are Project, Definition, Cash Flow, and Pro Forma. Where the Structured Finance module is active in the program (in other words, where the user is making more sophisticated and detailed assumptions about the sources and application of funds used in the project), a separate tab showing the finance cash flow appears (as shown in Figure 2-1). In addition, there are tabs for performance measures and the data checker, the latter a mechanism for identifying errors.

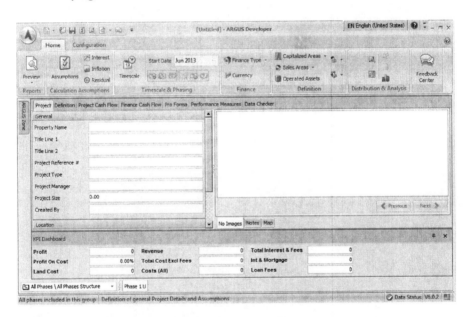

Figure 2-1. Argus Developer's initial screen: The User Dashboard

There is also a toolbar menu (Figure 2-2) that allows various functions of the program to be accessed. Each of the functions will be discussed as appropriate, but annotated diagrams of the icons are included in Figure 2-2.

Figure 2-2. Ribbon bar where program functions are accessed

In addition to the front part of the dashboard, there is a "backstage" view, accessed by clicking on the Argus symbol. This gives access to functions such as printing, saving, and file import and export (Figure 2-3). It also allows the user to check and define the preferences (things such as units of measurement—Figure 2-4) and configuration (currency and calculation preferences, for example, as shown in Figure 2-5).

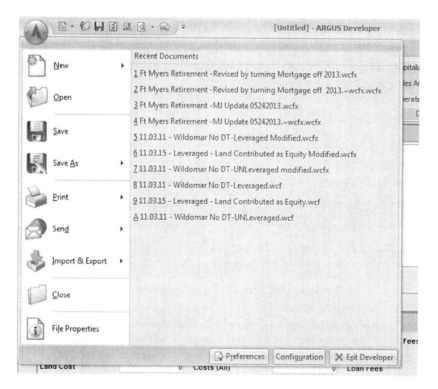

Figure 2-3. "Backstage" screen

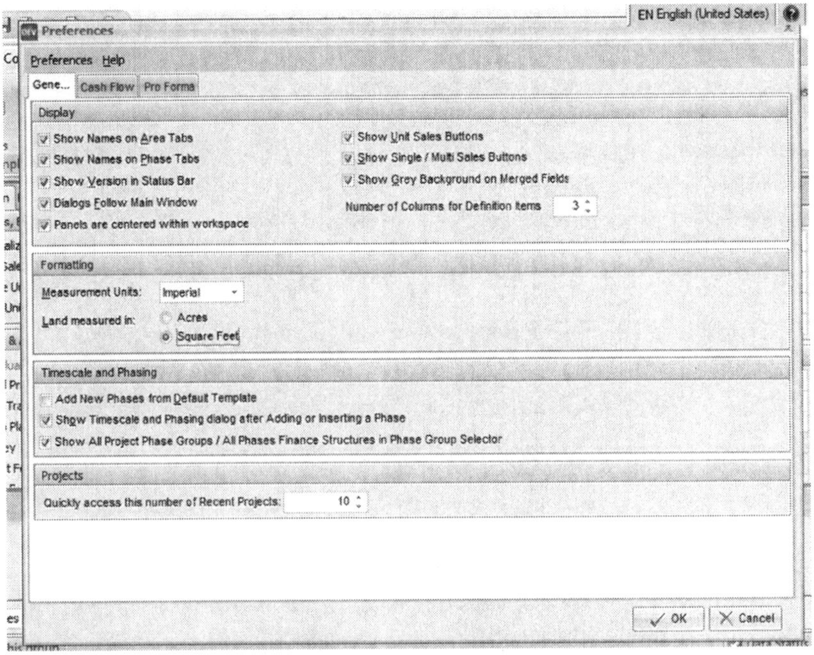

Figure 2-4. Preferences screen

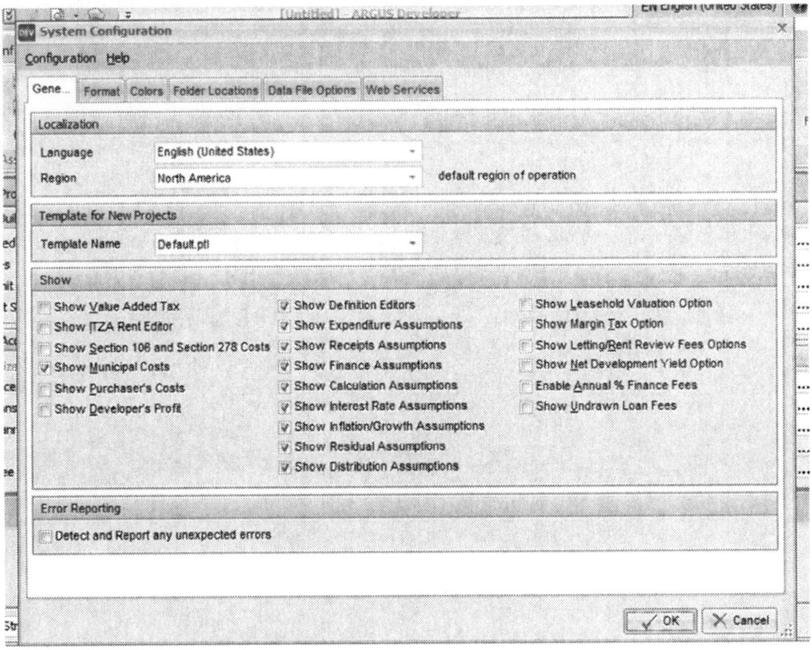

Figure 2-5. System configuration screen

Argus Developer has a preloaded template with a set of assumptions, preferences, and configurations already in place. These are designed to reflect the most commonly used requirements of the market into which the software has been loaded. Argus has created templates for the US, UK, Eurozone, and Middle Eastern markets, among others. You may wish to change the assumptions in your version of the software to suit your state or industry-specific requirements. It is possible to create a completely custom template to suit your exact requirements. For most circumstances, however, the default template is perfectly adequate and little prior setup of the program is required.

For this orientation section, we will work through the most used screens necessary for most appraisals, starting with the project screen.

Project Assumptions

Project is where the address details of the project are entered and also where the main calculation assumptions are made. As we shall see, these are broad, global assumptions that can be changed or overridden at any point during the calculation. They can be used to make broad assumptions where a quick calculation is required.

On the older versions of the software (before Version 6), the Project tab includes two shortcut buttons that take the user to key assumption elements. There is a third button for structured finance. This is an add-on module enabling the modeling of more complex financing such as partnerships and different sources and costs of finance. Unless this module option is taken, this option is grayed out.

Caution The Structured Finance module is standard on Version 6 of Argus Developer sold in the United States, but it's an add-on that must be purchased for previous versions and in some other markets.

In Version 6, the version illustrated in this book, onward the assumptions for calculation are accessed via the ribbon bar (Figure 2-6).

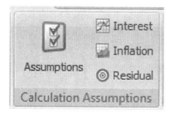

Figure 2-6. The assumptions for calculations shortcuts on the ribbon bar

Clicking the large icon will take you into the assumptions sections proper. You will observe that there are eight individual tabs in this section (Figure 2-7). As previously noted, Developer is preloaded with a template—essentially a default set of assumptions—that allows rapid appraisals to be carried out. These assumptions can be altered or just left at the default settings. For all appraisals, however, two areas must be visited by the appraiser: the Interest Sets sub-tab and the Residual sub-tab, which sets the mode of calculation. These will be covered in detail in the worked example section that follows.

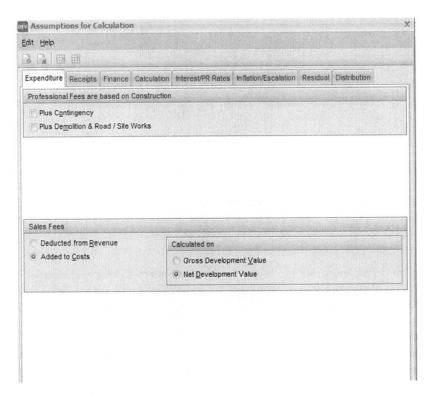

Figure 2-7. The Assumptions for Calculation tab showing the eight sub-tabs

Back on the user dashboard, to the right of the assumptions icon, is another sub-tab that takes the user to an important set of assumptions, the timescale and phasing section (Figure 2-8).

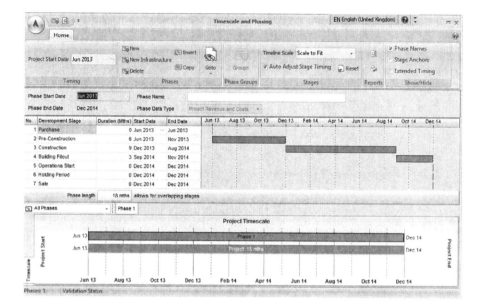

Figure 2-8. The Timescale and Phasing screen

The timescale assumptions are an essential part of an appraisal, and assumptions must be made here. The development is broken down into seven stages. The user does not have to define timescales for each of these stages, only those appropriate for the scheme.

Two things are important to know. First, the template the program comes preloaded with assigns activities and events to each of these stages. For example, any new construction work will be assigned to the construction phase with an automatic S-curve distribution.[2] Demolition work will be assumed to be a one-off event at the beginning of the construction phase and so on. The second thing to note, however, is that each individual event can be individually timed and distributed to suit the particular project. These pre-set assumptions can all be overridden.

Once the basic calculation assumptions and the timescale are set, the user would then normally go to the next tab, Definitions.

Definition Screen in Outline

The Definitions tab is the primary (but not the only) point for data entry. It is divided into groups of associated cost and income fields (Figure 2-9).

---

[2]An S-curve distribution follows most construction spending, where early spending is low, then builds, then flattens out again.

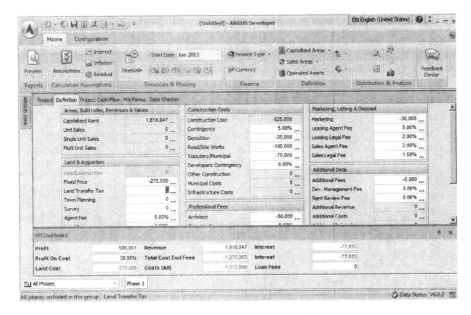

Figure 2-9. The Definitions tab

Most of the data entry can be carried out by typing values and assumptions straight into the relevant box, but there are some areas where it is necessary to drill down behind the box to make detailed entries. That is true of the four items in the upper-left part of the Definitions tab (Figure 2-10).

:ct	Definition	Project Cash Flow	Pro Forma	Data Checker
	Areas, Build rates, Revenues & Values			
	Capitalized Rent			1,818,047 ...
	Unit Sales			0 ...
	Single Unit Sales			0 ...
	Multi Unit Sales			0 ...

Figure 2-10. Detail of Definitions tab—the grouped project-type shortcuts

This is where the main value and construction cost elements are calculated. The Capitalized Rent box is designed mainly for income-producing commercial property while the three other boxes are for different types of residential development calculation.

In this case, drilling down behind the Capitalized Rent box (by clicking on the three dots) reveals the calculation that goes on behind (Figure 2-11).

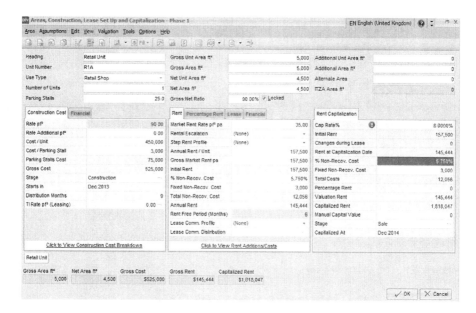

Figure 2-11. Drilling down behind to reveal the Capitalization of Income screens

There are other view options—including a schedule view—but this is the detailed view of the Areas, Construction, Lease Set Up, and Capitalization screen. Usually just called the "Commercial Areas" screen, it is divided into four broad parts. The top part is where the individual building type is defined and the built and net areas are provided. The lower-mid-left area is where the construction cost is calculated. The lower-mid-center area is where the income structure from the development is defined. The lower-mid-right area is where the capitalization of this income stream takes place.

There are no limits on the number of tabs that can be created in the Areas screen. The tab can handle both freehold and leasehold interests.

The results of all the calculations from these screens are taken back into the Definitions tab where there are displayed as grayed out boxes, in this case against Capitalized Rent and the Construction Cost boxes. (Refer to Figure 2-5.) An entry here is also reflected in the cash flow and the summary outcome sheet.

The remaining boxes in the Definitions tab allow all elements of the development to be costed or valued, and these elements are then placed in the relevant time frame. This can be done using the preloaded template or each individual cost and revenue element can be manually determined.

Take, for example, the Demolition element of this appraisal in the Construction Costs box (Figure 2-12). Demolition is grayed out, illustrating that there is more than one element to it. Drilling down into the box (using the button indicated by the three dots) reveals the detail of the calculation (Figure 2-13).

Construction Costs	
Construction Cost	-525,000
Contingency	5.00% ...
Demolition	-25,000 ...
Road/Site Works	-100,000 ...
Statutory/Municipal	-75,000 ...
Developers Contingency	0.00% ...
Other Construction	0 ...
Municipal Costs	0 ...
Infrastructure Costs	0 ...

Figure 2-12. Detail of Definitions tab: Construction Cost and related fields

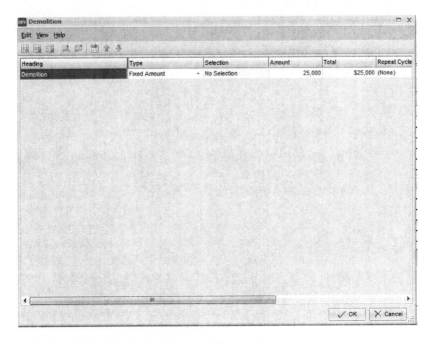

Figure 2-13. Drilling down behind the demolition section

As can be observed in Figure 2-14, there are two elements to the demolition. I created these extra elements by drilling down into this section and adding a new line for asbestos removal using the + symbol. As it happens, these items are both one-time cost items, but the program allows a number of different calculation options. For example, you can relate the cost to another element or elements or relate the cost to an area defined in the Commercial or Residential Areas screens. As you can see, the cost of asbestos removal is pegged to the Gross Land Area, which I previously set as 15,000 square feet.

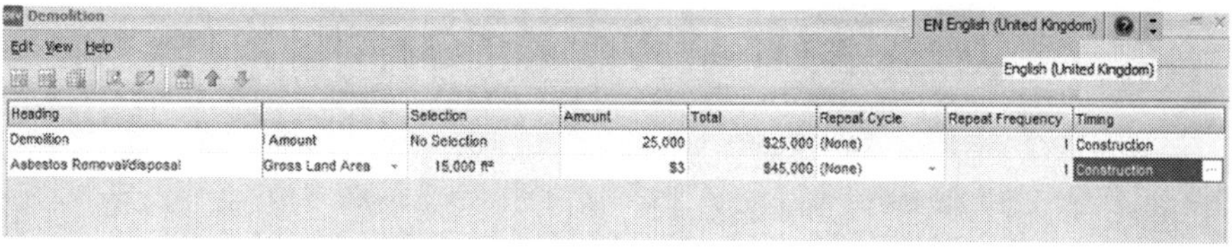

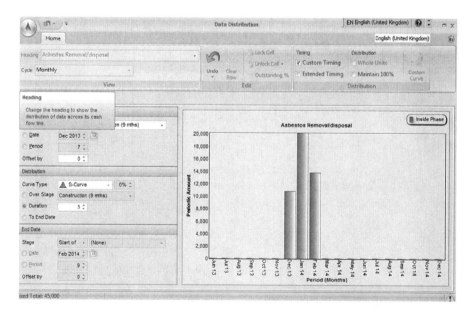

Figure 2-14. Detail of Demolition screen showing degree of variability/control possible with each element

As to timing, as previously noted, Developer assigns costs and revenues in accordance with the pre-existing template. In the case of the Demolition element, this is timed by default as a single cost item to the beginning of the construction stage of the project. This timing can be overridden by clicking on the relevant row in the timing column (Figure 2-15).

Figure 2-15. Adjusting the timing and distribution of an expenditure

Any distribution of an expense required can be modeled.

This, in essence, is the power of Developer as a program. It can, for instance, be used if a quick feasibility study is required because the template allows a rapid calculation of viability using reasonable approximations. It can, however, also be used as a finer tool with more in-depth assumptions that can vary with your unique needs. The program is also highly transparent. It can always be interrogated to discover exactly what assumptions have been made.

Once the data entry into the Definitions tab has been made, the appraisal is essentially complete. The results of the calculation can be seen in the results bar at the bottom of the screen, which gives an instant summary of the calculation and also in the Cash Flow and Summary tabs of the program.

I will quickly run through the remainder of the Definitions tab, which is, as noted before, grouped into related expenditure activities.

The first sub-area is for Land and Acquisition activities (Figure 2-16). As the name implies, this deals with all activities connected with the site itself, including the acquisition price, taxes on land transfers, any local planning charges or surveys required, agents and legal fees, and any other acquisition costs. A quick or approximate appraisal entry can be made into most of the boxes on the Definition screen itself or, if the acquisition is more complex or more information is available, the user can drill down behind the cells using the three dots to create an unlimited number of individual items in the background, the result of which is indicated on the Definition screen. Note that, as is the case with the Other Acquisition box, boxes with more than one calculation feeding into it are shaded and editing has to be done by drilling into the background detail. Using this function allows for the modeling of staged payments of the land, for example.

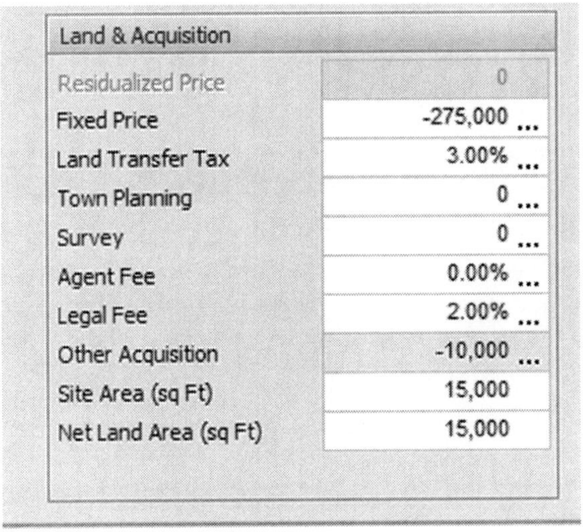

Land & Acquisition	
Residualized Price	0
Fixed Price	-275,000 ...
Land Transfer Tax	3.00% ...
Town Planning	0 ...
Survey	0 ...
Agent Fee	0.00% ...
Legal Fee	2.00% ...
Other Acquisition	-10,000 ...
Site Area (sq Ft)	15,000
Net Land Area (sq Ft)	15,000

Figure 2-16. Definitions screen: Land and Acquisition sub-area

Note that there is a shaded-out box headed Residualized Price at the top of this section. This is where the calculated land value is placed when Developer is run in the mode to calculate land value rather than development profitability. As this sum is calculated as a result of all the assumptions made elsewhere, it is not editable.

The next sub-area is Construction Costs (Figure 2-17). Note that the Construction Cost box itself is shaded, indicating that it cannot be edited. This is again because the figure has been calculated elsewhere and is just being reported here. In this case, the calculation has been done in the Capitalized Rent section.

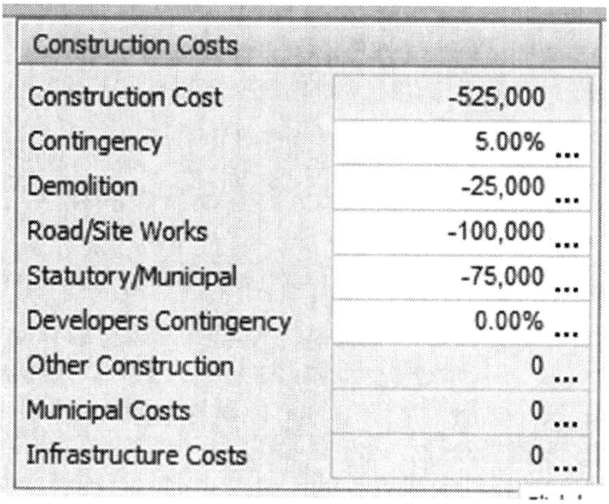

Construction Costs	
Construction Cost	-525,000
Contingency	5.00% ...
Demolition	-25,000 ...
Road/Site Works	-100,000 ...
Statutory/Municipal	-75,000 ...
Developers Contingency	0.00% ...
Other Construction	0 ...
Municipal Costs	0 ...
Infrastructure Costs	0 ...

Figure 2-17. Construction Cost sub-area

As we have already looked at this section in detail, we will move onto the next sub-area, Professional Fees (Figure 2-18).

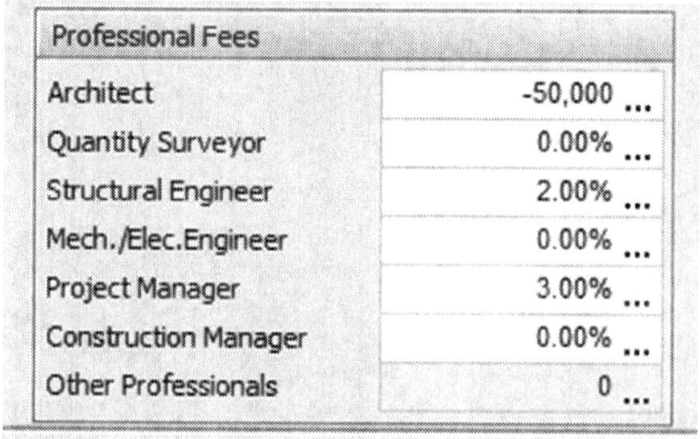

Professional Fees	
Architect	-50,000 ...
Quantity Surveyor	0.00% ...
Structural Engineer	2.00% ...
Mech./Elec.Engineer	0.00% ...
Project Manager	3.00% ...
Construction Manager	0.00% ...
Other Professionals	0 ...

Figure 2-18. Professional Fees sub-area

The headings for the Professional Fees sub-area is, like the rest of the Definitions screen, fully user-definable by double-clicking on the names. The default setting for this section is for percentages to be entered, the fees defaulting to being calculated from the construction costs. These settings can be overridden, either by entering a lump sum into the box on the Definitions screen or else by drilling down behind and either changing the association to the costs or else entering another set of calculation assumptions.

The final part of the Definitions screen covers Marketing, Letting, and Disposal (the top part of figure 2-19) along with an Additional Data section. This latter area is really a place where you can put unallocated costs and revenue.

Marketing, Letting & Disposal	
Marketing	-30,000 ...
Leasing Agent Fee	5.00% ...
Leasing Legal Fee	2.00% ...
Sales Agent Fee	2.00% ...
Sales Legal Fee	1.50% ...

Additional Data	
Additional Fees	-5,000 ...
Dev. Management Fee	3.00% ...
Rent Review Fee	0.00% ...
Additional Revenue	0 ...
Additional Costs	0 ...
Additional Related	0 ...
Rent Additions/Costs	0 ...
Sales Additions/Costs	0 ...

Figure 2-19. Disposal and Additional Data sub-areas

The Project Cash Flow

There are two Cash Flow screens, Project and Finance,[3] each of which can be viewed in different time cycles—monthly, quarterly, and so on. However, the finance cash flow only appears as a separate tab if the structured finance option

---

[3]The project cash flow shows all the items of expenditure and receipts, but it excludes financing costs. The finance cash flow details interest charges and accumulation as the project proceeds.

is selected. If, as is shown in this section, you take the simple interest set option, the finance calculation is shown at the bottom of the project cash flow.

The project cash flow shows the costs and revenues within the time frames defined either by the user or by default by the program template (Figure 2-20).

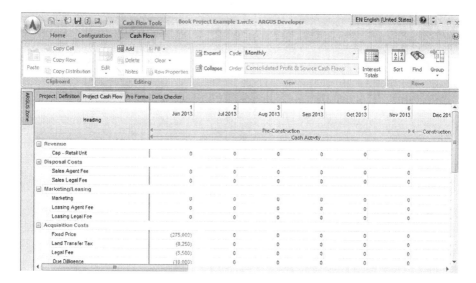

Figure 2-20. The Cash Flow tab, project view

Developer breaks down the project into subsets of revenue and expenditure. As well as the different time-view cycles (Figure 2-21), the user can also expand and collapse these subsets on the dashboard for ease of working (Figure 2-22).

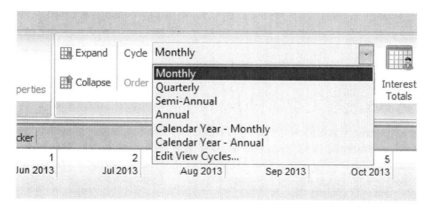

Figure 2-21. The Cash Flow tab—selecting the view cycle

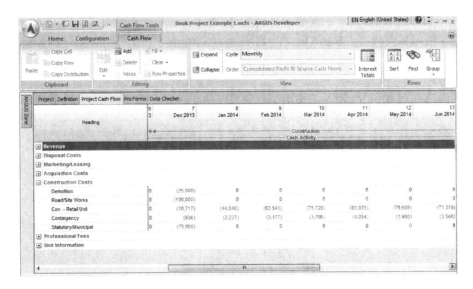

Figure 2-22. The Cash Flow tab, showing the ability to expand and collapse sections

Although the cash flow is an outcome of the program, it is also the primary calculation engine and the distribution of any of the lines within it can be reviewed and adjusted if required (Figure 2-23).

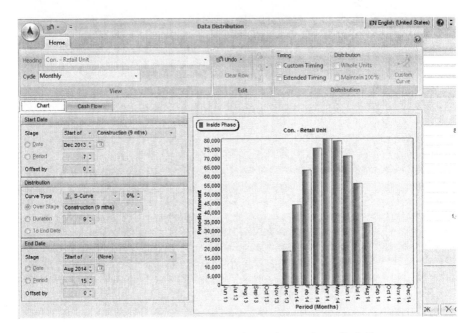

Figure 2-23. Adjustment of construction distribution line made via Cash Flow screen

New lines and new cost/revenue elements can be added directly into the cash flow. These automatically write back to the Definitions tab, keeping the records up-to-date. This ability to control and fine-tune underlines Developer's power and is something that we will explore further throughout this book.

The Finance Cash Flow

As noted above, Developer has two finance modes. First, there is the simple finance option (Figure 2-24), which allows you to define interest rate sets[4] and uses them to take into account the time value of money (that is, the impact of time on the project's revenue.) Second, there is the structured finance option, which allows you to model the effect of different sources of finance. For example, a project might be funded by equity, primary debt, mezzanine finance, long-term mortgages, or any combination of funding sources with differences in the timing of draw down and repayments.

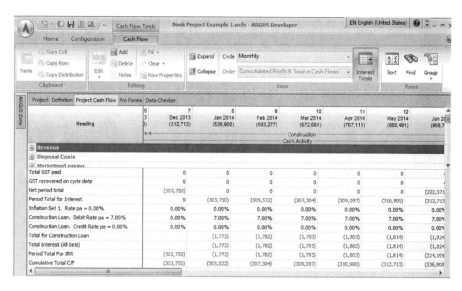

Figure 2-24. The finance cash flow in the simple finance mode

Obviously, the latter is more realistic in today's market and is often critical to the success of a project. It is also the default setting of the program in the US market. However, I would personally recommend, when doing a development feasibility study, to run the program in the simple finance mode. Doing so will

---

[4]Developer requires the user to define interest rate "sets"—a schedule of interest rates and time assumptions—which are stored in a library once created and can be referred to and linked to elements in the feasibility study as required.

give the best indication of the basic soundness (or not) of the project. Once the calculation has been done, the software can be switched to the structured finance mode. (We will look at the Structured Finance module in detail in the next section.)

Look again at Figure 2-24. When the program is run in the simple finance mode, the finance cash flow is shown by clicking on the icon Interest Totals while on the Cash Flow screen.

Tip Even though the structured finance mode gives you greater capabilities, at first you should run the appraisal in the simple finance mode. It will provide quick feedback on whether your project is financially sound. Then you can move into the Structured Finance module to refine your calculations.

Pro Forma Output

The final tab, other than the data checker, is the Pro Forma (summary) screen (Figure 2-25). As has been noted, this is laid out as a traditional residual appraisal and gives a quick, concise, and clear overview of the development.

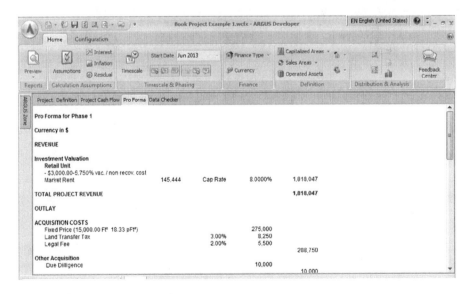

Figure 2-25. The Pro Forma tab

The summary can be printed directly from this tab or converted to PDF format for easy transmission. It can also be printed via the Reporting module and exported into Word.

A sample pro forma output is illustrated in Figure 2-26.

Pro Forma for Phase 1

Currency in $

REVENUE

Investment Valuation
  Retail Unit
  - $3,000.00-5.750% vac. / non recov. cost

Market Rent	145,444	Cap Rate	8.0000%	1,818,047

TOTAL PROJECT REVENUE   **1,818,047**

OUTLAY

ACQUISITION COSTS

	ft²	Rate ft²	Cost	
Fixed Price (15,000.00 Ft²_18.33 pFt²)			275,000	
Land Transfer Tax		3.00%	8,250	
Legal Fee		2.00%	5,500	
				288,750

Other Acquisition

Due Dilligence	10,000	
		10,000

CONSTRUCTION COSTS

Construction	ft²	Rate ft²	Cost	
Retail Unit	5,000 ft²	90 pf²	450,000	
Retail Unit (Parking Stalls)	25	3,000.00	75,000	**525,000**
Contingency		5.00%	26,250	
Demolition			25,000	
Road/Site Works			100,000	
Statutory/Municipal			75,000	
				226,250

PROFESSIONAL FEES

Architect		50,000	
Structural Engineer	2.00%	10,500	
Project Manager	3.00%	15,750	
			76,250

MARKETING & LEASING

Marketing		30,000	
Leasing Agent Fee	5.00%	7,272	
Leasing Legal Fee	2.00%	2,909	
			40,181

DISPOSAL FEES

Sales Agent Fee	2.00%	36,361	
Sales Legal Fee	1.50%	27,271	
			63,632

Additional Costs

Additional Fees	5,000	
		5,000

FINANCE
  Debit Rate 7.00% Credit Rate 0.00% (Nominal)

Total Finance Cost	77,033

TOTAL COSTS   **1,312,096**

PROFIT   **505,951**

Performance Measures

Profit on Cost%	38.56%
Profit on GDV%	27.83%
Profit on NDV%	27.83%
Development Yield% (on Rent)	11.08%
IRR	44.99%
Rent Cover	3 yrs 6 mths
Profit Erosion (finance rate 7.000%)	4 yrs 8 mths

Figure 2-26. The pro forma, which summarizes all the variables you've plugged into Argus Developer

Reporting

The program has a number of other features including a quick and a full Reporting module. Access it by hitting Preview in the upper-left part of the screen (Figure 2-27).

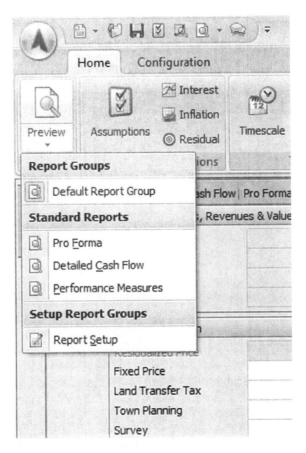

Figure 2-27. The Reporting module shortcut

We will be exploring many of these other features later in the book, but the Reporting module needs to be looked at here.

Reporting the outcome of a feasibility study to partners, the company's board of directors, the project manager, or a potential financial backer is an essential function. This is another area where Developer is superior to, say, self-created Excel sheets. The program packages the key outputs of the calculation and presents them in a way that these key decision makers need to properly evaluate a development project.

Developer has a series of pre-prepared reporting outputs—a Pro Forma sheet, a Cash Flow sheet, and the main Performance Measures sheet (Figure 2-27) or, alternatively, the user can assemble a more comprehensive set of reports using the full Reporting module (Figure 2-28).

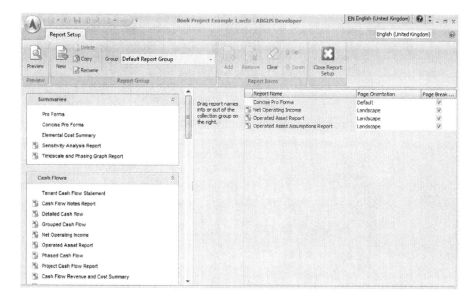

Figure 2-28. The Reporting module: Backstage view showing potential for a "build up" of a report specific for the user's needs

Summary

This chapter is intended to give a broad overview of the basics of Argus Developer and to act as an orientation for the user. A more in-depth appreciation of its use and power will be given in later sections of the book.

In the next section, we will look at some of the more advanced features of the program. This includes the Structured Finance module and, very importantly given the nature of development, the Sensitivity Analysis module. This is a powerful tool, although it is perhaps the least well developed and, from my observation, the least well used in practice of the elements of the program. We will examine the best use of this module later in the book, but we will introduce it in the next chapter.

I think it can be seen already, however, that Argus Developer is a powerful, comprehensive, and complete appraisal tool. It has very distinct advantages over self-created Excel models, as it is reliable, flexible, and consistent.

Argus Developer: Advanced Features

Three Key Modules

In this section, we will look at additional features of the program—those that are outside of its core operation.

Additional Features of Argus Developer

In addition to the basic features of the program, Developer—thanks to its long period of use and feedback from users from all parts of the world—has added many sophisticated features that are essential for accurately modeling projects. I will highlight three in this chapter: the Sensitivity Analysis module, the Structured Finance module, and the Operated Asset module. They are all important for different reasons.

As I have already discussed in Chapter 1, development feasibility studies involve modeling uncertain future events. A single development appraisal conducted prior to a development scheme's starting is going to represent one view about how the future might pan out. One thing is certain about this appraisal; it will be wrong!

Hopefully, the appraisal will be the best, most reasoned assessment of the outcome, but it is almost inevitable that at least some of the assumptions within it will prove to be inaccurate. If, however, some of the key variables—the ones that have the most impact on value or profitability—vary (usually the rental income stream, the capitalization yield, sale prices, construction costs, and project duration), then the impact on the bottom line can be very significant. Even a fairly small variation to some of these items can be fatal to the project.

It is, therefore, vitally important for the developers to understand how exposed they are to these potential variations. If they do so, the developers will have a much better understanding of the level of risk they are taking. They will be able to judge whether the level of return they expect will adequately compensate them for this risk. Exploring the risk will give developers the opportunity to accept the risk and take steps to mitigate it or, ultimately, to walk away from the project in its entirety. Proper risk analysis requires a powerful sensitivity analysis/risk appraisal module. Indeed, this is essential for development-appraisal software.

Note   Any good real estate development program must have the ability to assess risk. The Sensitivity Analysis module in Argus Developers provides that capability admirably.

Similarly, it is now essential for development appraisal software to reflect the sophisticated financing arrangements that are typical of many development projects. The viability of many projects goes way beyond the simple real estate fundamentals to the ability to finance the project in a way that it is still profitable. Traditionally, many development appraisals were done with the assumption that the project was 100% debt-financed. Today this never happens.

A minimum requirement of development appraisal software is that it be able to distinguish (and measure the return to) equity and debt sources of finance. Many projects, however, involve multiple sources of both debt and equity, and it is important to be able to model the flows of these funds through the project—how and when they are drawn down, how they are repaid, how their different cost structures are assembled, and how and when the profit is distributed to stakeholders. Getting these structures right can have a huge impact on development viability, so the software must be able to do more than model this area. Yet this model cannot be static; users must be able to modify and test it. Argus Developer used to be weak in this area, reflecting perhaps its roots in a market where finance on development projects was less sophisticated, but it has taken huge strides in developing this area, mainly due to such needs in the US market.

■ **Note** Given today's financing realities, real estate development programs must be able to account for different financing schemes including debt of all kinds and equity. The Structured Finance module in Argus Developer can handle all manner of financing schemes.

Finally, the last additional feature I want to look at is the Operated Assets module. Initially, Developer was primarily aimed at serving the developers of the most common property types in the commercial sector—retail, office, and industrial—as well as the residential sector. It neglected the more specialized kinds of income-producing property, the ones where the value, in many respects, related less to the pure real estate qualities (area, rent and cap rate) and more to business issues (income streams less fixed and variable operating costs). These businesses, or "operated assets," include hotels, golf courses, marinas, care homes, and the like. They have become increasingly important to the real estate development sector. As a result, it is increasingly important that the appraisal tools used by the industry are able to deal with their special features.

I will return to the detailed use of these modules in practice throughout this book, but it is important that we introduce them here.

The Sensitivity Analysis Module

A sensitivity module has been part of Developer from its earliest versions. It has, however, become more sophisticated over the years.

One thing has remained constant, however—the sensitivity analysis must be done after the appraisal has been completed. This is because it draws on the components of the appraisal in order to be able to do the analysis.

The module is accessed via an icon on the dashboard. This produces the initial screen where you select the variables to be tested (Figure 3-1).

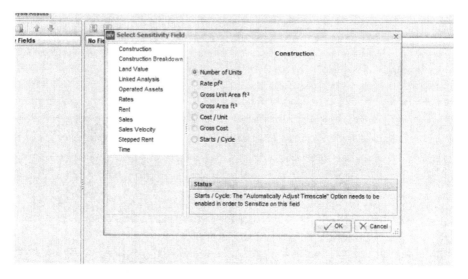

Figure 3-1. The initial screen for the Sensitivity Analysis module

Developer allows three groups of factors to be tested as part of an analysis scenario. A fourth, time-related factor can be added to the three groups.

Within the broad factors selected (such as rent, construction cost, and interest rates), you can choose all of the items within the group or select individual items you feel are particularly important (Figures 3-2, 3-3, and 3-4).

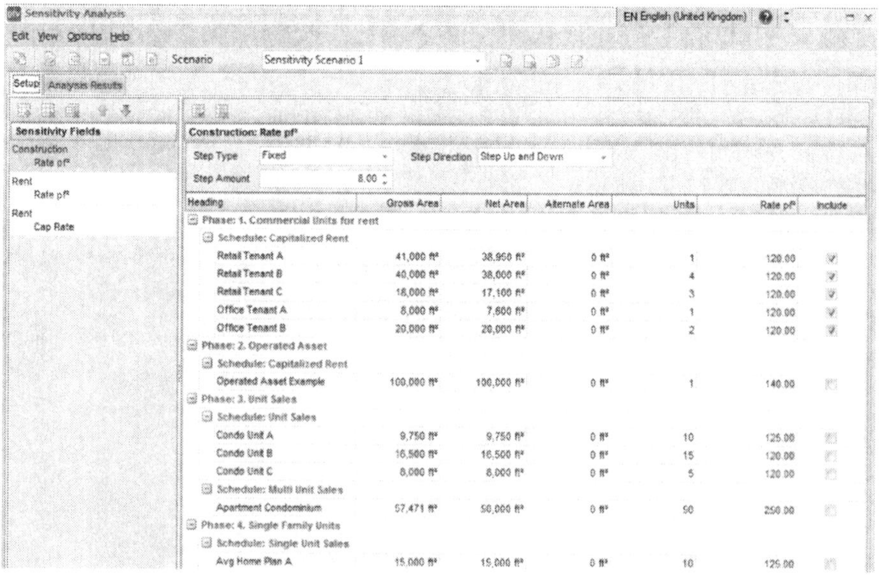

Figure 3-2. Selection of items within the broad area, in this case construction costs

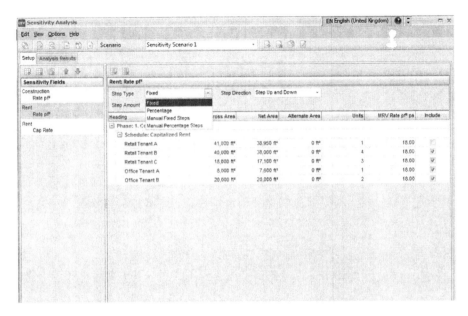

Figure 3-3. Selection of items within the broad area, in this case rental value

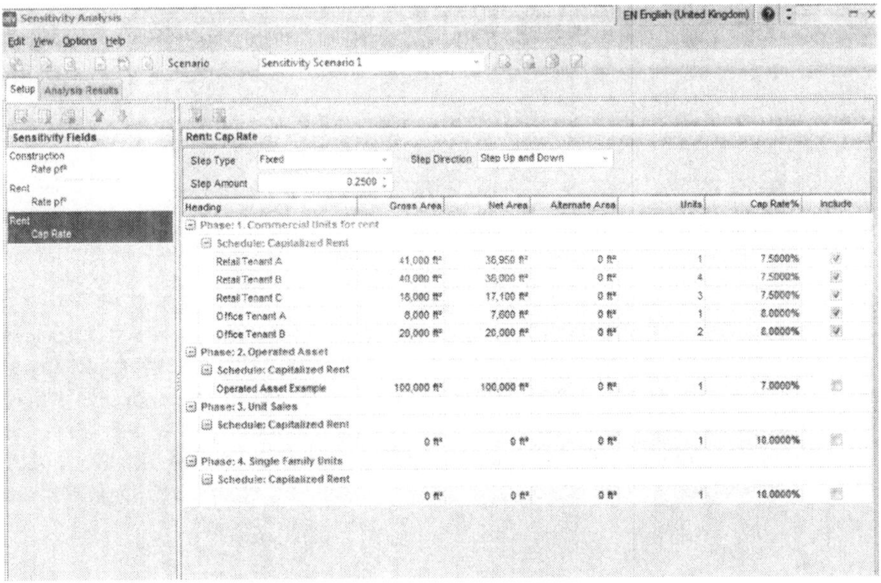

Figure 3-4. Selection of items within the broad area, in this case capitalization rates

In the cases illustrated here, the user has selected construction costs, rental values, and capitalization rates. Note that the user can define the step type[1] (fixed, percentage, manual fixed steps, or manual percentage steps), whether the analysis is unidirectional (in other words, just testing the downside or upside risk of a project), or if it tests the impact of market movement upward and downward. The user can also define the step amount.

Once the sensitivity analysis has been set up to your satisfaction, the analysis can be run by clicking into the tab behind the setup screen, Analysis Results (Figure 3-5).

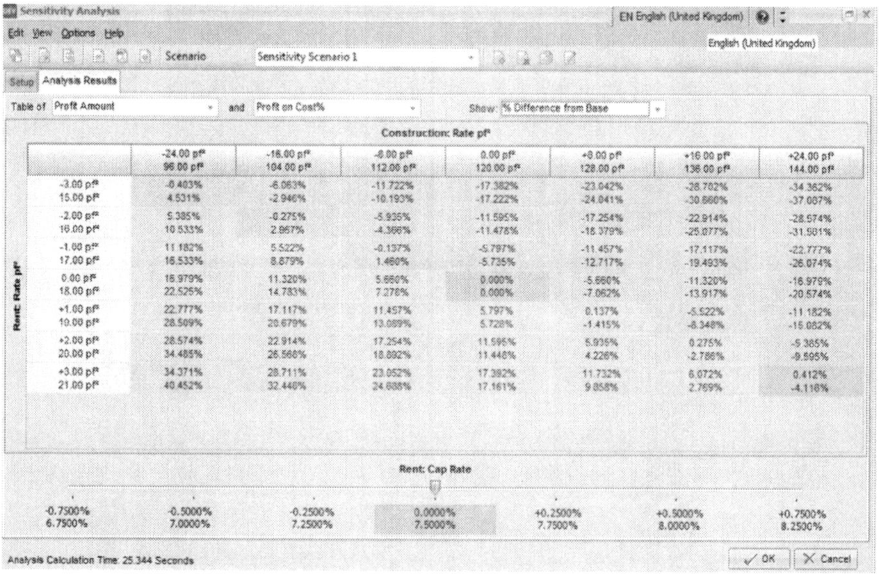

Figure 3-5. Sensitivity analysis results

As can be seen, the results are presented in a table. The analysis output is user-definable; it is possible to look at land value, profitability, internal rate of return, costs, and so on. The first two items selected in the setup are presented as the vertical and horizontal scale, while the third variable (here the Cap Rate) is displayed on a sliding scale at the bottom of the results screen. Moving the slider to the step value points displayed changes the presented values in the table.

---

[1]Steps are the variation in values of the variables, up and down either side of the values estimated in the original appraisal, which test the effect of those values on the land value or profitability.

All the results displayed onscreen can be exported into reports or printed off directly, either in .rtf or PDF format.

The sensitivity analysis module of Developer is a very useable function. However, it is not without aspects that might be criticized. For example, it enables the users to explore the basic sensitivity of their appraisal to market fluctuations. Simple sensitivity tests one variable at a time to determine the impact on returns or values. This can be done with Developer, although it is invariably the same few factors that always impact on the outcome of the appraisal. These include anything to do with value—rents, yields, sale values, and so forth—that the appraiser needs to pay the greatest attention to.

In reality, the chance of single variables changing in isolation is limited; variables inevitably will tend to move together. For example, in an economic downturn, the project duration tends to increase because it might be harder to find tenants or sell units. At the same time, rental values tend to fall because of the decrease in demand. As rents fall, so do capital values. That is not only because of the reduced income, but also because yields increase as investors seek higher initial returns to compensate them for increased risk and lower future rental growth. On the upside, construction costs tend to fall in these conditions as contractors compete more strongly for what little work is available. (Although of course this can only apply to construction work for which contracts have not yet been awarded.)

The nature of the development environment thus suits the use of scenarios. However, as I've just shown, Developer is slightly limited by allowing only the three variables to be compared at any one time. In real situations, more variables will move together. The technical limits of Developer prevent these more complete scenarios to run.

Another issue is that the program doesn't allow you to weight the resulting outcomes according to the probability of any of the scenarios actually occurring. In reality, the probability of any one of them occurring is not likely to be 50/50; extreme market movements, either upward or downward, may well have only a 2% or 3% chance of actually happening. You can weight the outcomes outside the system in an additional analysis, but it does represent a weakness in the system. The usability, flexibility (within the limits identified), and accessibility of the sensitivity module within the program do, however, go a long way toward mitigating these weaknesses.

The Structured Finance Module

Prior to 2005–6, the greatest weakness of Argus (or as it was then called, Circle) Developer was the lack of a sophisticated finance module. The program had the ability to define multiple interest and finance sets, to ascribe different interest sources and costs to any cost or income line within the cash flow, and to do a limited degree of analysis for joint venture or partnership arrangements. It was not possible to easily model finance flowing into a development from multiple sources, equity and debt, nor model the types of multiple layers of profit distribution that were becoming more common in projects. Although the actual structure and workings of the pure project modeling section was excellent, the lack of a finance module with real power and flexibility was a major flaw, particularly for the North American market. From Developer 3 onward, this weakness was corrected with the addition of the Structured Finance module.

Access the module by clicking into the Finance Type icon on the ribbon bar (Figure 3-6). As was mentioned in the introduction, there are two finance modules available in Developer, including a simple finance module.

Figure 3-6. Accessing the Finance Type icon (in the middle) from the ribbon bar

---

■ **Tip** I always run an initial appraisal using the simple finance module because it provides a much better idea of the underlying soundness of the project fundamentals. That done, I turn to the Structured Finance module for a more sophisticated look at the possible financing configurations.

For illustration, I will select the Structured Finance module. Note that in the US market this is the default setting. International users may find that the program defaults to the simple option. Clicking into Structured Finance produces the screen shown in Figure 3-7.

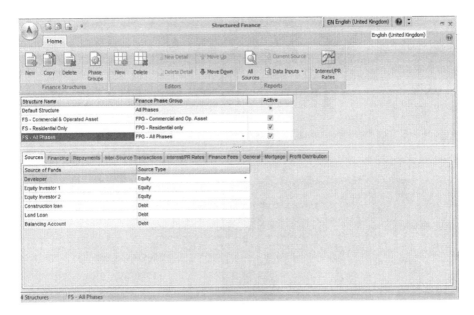

Figure 3-7. The Structured Finance opening screen

Developer allows you to define and test multiple financial structures. You can define different finance structures for different parts of projects, such as different phases, and each can be made active or inactive as appropriate. (Inactive in this case means that the structure is not applied within the project but is retained in a library form.) The opening screen shows the financial structures within the system at the middle top of the screen. At the bottom, the finance sources are shown. These can be defined as being debt or equity sources. Create or delete the financial structures using the icons to the left of the ribbon bar; create or delete the finance sources using the icons in the left-center of the ribbon.

In the center part of the screen, where the sources of funds are listed, you'll find nine sub-tabs. This is where the details of the financial structure are defined.

The second of the sub-tabs is the Financing screen shown in Figures 3-8 and 3-9. Note that these are shown in two diagrams because there are too many columns to show them in a single screenshot.

Sources			Contributions							
Source of Funds	Source Type	Order	Contribution % of Cost	Contribution Cap	Fixed Contribution	Contribution Shortfall %	Contribution Inc. Interest	Proportionate	Earliest Contribution Date	Interest/PR Rates
Developer	Equity	1	0.00%	0	1,000,000	0.00%	☐	☐	Project Start	(None)
Equity Investor 1	Equity	2	15.00%	0	0	0.00%	☐	☑	Project Start	(None)
Equity Investor 2	Equity	2	15.00%	0	0	0.00%	☐	☑	Project Start	(None)
Construction loan	Debt	3	70.00%	0	0	0.00%	☐	☐	Project Start	Construction Loan
Balancing Account	Debt	4	0.00%	0	0	100.00%	☑	☑	N/A	(None)

Figure 3-8. The Financing sub-tab, left side

Sources						Finance Costs				
Source of Funds	Source Type	Contribution Inc. Interest	Proportionate	Earliest Contribution Date	Interest/PR Rates	Finance Fees	Project Funds Interest	Project Funds Fees	Fees based on Contribution only	
Developer	Equity	☐	☐	Project Start	(None)	(None)	☐	☐	☐	
Equity Investor 1	Equity	☐	☑	Project Start	(None)	(None)	☐	☐	☐	
Equity Investor 2	Equity	☐	☑	Project Start	(None)	(None)	☐	☐	☐	
Construction loan	Debt	☐	☐	Project Start	Construction Loan	Const. Loan Fees	☐	☐	☐	
Balancing Account	Debt	☑	☑	N/A	(None)	(None)	☑	☐	☐	

Figure 3-9. The Financing sub-tab, right side

The Financing sub-tab allows the user to define where the money to undertake the project is sourced from; how the finance is to be drawn down from these sources; what, if any, limits there are to the finance from each source (an upper limit to contributions from a particular source, for example); the order each source is to be drawn down (this can be consecutive or side-by-side); and the cost of each source (interest rates and finance charges such as arrangement fees). The cost elements are defined by reference to two other sub-tabs, Interest/PR Rates (Figures 3-10 and 3-11) and Finance Fees (Figure 3-12). PR stands for *Profit Rates*.

Description	Interest/PR Rates	Nominal Rates	In Advance	Compounding Period
Construction Loan	Constr Loan	☑		None
12% Preferred Return	12% Pref Return	☑	☐	Monthly
10% Preferred Return	10% Pref Return	☑	☐	Monthly

Figure 3-10. Interest/PR Rates sub-tab

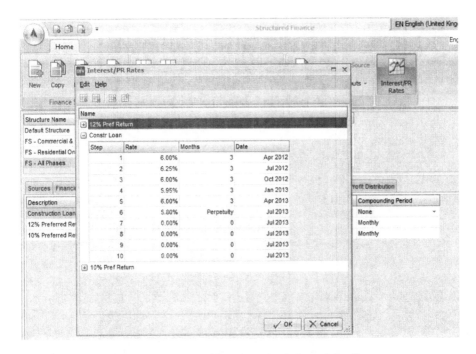

Figure 3-11. Source tables for Interest/PR Rates sub-tab (user-defined)

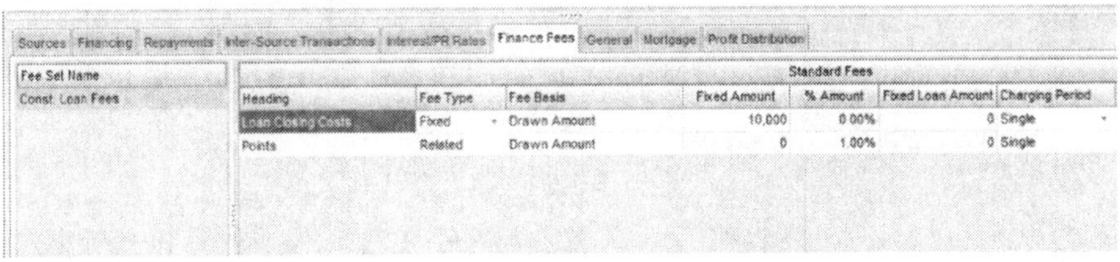

Figure 3-12. Finance Fees sub-tab

If the Financing sub-tab can be seen to be where the "money in" to the project is identified and its details defined, then the Repayment sub-tab (Figure 3-13) is how the finance sources drawn down are repaid, excluding any profit distribution.

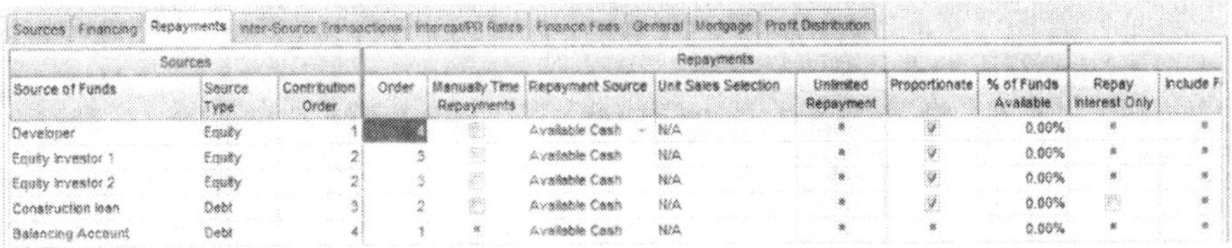

Figure 3-13. Repayments sub-tab

Again, this section is comprehensive enough to give the user sufficient control to accurately model very complex financial arrangements in projects. These include the order each source is to be repaid, the priority of payment, where the finance is to be sourced to fund the repayment—note the software allows inter-source transactions to be modeled using a separate sub-tab, not shown here—and the timing of repayment. Note also that in the Finance Cash Flow screen, accessible from the main dashboard, it is possible to manually override both drawdown and repayment using separate lines available for each source. This allows even further customization of financing for the user.

In addition to the pure project (that is, short-term) finance, the Structured Finance module allows you to incorporate long-term mortgage finance (Figure 3-14). This can be calculated by reference to the stabilized income produced from the property, or it can be manually calculated. The timing of the mortgage is also defined by the user both in terms of the loan duration and the time when it is assumed to become "live."

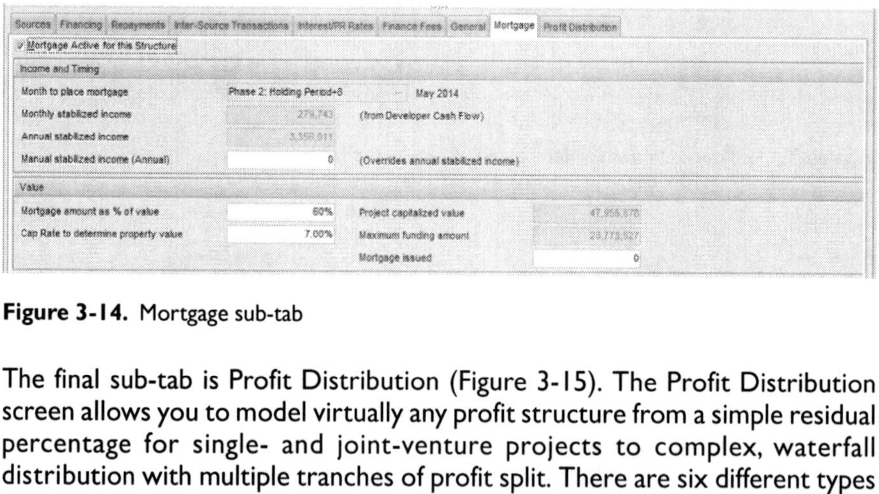

Figure 3-14. Mortgage sub-tab

The final sub-tab is Profit Distribution (Figure 3-15). The Profit Distribution screen allows you to model virtually any profit structure from a simple residual percentage for single- and joint-venture projects to complex, waterfall distribution with multiple tranches of profit split. There are six different types of profits that can be applied, and the setup screen allows the user fine control of the definition, order, and timing of each.

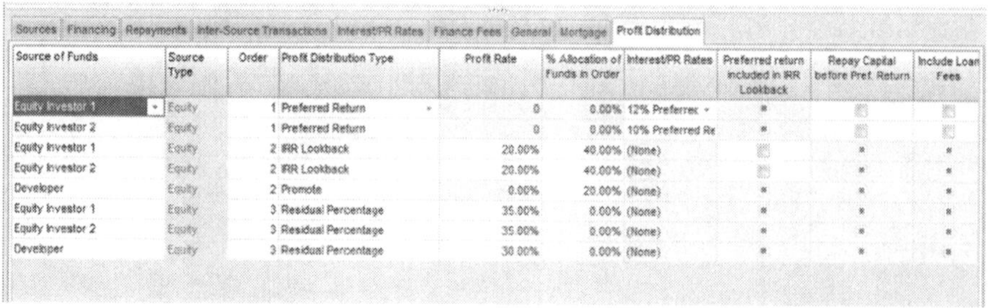

Figure 3-15. Profit Distribution sub-tab

The Structured Finance module feeds into the separate finance cash flow, referred to previously. It also has its own separate reporting module. You can also incorporate the finance report into the full reporting module.

The Structured Finance module can be daunting to new users of the software. However, its abilities, power, and flexibility have transformed Developer's capabilities in this area. It is an essential part of the software and offers a more complete solution to the developer. Its integration with the pure real estate elements of the system gives you a consistent and reliable tool for all aspects of the project that is only achievable in, say, self-created Excel models after considerable investment in time and after exhaustive and continuing auditing. Developer provides an off-the-shelf solution that a user can trust and apply to project after project.

■ **Tip**   Get to know the Structured Finance module. Its powerful capabilities can save you hours and hours of custom work you would otherwise have to do in an Excel spreadsheet created from scratch.

The Operated Assets Module

As noted in the introduction to this chapter, a deficiency in the early versions of Developer was an inability to model certain specialized types of real estate, particularly "operated assets" such as hotels, golf courses, and marinas. The Operated Assets module, introduced in Developer 4 in 2008, corrected this deficiency.

The Operated Assets module can be accessed either from the area tab in the Capitalized Income screen or from the ribbon bar on the control dashboard. The icon there is the third under the Definition group (Figure 3-16).

Figure 3-16. The ribbon bar showing the Operated Asset icon in the Definition group (right of center)

Clicking on this icon brings up a screen that allows the user to create a new operated asset profile. A completed profile is shown over the next few pages.

The Occupancy and Rates tabs allow the user to create a series of interrelated screens that, together, calculates the core income from the asset over a given time frame. In Figures 3-17, 3-18, and 3-19, the user has created such a set for a hotel. The first screen projects the expected occupancy percentage over the first eight years following completion. This can be defined as an average annual rate or as a month-by-month rate. The second screen lays out the number of rooms available to let; this is particular pertinent where the development is phased and completed rooms become income-producing over a longer period of time. Finally, the user defines a monthly Average Room Rate (AVR). The combination of these three will clearly give a good forecast of room income.

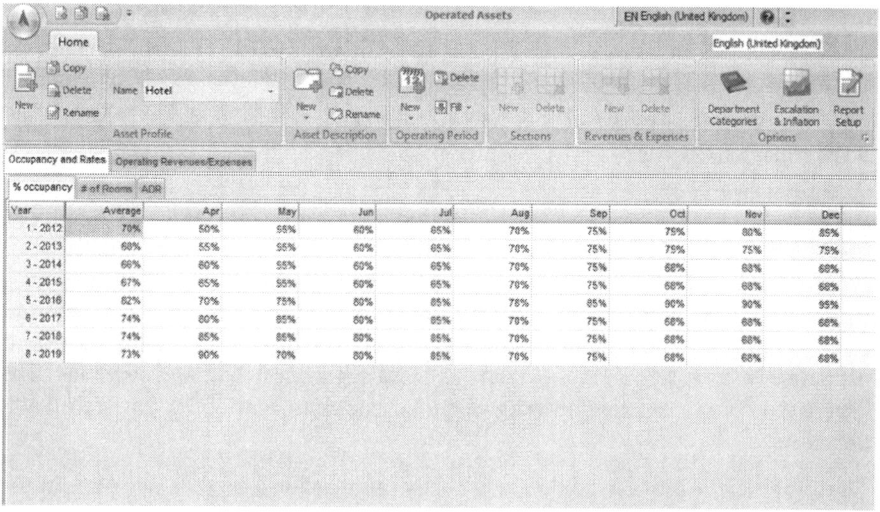

Year	Average	Apr	May	Jun	Jul	Aug	Sep	Oct	Nov	Dec
1 - 2012	70%	50%	55%	60%	65%	70%	75%	75%	80%	85%
2 - 2013	68%	55%	55%	60%	65%	70%	75%	75%	75%	75%
3 - 2014	66%	60%	55%	60%	65%	70%	75%	68%	68%	68%
4 - 2015	67%	65%	55%	60%	65%	70%	75%	68%	68%	68%
5 - 2016	82%	70%	75%	80%	85%	78%	85%	90%	90%	95%
6 - 2017	74%	80%	85%	80%	85%	70%	75%	68%	68%	68%
7 - 2018	74%	85%	85%	80%	85%	70%	75%	68%	68%	68%
8 - 2019	73%	90%	70%	80%	85%	70%	75%	68%	68%	68%

Figure 3-17. Example of Occupancy and Rates screen, percentage occupancy

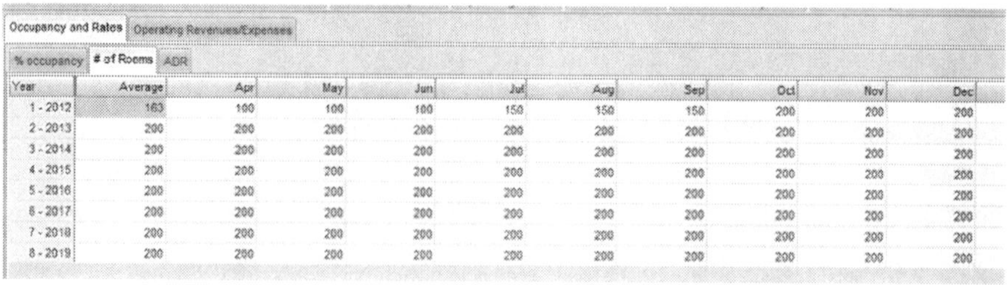

Year	Average	Apr	May	Jun	Jul	Aug	Sep	Oct	Nov	Dec
1 - 2012	163	100	100	100	150	150	150	200	200	200
2 - 2013	200	200	200	200	200	200	200	200	200	200
3 - 2014	200	200	200	200	200	200	200	200	200	200
4 - 2015	200	200	200	200	200	200	200	200	200	200
5 - 2016	200	200	200	200	200	200	200	200	200	200
6 - 2017	200	200	200	200	200	200	200	200	200	200
7 - 2018	200	200	200	200	200	200	200	200	200	200
8 - 2019	200	200	200	200	200	200	200	200	200	200

Figure 3-18. Example of Occupancy and Rates screen, number of rooms

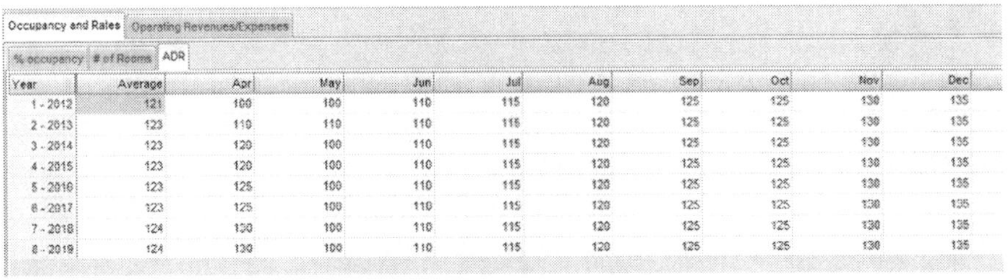

Year	Average	Apr	May	Jun	Jul	Aug	Sep	Oct	Nov	Dec
1 - 2012	121	100	100	110	115	120	125	125	130	135
2 - 2013	123	110	110	110	115	120	125	125	130	135
3 - 2014	123	120	100	110	115	120	125	125	130	135
4 - 2015	123	120	100	110	115	120	125	125	130	135
5 - 2016	123	125	100	110	115	120	125	125	130	135
6 - 2017	123	125	100	110	115	120	125	125	130	135
7 - 2018	124	130	100	110	115	120	125	125	130	135
8 - 2019	124	130	100	110	115	120	125	125	130	135

Figure 3-19. Example of Occupancy and Rates screen, average room rate

All of this will not, however, give you the true income figure for the development. In an operated asset, there will be other elements that earn income—food and bar income in the case of a hotel—and there will also be the running and variable costs such as staff, administrative overheads, depreciation, and so forth. All of this will have to be taken into account, and this is what the second sub-tab, Operating Revenues/Expenses, allows you to forecast.

Excerpts from the example are illustrated in Figures 3-20, 3-21, and 3-22. You can define any number of individual elements, and each one can have multiple expense and income lines attached to it. For example the Room Revenue line (shown over two figures here so the detail can be more easily seen) has four different revenue streams—three that arise from the different types of rooms in the hotel and the fourth from the food income that is tied to the level of room occupation. Similarly, the category of room expenses (Figure 3-22) has six different cost elements, some of which are occupancy dependent (in other words, the more rooms occupied, the more cleaning/servicing and other costs will increase).

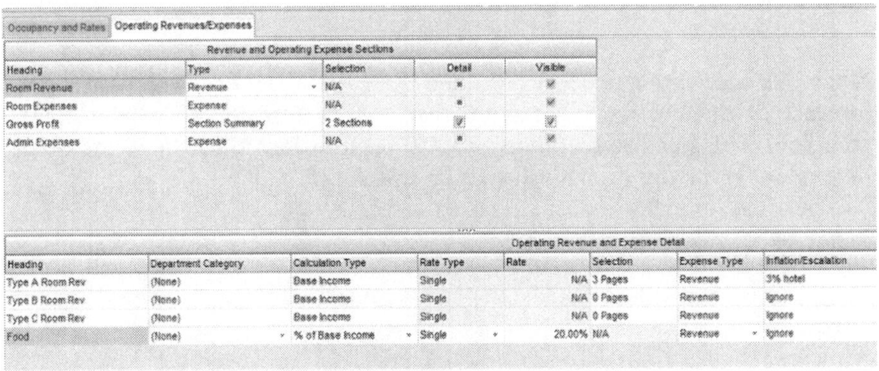

Revenue and Operating Expense Sections				
Heading	Type	Selection	Detail	Visible
Room Revenue	Revenue	N/A	*	✓
Room Expenses	Expense	N/A	*	✓
Gross Profit	Section Summary	2 Sections	✓	✓
Admin Expenses	Expense	N/A	*	✓

Operating Revenue and Expense Detail							
Heading	Department Category	Calculation Type	Rate Type	Rate	Selection	Expense Type	Inflation/Escalation
Type A Room Rev	(None)	Base Income	Single	N/A	3 Pages	Revenue	3% hotel
Type B Room Rev	(None)	Base Income	Single	N/A	0 Pages	Revenue	Ignore
Type C Room Rev	(None)	Base Income	Single	N/A	0 Pages	Revenue	Ignore
Food	(None)	% of Base Income	Single	20.00%	N/A	Revenue	Ignore

Figure 3-20. Operating Revenues/Expenses screen, Room Revenue left

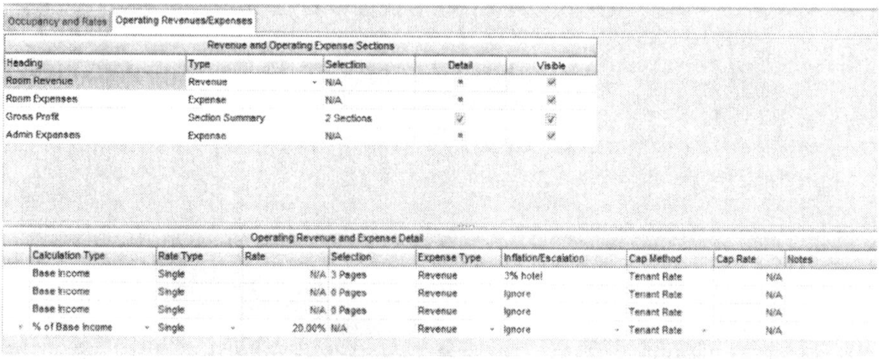

Figure 3-21. Operating Revenues/Expenses screen, Room Revenue right

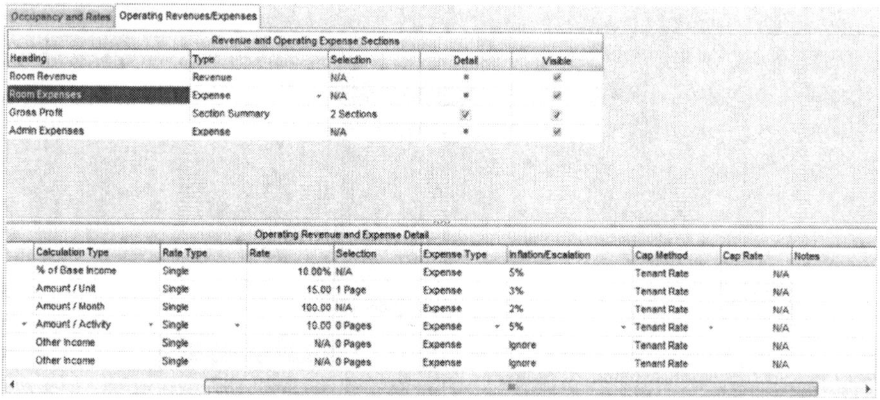

Figure 3-22. Operating Revenues/Expenses screen, Room Expenses

Once this accounting process has been completed, the user will have a good forecast of the net income stream that will be transferred to the project cash flow. The stabilized income will also be transferred to the Areas screen (Figure 3-23) for the capital value to be calculated.

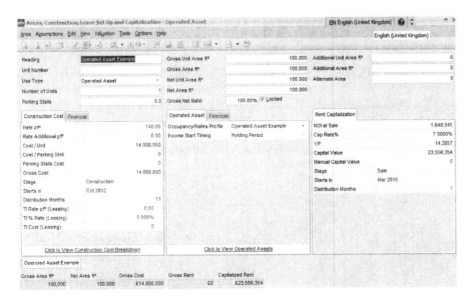

Figure 3-23. Transfer of calculated operated asset income to Area screen in Definitions tab

This is just a taste of how the Operated Asset module works, but even from this brief introduction it should be apparent how capable the module is and how it has opened up Developer to being able to model the development of virtually all categories of real estate. Later in the book, I will look in more detail at the appraisal of a pay-and-play golf course, which will give a more detailed step-through of the construction of an operated asset development appraisal.

Summary

Two of the three modules covered in this section, the Operated Assets module and the Structured Finance module, are relatively recent additions to the program, while the third, the Sensitivity Analysis module, has existed in some form from the very start. The latter is perhaps not used as much as it should be. All modules are, I believe, essential for the future success of the software and underline its position as the "go-to" tool for anyone wanting to conduct a development appraisal.

We will look at all three modules again in more detail as we work through examples later in this book.

Now we have looked at the main components of Developer. Over the next few chapters, we will look at it in action, examining how it can easily model the development of a range of real estate types and complexities of projects.

Commercial Feasibility Studies

Argus Developer Case Studies

The appraisal of commercial development projects is one of the primary activities for professionals involved in appraisal and development consultancies. The types of real estate involved are varied; they include offices, retail units, industrial buildings, and warehousing. One common feature is that they are income producing—or at least potentially so in the case of owner-occupied buildings—and their value is determined by reference to this income stream and the value that potential investors place upon them. This assessment is reflected in the capitalization rate and discount rates applied to this income stream. This relationship, and the projects themselves, can be complex and involved. It was exactly this type of project that Developer was designed to deal with.

We will start with some relatively simple projects in order to understand the workings of the software. Later, we will look at the appraisal of more complex projects.

Simple One Building/One Type/One Phase Commercial Project

The initial project we will be appraising is the development of a speculative single, three-level office building on a greenfield site. Here are the details:

- The site is clear and flat and has an area of 10,000 square feet.

- The building will have a plan area of 3,000 square feet and will be steel-framed with concrete floors, brick and block walls, and casement windows. It will be ventilated naturally.

- Eighty percent of the grounds of the building will be given over to car parking. The remainder of the area will be landscaped.

- The construction will start three months after the completion of the land purchase. Construction will take six months, and we will assume an additional six months to rent all the spaces.

- Tenants will expect to receive a three-month, rent-free period on five-year leases.

- Current interest rates for development loans are 6 percent.

- The developer will sell the building on leasing.

For this development only, we will do the calculation both for land residual, (in other words, land price or valuation) and for profitability.

Land Bid Calculation

The first step in appraising this project is to fill in the identification information on the Project screen and to create a Save file for the project (Figure 4-1). Developer does not automatically save the data although, like Excel, it has a recovery save function. It will also prompt you to save upon closing the program.

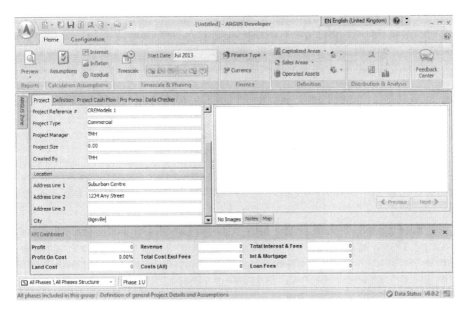

Figure 4-1. Project screen

Once we have entered the address data, we can save the project. I recommend that you save the project file regularly as data is entered (Figure 4-2).

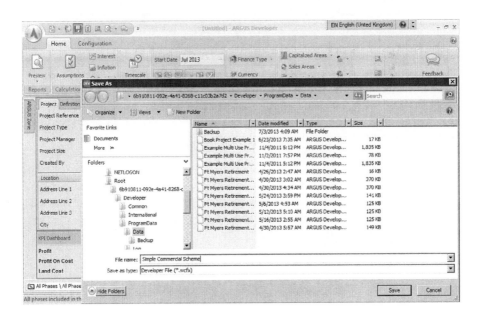

Figure 4-2. Saving the project in Argus Developer

■ **Tip** Save regularly. Though Developer has an automatic save feature, you may lose some data in a power outage or crash.

Assumptions

The next step is to review the assumptions for calculations and to make the necessary entries for interest costs and mode of calculation.

You can access the assumption options from the drop-down menu, the button on the icon ribbon, or else the button on the Project tab itself. All take you to the same screen.

As I have already noted in the introduction, Developer has a template pre-loaded. The template uses reasonable assumptions that are derived from market experience and are applicable to many projects. The user can adjust all of the pre-set assumptions in the template.

Over the next few pages, I show the assumptions for each individual sub-tab and will outline what each of the options are.

■ **Note** I will not do an appraisal in such detail later in this book. Therefore, do your best to understand the preliminary setup procedures now.

Expenditure Assumptions

The expenditure assumptions contained within the template (Figure 4-3) are, as with other aspects, those that are most commonly used in the development market, with the most popular alternative options available by checking the appropriate button. This section deals with the calculation of professional fees, the treatment of the purchaser's costs, and sale fees.

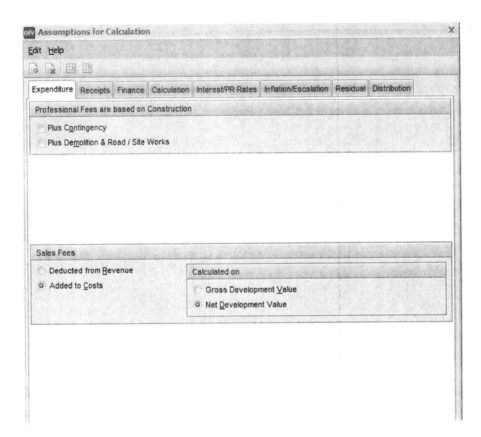

Figure 4-3. Expenditure assumptions

The default settings for professional fees are for them to be calculated against the build cost, which is the more common option in projects. However, this definition can be widened if the professional team has wider responsibilities. Again, this is only the global setup; any individual item of expenditure or receipts in Developer can be individually defined later in the program. Here the default is to set professional fees as a percentage of the costs expended, but the user can define the professional fees as, say, a lump sum if required.

Similar switching options are available for the treatment of (incoming) purchaser's costs and sale fees (that is, the developer's cost of disposal). With the former, the default is to deduct the costs from the sale receipts. However, for lending and performance reasons, some developers prefer to add the purchaser's costs to the development costs.

Receipts Assumptions

The next setup assumptions deal with receipts (Figure 4-4).

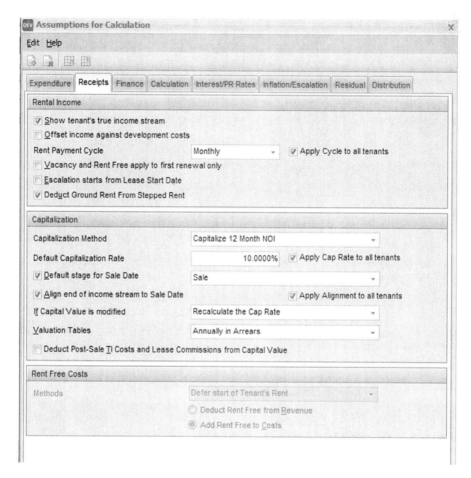

Figure 4-4. Receipts standard assumptions

The receipts section is similarly set up with the industry norms (for the UK market, at least) in mind. It is divided into two sections, the first dealing with the rental income stream, and the second with the capitalization assumptions.

There is a third, grayed-out section, which allows an alternative treatment of any rent-free period in the development calculation. This section is made live by unchecking "Show tenants true income stream" in the Rental Income section. The user would normally do this to switch the rent-free period to a development cost rather than as a deduction from capital value, a common choice for developers as it gives them financing advantages by maximizing the projected end value of the scheme.

The top part of the screen deals with the income stream that the development produces. Options available include switching the income cycle from the default setting, which is usually monthly, to perhaps a quarterly or semi-annual income cycle. For residential investments, for example, it would be more appropriate to select a monthly income pattern. Note, however, that these changes will only have a significant impact if there is a substantial "hold" period envisaged.

The lower half of the tab deals with the capitalization of this income stream. The capitalization of income is normally calculated and defined within the Area sheets accessed from the Definitions tab. However, it is possible to set a global capitalization rate. In practice, this option is rarely used.

Finance Assumptions

The third of the assumption screen tabs deals with finance (Figures 4-5 and 4-6).

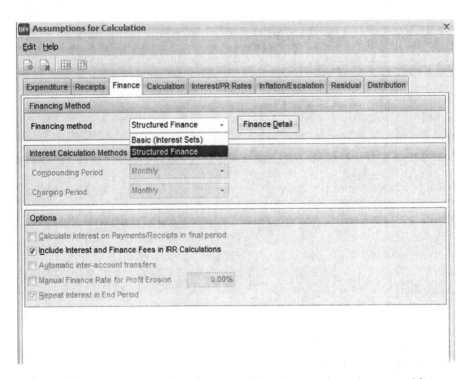

Figure 4-5. Switching between basic finance module and more advanced, structured finance assumptions in Developer

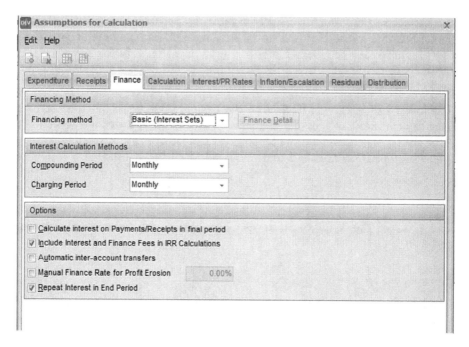

Figure 4-6. Finance standard assumptions

Argus Developer's base version, in which all the models presented in this chapter are constructed, has a relatively simple finance module, although it can be used in quite a sophisticated way with the ability to set multiple rates and to tie any loan into any element of the project. To do proper debt/equity analysis, however, you must purchase the structured finance module (except in the United States, where it comes standard with the program). This is a very sophisticated tool, allowing the modeling of complex financing and joint-venture arrangements.

As you'll see, the standard module allows you to make a global change to the compounding and charging periods. You can also choose whether the interest is nominal or effective—in other words, the program can take account of the number of charging periods in the year.

You'll find five switching options at the bottom of this screen, which allow for fine-tuning the finance assumptions. Normally, these would all remain unchecked. However, in our scenario, the client has requested specific assumptions to be made.

Other than this, I'm using the normal setup; the only option I feel that should be made is to switch the quarterly compounding period to monthly because it is far more common in today's market.

Inflation/Escalation Assumptions

Argus Developer allows you to model changes in costs (inflation) and values (growth) (Figure 4-7). Users can create a number of modeled sets. The mere creation of these sets will not, in themselves, make any changes to the appraisal. The assumptions have to be manually ascribed to elements in the appraisal (using the drill-down function as outlined in the software summary). This is sensible, as these assumptions can make the appraisal extremely volatile.

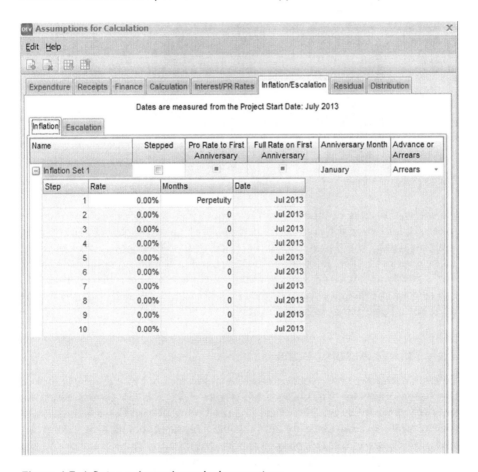

Figure 4-7. Inflation and growth standard assumptions

Distribution Assumptions

The next section to consider concerns the distribution of payments and receipts (Figure 4-8).

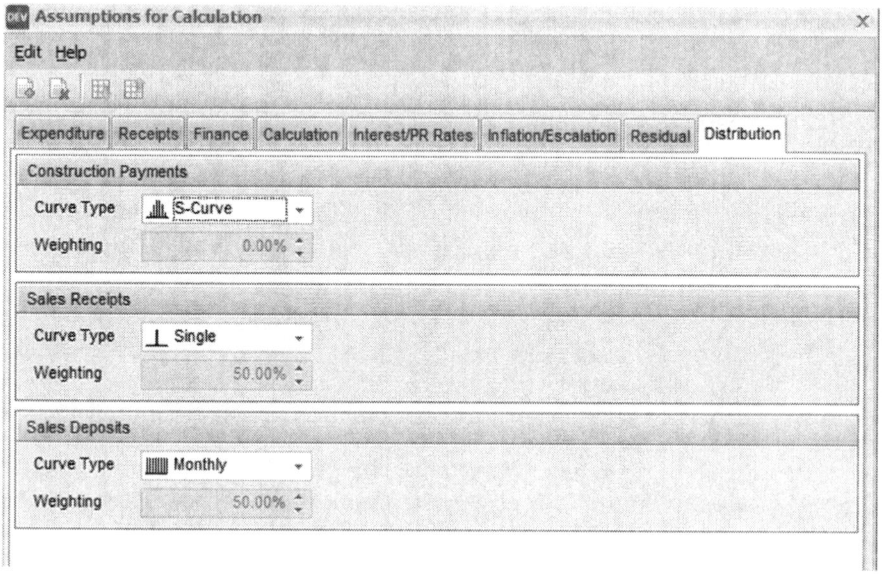

Figure 4-8. Distribution standard assumptions

As with all aspects of inputs into Developer, you can model all distributions manually. However, for convenience, there are the most popular distribution options within the assumptions for calculation, allowing you to construct quick appraisals. The template is built around a simple commercial project. For a residential scheme, with multiple sales over a longer time period, you can select a more appropriate distribution, though this would normally just be done for a basic, initial feasibility study.

Calculation Assumptions

Before dealing with the sections where changes must be made, we will look at the Assumptions for Calculations tab (Figure 4-9). This tab covers details on how you treat the mechanics regarding the timing of cash flows in and out, as well as how you'll calculate IRR, and the like. This tab contains a lot of information, reflecting the transparency of the program to the user, and showing just how it is set up to calculate and allow fine tuning.

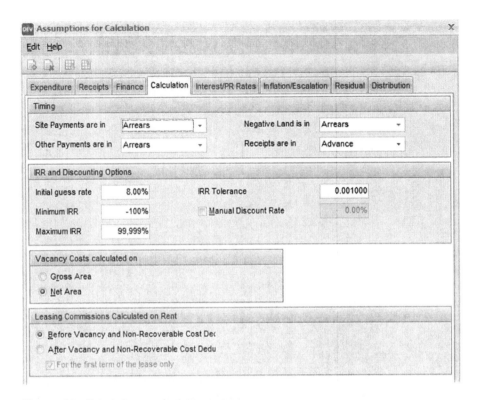

Figure 4-9. Calculation standard assumptions

I am content to let the standard assumptions run for this appraisal.

Interest Rate and Residual Assumptions

There are, however, two entries that must be made, and these entries are found on the tabs that I have not yet reviewed. The items we must address in this appraisal are the Interest Sets (Figure 4-10) and the Mode of Calculation, found on the Residual tab (Figure 4-11).

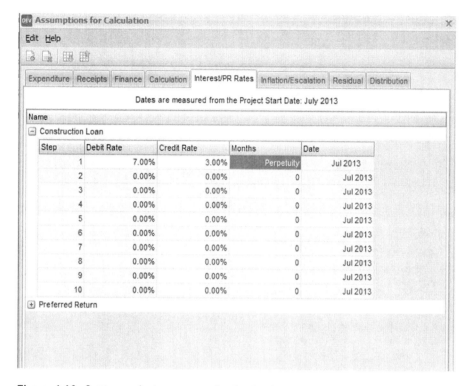

Figure 4-10. Setting up the interest sets for the development

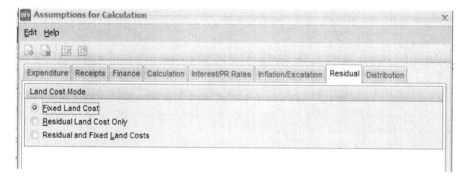

Figure 4-11. The standard Residual tab setup

Developer needs at least one entry in the Interest Sets section. Multiple sets can be created but the program, by default, only reads the first one on the list; any subsequent ones have to be allocated to specific items in the Definitions tab. You will note that there are two columns in the basic interest sets module; the debit column is the rate of interest on borrowed money, while the credit column deals with interest earned on project surpluses. The only requirement is to make an entry into the debit column, as shown here.

Note also the column with the heading Months. This column allows the modeling of variable interest rates, so it is possible to have, say 6% applying for 12 months and then 5.75% thereafter. I advise that, when you create these structured interest sets, you put a rate of zero in the final spot in the Months column and "perpetuity" in the first spot as shown. This has the meaning of "and thereafter" in Developer and avoids the interest rate charged on the development dropping to zero after the modeled structured element has expired.

I will cover the use of structured and multiple interest sets in later sections and examples.

The final area that we need to address at the assumptions stage is the mode of calculation.

As noted in the introduction, development appraisal/feasibility studies are undertaken to answer one of two alternative questions. First, what amount can be bid for the land while meeting the required target return? Second, where the cost of the land is known, what profit (or loss) will the project generate? Quite frequently a developer may well run the calculation in one mode in order to inform their bid to secure the site, and then later in the other mode as a development-monitoring and project-design tool.

Note that Developer also has a third option, a part residual land value/part profits calculation mode used only in special circumstances.

Because we are doing a land residual calculation, we need to change the setup of the program, as the default setting is to calculate development profitability against a known land value.

Clicking the Residualized Land Value Only option (Figure 4-12) allows assumptions to be made regarding the required developer's profit, the element that has to be fixed as a target so that the unknown element in the development appraisal—the land value—can be calculated.

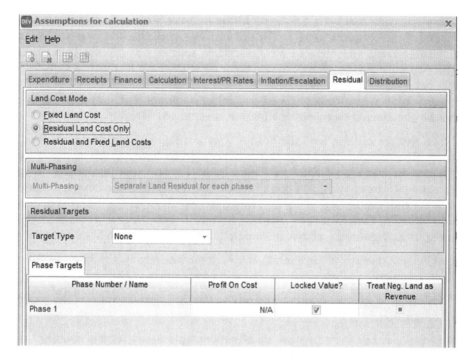

Figure 4-12. The Residual screen with Residual Land Cost Only selected

Developer has five options for developer's profit (Figure 4-13). The most commonly used is Profit on Cost, the total sums actually expended on the project. The alternatives are less frequently used. Profit on GDV (Gross Development Value) is profit related to the end value of the scheme. It excludes the costs involved in selling the building. IRR is Internal Rate of Return, the standard tool for measuring the returns from an investment. Because development is a form of investment, sometimes using this measure is more appropriate. Development Yield allows the developer to define a yield, or return that the scheme must produce in terms of income on completion relative to the costs of completing it. Similarly, developers simply want to make a particular sum, and the program is flexible enough to allow you to calculate this option (Profit Amount).

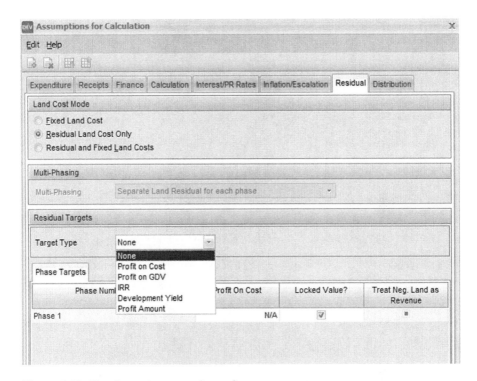

Figure 4-13. The alternative targets for profit

In this example, we will stick to return on cost, as this is the most common benchmark used (Figure 4-14). We will use a rate of 20 percent, which may appear high to the layman but is a normal benchmark for a commercial scheme. We shall see later that the geared nature of appraisal (the relationship between end value and input costs) means that development is a high-risk endeavor and such wide margins are necessary to cover the risk elements.

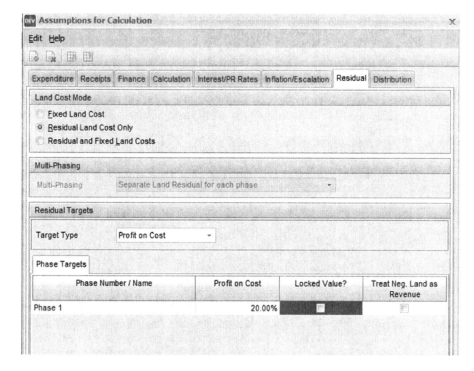

Figure 4-14. The Residual screen final setup

Note that the Locked Value and Treat Negative Land Value as Revenue should remain unchecked at this stage.

Once this screen is closed, you'll receive a warning that the mode of calculation has been changed (Figure 4-15). Often, too, the data checker reports that no land value can be calculated (Figure 4-16). This is perfectly normal at this stage, and you can ignore it.

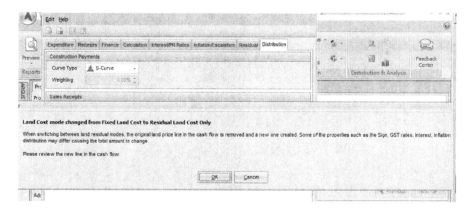

Figure 4-15. Data check warning screen, which can be ignored at this stage

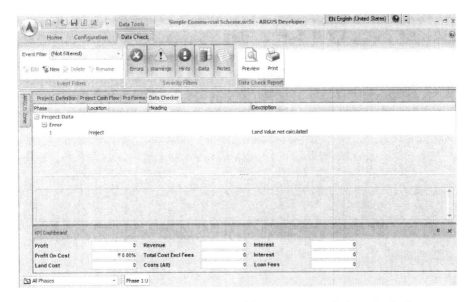

Figure 4-16. Don't worry about the inability of the program to calculate a land value at this stage

Timescale and Phasing

The next element we must deal with is timescale. The Timescale and Phasing section of the program is intended to set up the broad timings only. The cash flow template preloaded into development has elements of the project associated with certain time elements, and setting up the timescales allows these to work. These assumptions can be viewed by selecting File/Administration/View Cash Flow Templates from the drop-down menus (Figures 4-17, 4-18, and 4-19).

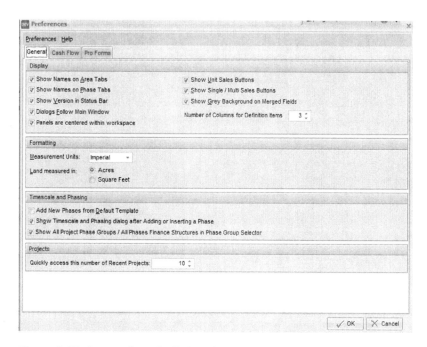

Figure 4-17. Extracts from the Default Cash Flow Template showing associations and timings (1)

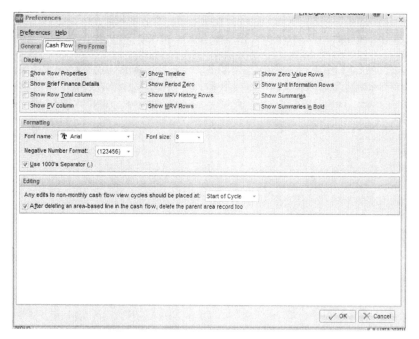

Figure 4-18. Extracts from the Default Cash Flow Template showing associations and timings (2)

Preferences

Preferences Help

General Cash Flow Pro Forma

Show Itemized Schedules

- [ ] Rental Area Summary
- [x] Investment Valuation
- [x] Itemized Tenant Income
- [ ] Itemized Rent Free Costs
- [x] Itemized Additional Revenue

- [x] Itemized Fixed Acquisition Costs
- [x] Itemized Other Acquisition Costs
- [x] Itemized Construction Costs
- [x] Itemized Other Construction Costs
- [x] Itemized Other Professional Fees

- [x] Itemized Additional Costs
- [x] Itemized Inflation/Escalation Schedule
- [ ] Timescale

Show Performance Measures

- [x] Pre-Finance IRR
- [x] IRR
- [x] Equity IRR (Composite)
- [x] Return on Equity (Composite)
- [ ] IRR Scenario Dates
- [x] NPV (at Manual Discount Rate)
- [x] After Tax IRR
- [x] After Tax Equity IRR (Composite)
- [x] After Tax Return on Equity (Composite)

- [x] Profit on Cost
- [x] Profit on GDV
- [x] Profit on NDV
- [x] Development Yield
- [x] Rent Cover
- [x] Profit Erosion

- [x] Equivalent Yield (True)
- [x] Equivalent Yield (Nominal)
- [ ] Gross Initial Yield
- [ ] Net Initial Yield
- [ ] Capitalized Rent per Net ft²
- [ ] Cost per Gross ft²
- [ ] Cost per Net ft²
- [ ] Floor Area Ratio
- [ ] Land Cost per Acre

Formatting

Visible Columns:	7	Font name: Arial	Font size:	9
Heading Column Width (Pixels):	200			
Data Column Width (Pixels):	100			
Number of Decimals:	2			

✓ OK   ✗ Cancel

Figure 4-19. Extracts from the Default Cash Flow Template showing associations and timings (3)

Developer allows you to save separate assumptions for different user-defined projects as a template. (How to do so is beyond the scope of this book.)

■ **Note** Remember, the assumptions made for any individual cost or value element can be overridden by the user.

Pressing the shortcut button (Figure 4-20) from the main project screen brings up the setup screen for Timescale and Phasing (Figure 4-21).

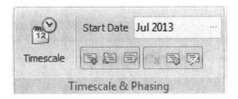

Figure 4-20. The Timescale and Phasing shortcut

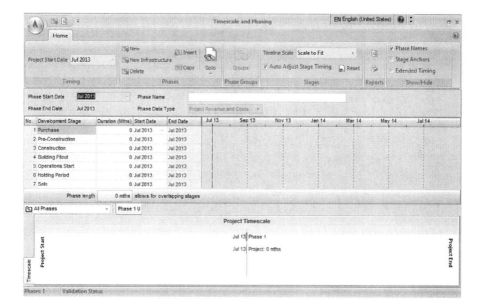

Figure 4-21. Timescale and Phasing screen

Development Stages

As you can see, Developer uses seven broad development stages. These cannot be increased, although the names of each stage can be changed. Not all the stages need to have a time set against them, only those that are appropriate.

Some users on first introduction to this section of the program are surprised that only seven stages are defined. To them, this seems to be oversimplifying and restrictive. In practice, however, it is not. As noted, these are just broadbrush timings. Any individual item can be separately timed, the stages can overlap, and the ability to add phases that can be consecutive or concurrent (or, indeed, both) means that the program can deal with the vast majority (if not all) of specific timing requirements. The Timescale and Phasing tab is essentially a visualization tool, albeit with key expenditure and receipts tied to it via the default template.

In our case, we will be using only three of the sections: The three-month planning period, the sixth-month construction phase, and the sixth-month rental phase (Figure 4-22).

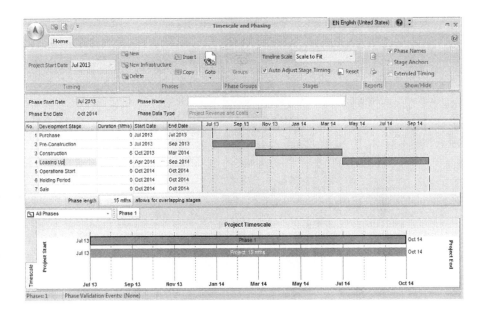

Figure 4-22. The Timescale and Phasing screen as set up for our development

---

Tip You can obtain data on timescales for projects from a number of sources including the client, architect, or surveyor, as well as from experience of other, similar projects. Sometimes, however, particularly at the feasibility stage of a project, a surveyor may have to simply form a reasoned judgment on timings.

The Purchase stage allows for a delayed, or staged, land purchase; Operations Start is designed for a snagging (fixing problems) and fitting-out period best suited to the development of a building for a known end user; Holding Period is for retained investments; and Sale allows the modeling of a longer sale period (usually) for multiple units as is found with residential schemes. As you can see, none of these stages are really appropriate for our simple speculative scheme produced by a developer-trader.

Developer is now set up to receive data. We can, therefore, move onto the Definitions tab (Figure 4-23), remembering to save our project.

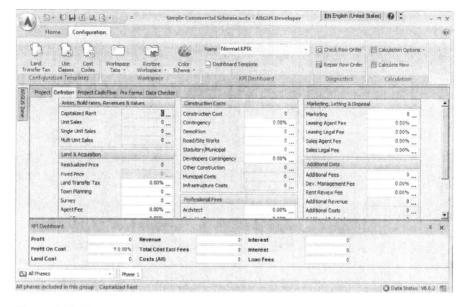

Figure 4-23. The Definitions tab for our project

Project Definitions

The starting point for our project on this screen is to drill behind the Capitalized Rent box, double-clicking the three dots (Figure 4-24) to open up the Area screen. This is where the majority of the cost and value assumptions will be made.

Project	Definition	Project Cash Flow	Pro Forma	Data Checker
	Areas, Build rates, Revenues & Values			
	Capitalized Rent			⬛ ...
	Unit Sales			0 ...
	Single Unit Sales			0 ...
	Multi Unit Sales			0 ...

Figure 4-24. The shortcuts to the Area screens

The commercial Area screen can be viewed in different modes in the program, but the most common view used is the detailed screen shown in Figure 4-25.

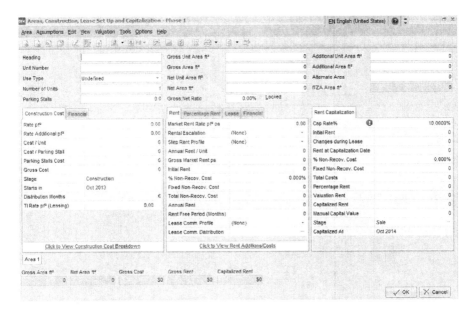

Figure 4-25. The Capitalized Rent Area screen

The Area screen is divided into four functional areas. The top part of the screen defines the use type (mostly used for the reporting and sensitivity elements) and allows the setting of areas, both the Gross Area (that is, the built area) and the Net Area (the Net Rentable Area). The latter can be entered directly or else estimated using the Gross to Net Ratio function. Note the program allows the modeling of multiple units of the same size/type (Number of Units). You can define other areas such as parking spaces and. In this case, I am using the additional areas for the landscaping and car park areas, which will be costed later in the appraisal.

The mid-left area of the screen is where the main construction cost calculation and modeling takes place (Figure 4-26; detail in 4-27). The construction frame takes the measurement data entered into the program, using the Gross Area to calculate the costs plus any entry for parking spaces and the like. The cost data can be entered in one of four ways: a rate per unit of measurement (in this case cost per square foot), a cost per unit, the overall unit cost, or a detailed construction cost breakdown if a detailed estimate is available.

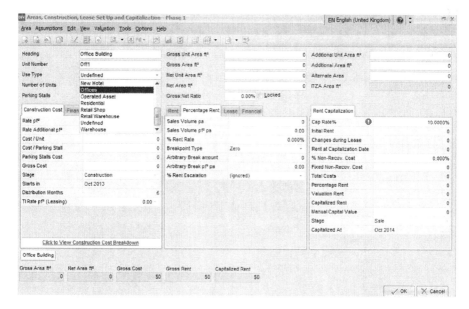

Figure 4-26. Use type and areas

Construction Cost	Financial	
Rate pf²		140.00
Rate Additional pf²		0.00
Cost / Unit		1,260,000
Cost / Parking Stall		0
Parking Stalls Cost		0
Gross Cost		1,260,000
Stage	Construction	...
Starts in	Oct 2013	
Distribution Months		6
TI Rate pf² (Leasing)		0.00 ...

Click to View Construction Cost Breakdown

Figure 4-27. Construction calculation frame

Note that the TI boxes in the bottom part of this frame relate to tenant improvements, works that can be scheduled to meet the requirements of an individual tenant and where a separate cost estimate is required.

Construction cost information can be surprisingly hard to obtain. Most up-to-date cost information is collected and sold by commercial organizations. The situation is made more complex by the extremes in the range in costs displayed in construction. Similarly specified buildings, for example, have very different construction costs depending on whether they are located in the center of a major city, or in a greenfield, edge-of-town location. The cost of constructing an office can easily range from a few tens of dollars to several hundred dollars per square foot depending on type, specification, and location.

Tip Anyone conducting a development appraisal is well advised to consult a construction cost specialist and to look at the specifications and location very carefully.

The timing and distribution of the construction costs can be viewed by pressing the shortcut button on the Stage row (Figure 4-28). The timing and distribution can be amended by checking Custom Timing (Figure 4-29).

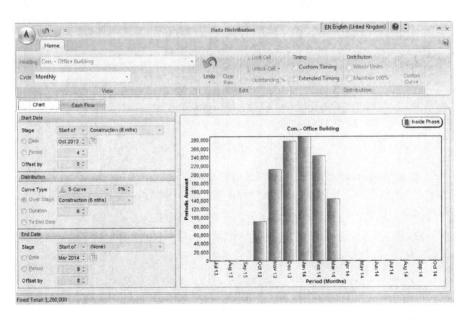

Figure 4-28. Construction cost distribution details indicating level of control possible summary

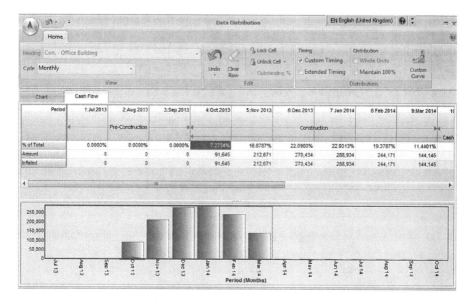

Figure 4-29. Construction cost distribution details indicating level of control possible detail

You can then manipulate the data using the three edit boxes available or by clicking into the data distribution editor, which opens up a mini-spreadsheet. A fifth amendment option is to do the revisions in the Cash Flow tab of the program. It should be noted that the amendments made to any individual item do not affect the global timing assumptions. Thus, it is easily possible to adjust the timing of just one building among a group of buildings in isolation.

In this case, I am content with the distribution that the program has given me and I will make no adjustments.

Note that there is a second frame behind the calculation area in Figure 4-28 that deals with finance. This allows the allocation of a different interest set and the individual (rather than global) treatment of GST. There is no absolute need to adjust these values and I will leave them in the default setting for this appraisal.

The lower center part of the Area screen (Figure 4-30) is where the income screen for the developed property is calculated. There are three possible modes of data entry: a rate per unit area, annual rent per unit, or gross annual rent (which is the same as the previous when there is only one unit).

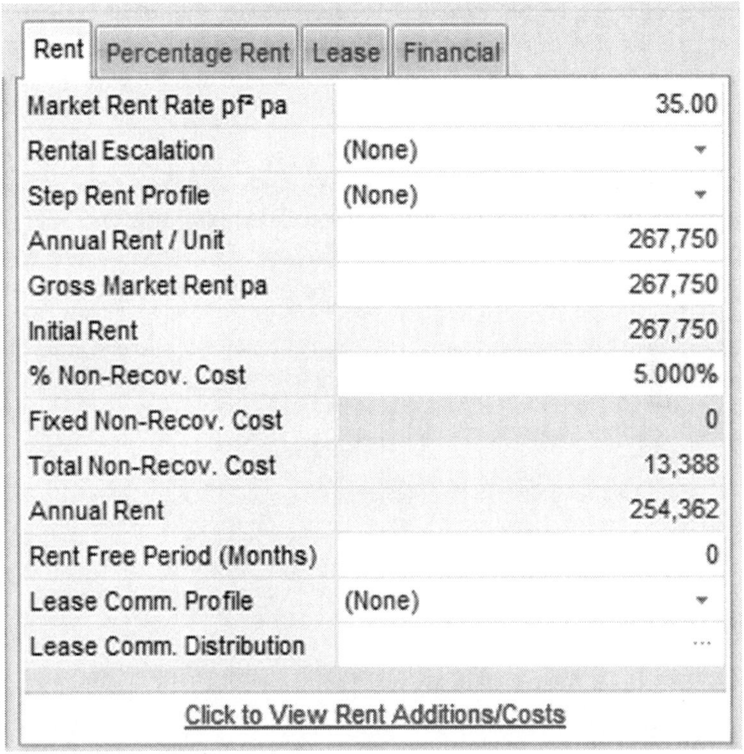

Rent	Percentage Rent	Lease	Financial
Market Rent Rate pf² pa		35.00
Rental Escalation	(None)	▼
Step Rent Profile	(None)	▼
Annual Rent / Unit		267,750
Gross Market Rent pa		267,750
Initial Rent		267,750
% Non-Recov. Cost		5.000%
Fixed Non-Recov. Cost		0
Total Non-Recov. Cost		13,388
Annual Rent		254,362
Rent Free Period (Months)		0
Lease Comm. Profile	(None)	▼
Lease Comm. Distribution		...

Click to View Rent Additions/Costs

Figure 4-30. Rental calculation frame

Rental value is determined by what tenants will pay to lease property of a similar standard and in similar locations in the open market. In active markets, this can be relatively easy to determine, other than the fact that the development will be completed at some time in the future, during which time the economy and local market conditions may have changed radically. In other places and times it can be hard to find good evidence for rental values, such as where the building being developed is unusual for the area or when market conditions are difficult. In the downturns of 1990–93 and 2008 onward, property owners were offering such high rental incentives (rent-frees and the like) that it was very hard to determine the true level of rental value in many markets.

The frame allows adjustment for rental growth or escalation (which has to be defined in the Assumptions tab), a step rent profile (which has also to be defined but this is done within the Area screen via the drop-down menus), and any deductions for non-recoverable parts of the income stream.

It will be observed that there are three other calculation frames behind the main calculation frame. The first allows turnover rents, most commonly found in shopping centers, to be modeled. In the second, the lease assumptions in the template are laid out. These would only need to be altered if a long-term holding of the property were envisaged, or if some special arrangement (like a rent holiday) had been made with a tenant.

The center lower right part of the Area screen is given over to the calculation of income frame (Figure 4-31). This is where the data from the income stream frame (Figure 4-30) is capitalized to determine the end value of this part of the development output. By default, Developer assumes that the interest is freehold, but you can switch the program via the drop-down menu to a leasehold interest. This creates a frame behind the front screen that allows the entry of the head lease details such as rent, review pattern, and duration. However, in this case, we are dealing with a freehold property.

Rent Capitalization		
Cap Rate%		7.0000%
Initial Rent		267,750
Changes during Lease		0
Rent at Capitalization Date		254,362
% Non-Recov. Cost		5.000%
Fixed Non-Recov. Cost		0
Total Costs		13,388
Percentage Rent		0
Valuation Rent		254,362
Capitalized Rent		3,633,750
Manual Capital Value		0
Stage	Sale	...
Capitalized At	Oct 2014	

Figure 4-31. The capitalization of income frame

There are two modes of calculating the capital value of the freehold interest. You can either enter a cap rate yield into the appropriate box or enter a figure in Manual Capital Value. The latter might be required where a presale agreement had been entered into.

Yield, like rental value, is market-determined. It is essentially the annual return that the investment owner will accept given the quality of the income stream (determined by a complex combination of the quality of the tenant, the length and quality of the lease, the quality of the building, and the attractiveness of the location, among other things) and the returns obtainable on rival investments, both property and others. Office yields have as broad a range as office rents and office costs. Careful research is required to place the completed investment in its correct standing in the market.

As with all elements of Developer, it is possible to adjust the timing and distribution of the projected sale receipts by clicking the three dots next to the Stage row in Figure 4-31 and bringing up the distribution screen. The same options for altering the distribution and timing as were available with the construction section are available here and, indeed, with all other elements of the appraisal (Figure 4-32).

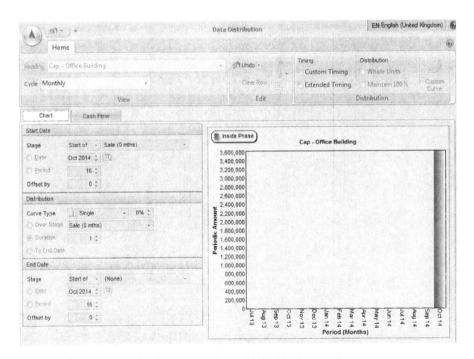

Figure 4-32. The Data Distribution screen for the disposal of the freehold interest

Figure 4-33 shows the Areas screen with all the assumptions for our project in place.

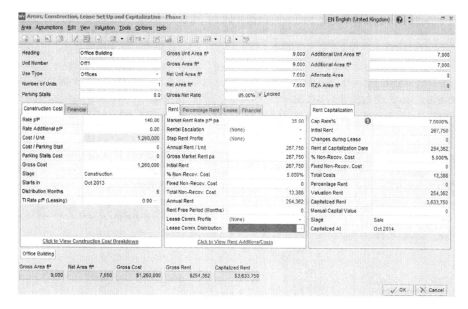

Figure 4-33. The completed Area tab for our development

When you have completed the Areas screen, click the green OK button to save the assumptions made. This returns us to the Definitions tab (Figure 4-34).

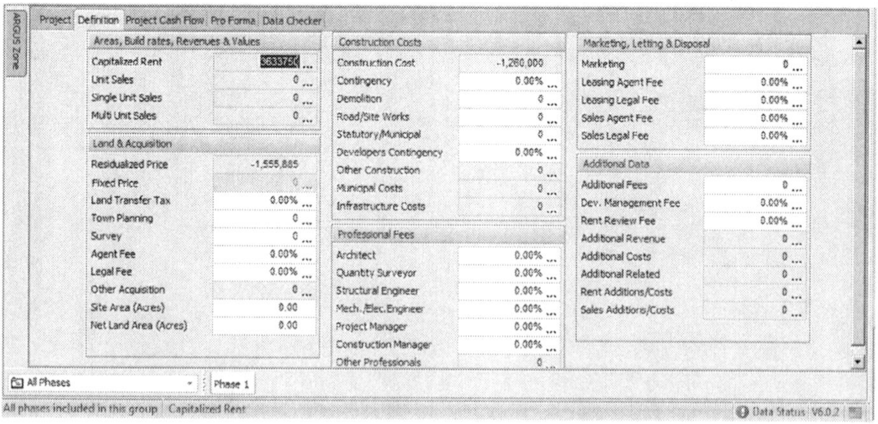

Figure 4-34. Definition tab after the Areas screen has been completed

You will note that the key values from the Areas screen have been imported in summary to the Definition tab, namely the construction costs and completed value (Residualized Price). Both boxes have been grayed out to indicate that they have been calculated outside of the definitions tab itself. No direct edit of these values is possible from here. Any changes have to be made by clicking back into the Area tab or else adjusting the values and distribution directly in the cash flow.

You complete the appraisal by entering the required values in the Definition tab. You can do this in one of two ways. The first approach is to enter figures directly into the appropriate open box on this screen and let the program distribute the values according to the template. Use this method when you need a quick appraisal, or if there are limited details of the scheme available as in an early stage feasibility study. With the second approach, you can drill down into each box and enter the details of the expenditure or receipts.

In this case, I have used the quick appraisal approach with the exception of the Road/Site Works box, where I have modeled the hard and soft landscaping by reference to the additional area I defined in the Area tab. The default setting in the template is a single lump sum item tied to the beginning of the construction stage. Here I have overridden the default (Figures 4-35 and 4-36), turning the item into a cost related to the alternative area, Landscaping. I have also adjusted the timing so that the expenditure occurs toward the end of the construction stage, as would occur in practice (Figure 4-37; indeed, I have allowed the Landscaping to run on into the Rental Phase).

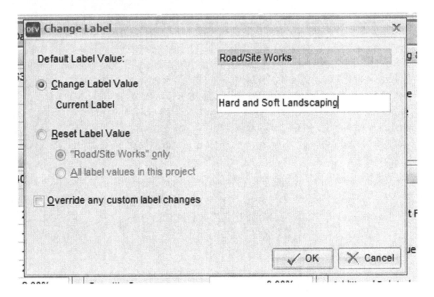

Figure 4-35. Changing the label from Road/Site Works to Hard and Soft Landscaping

Figure 4-36. Detail of the Hard and Soft Landscaping assumptions override

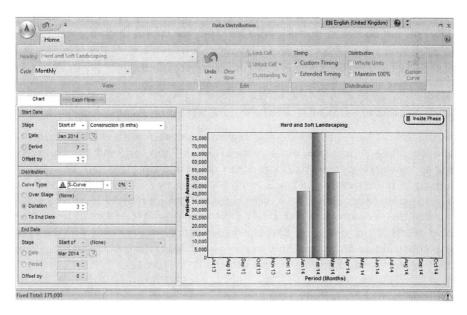

Figure 4-37. Overriding the related items set up

In all this I can illustrate the flexibility and power of Developer. You can use the program in its default mode and it will produce a quick and reasonably accurate appraisal. Or, if you have more information or there are some special assumptions, you can take control of any or all of the items making up the development and produce a tailored, more accurate model of the actual development project.

Note that the Definition tab is itself divided into functional areas for ease of calculation (Figure 4-38). The area to the bottom-left of the screen is generally connected with the site, its acquisition, and any investigations required pre and post purchase. There is also a section dealing with the costs of getting planning consent.

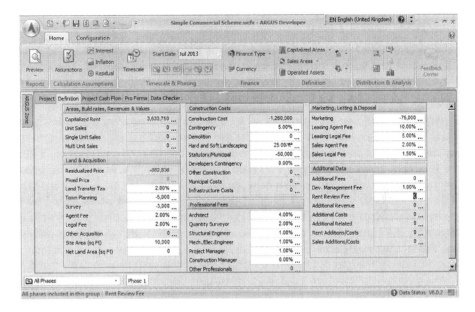

Figure 4-38. The resulting entry in the Definition screen

The upper-middle part of the Definition tab is where the main construction cost is reported and where any additional construction cost items are located. There are two contingency cells where you can make allowances for uncertainty in construction and other aspects of the development. There is also a section that deals with municipal fees. You often have to enable this in the software (under File/Administration/System Configuration/Country).

The lower-center part of the Definition tab is where the cost of the construction professional team is calculated. The default setting is that these are related to the construction costs, both those defined in the Area screen and any additional costs. These settings can be overridden by drilling down into the calculation screen behind the cell. This might be required where the professional team is working to fixed fees or where some special arrangement is required.

The top-right part of the Definition tab is where the disposal of the development is modeled. This includes cells for marketing, leasing, sale fees, and so on.

The lower-right part of the Definition tab is mainly a sweep-up area where any other costs or revenue streams not accounted for elsewhere can be modeled. It is worth noting once again that Developer's flexibility allows for most of the cells on the Definition tab to be renamed or tailored to meet the specific requirements of the scheme being appraised.

Project Cash Flow

The data entered into the Definition tab is automatically placed in the cash flow according to the template. Each data entry creates its own line in the cash flow and it is to the cash flow that we would normally go to once all the data has been input into the Distribution tab.

There have traditionally been two cash flows in Developer: the project cash flow and the finance cash flow. In the base, non-structured finance version of the program that we are initially examining, the finance cash flow is a set of summary rows that can be accessed via the View menu. In the structured finance version, the finance cash flow appears automatically on a separate tab. The project cash flow shows each of the individual income and expenditure items in the assumed time frame and distribution either according to that laid down by the template or according to the individual distribution determined by the modeler (Figures 4-39 and 4-40). These cash flows are, in the main, open to be altered; as noted in the introduction, the cash flow in the program is the primary calculation tool. It is an output, but it is also a tool for fine-tuning the appraisal model.

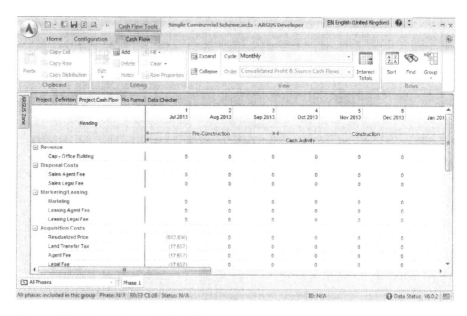

Figure 4-39. Extract from the Cash Flow screen

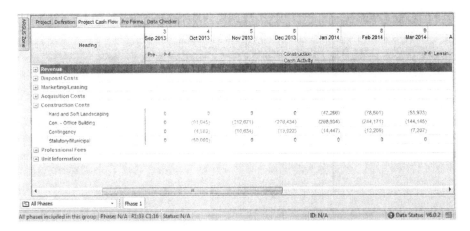

Figure 4-40. Detail of the Cash Flow tab

This can be illustrated using the marketing line. The standard template puts the marketing expenditure into the beginning of the leasing period, which is not unreasonable for an initial feasibility study. It would be more accurate, however, to spread the expenditure over part of the construction phase, as it is almost certain that the marketing campaign would start far earlier than this to ensure that the income stream would start as soon as possible.

Note There is a strong imperative for the developer/trader of a speculative development to achieve a full leasing as the investment is not sellable unless it is 100 percent let. Without the sale, a developer/trader cannot recoup their development costs and realize their profits.

You can alter the distribution of this line in the Definition tab, but you can also adjust it via the cash flow. You can do this in two ways. One way is to click into the line and select Data Distribution from the drop-down menu (Figure 4-41).

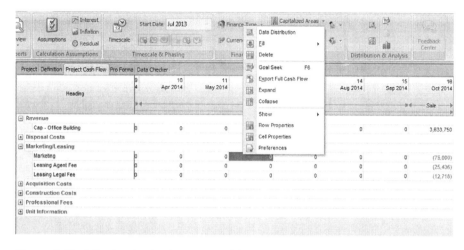

Figure 4-41. Adjusting the development model via the cash flow

This opens up the Data Distribution screen pertinent to this line (Figure 4-42); the process for adjustment is as discussed in earlier sections.

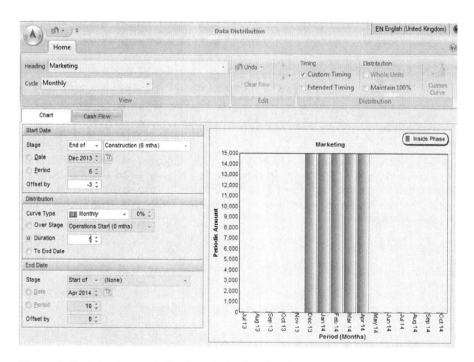

Figure 4-42. Adjusting a cash flow line via the data distribution

The alternative way of adjusting the distribution is to type directly into the cash flow. This is only possible for lines that are not dependent ones, that is, those not calculated by reference to some other line, as is the case with marketing expenditure (Figure 4-43).

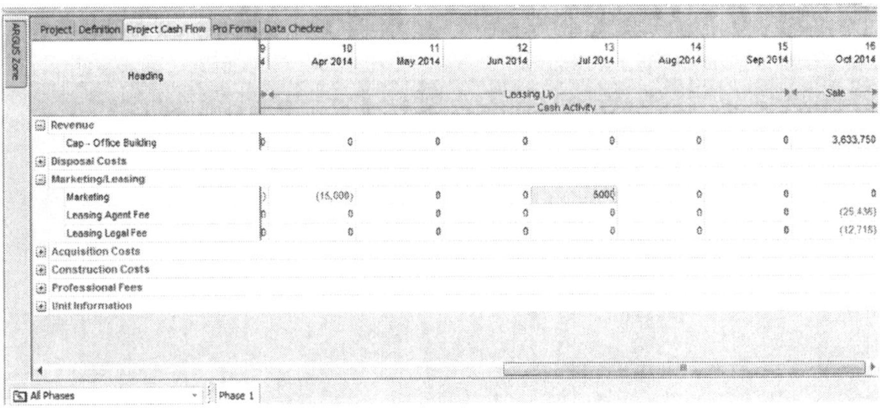

Figure 4-43. Adjusting a cash flow line manually

This is relatively simple with a single cost item because the sums can be adjusted manually. The sums do not automatically self-adjust when alterations are made directly into the cash flow, though they do when the data distribution route is taken. This allows a direct adjustment to the sums originally modeled, which may be useful when more information on the project is received or new estimates made. The sum assessed may well go up or down, and it can create problems where the item being adjusted is complex. Nonetheless, this remains a very useful modeling tool.

Finance Cash Flow

The second cash flow is the finance cash flow (Figure 4-44). This shows the results of the cash flow "below the line"—in other words, the result of the cash flow calculations, including interest calculations and taxes (if allowed for in the calculation). The cash flow items in this section are not adjustable.

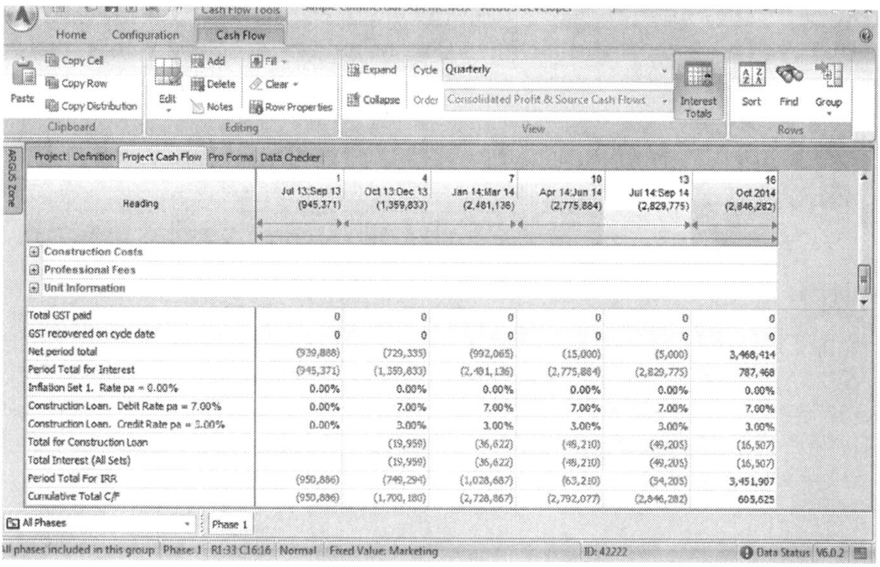

Figure 4-44. The finance cash flow summary in the Simple Finance option of Developer

Once the cash flow has been reviewed and adjusted, if required, then it is normal to go to the appraisal summary, which, as noted, is the standard output of the appraisal, summarizing the project in a simple and clear manner. You can be either print this off directly or else incorporate it into the reporting module. The appraisal summary, or pro forma, for our development is displayed in Figure 4-45. You can choose to see the print preview (Figure 4-46) before printing it out (Figure 4-47).

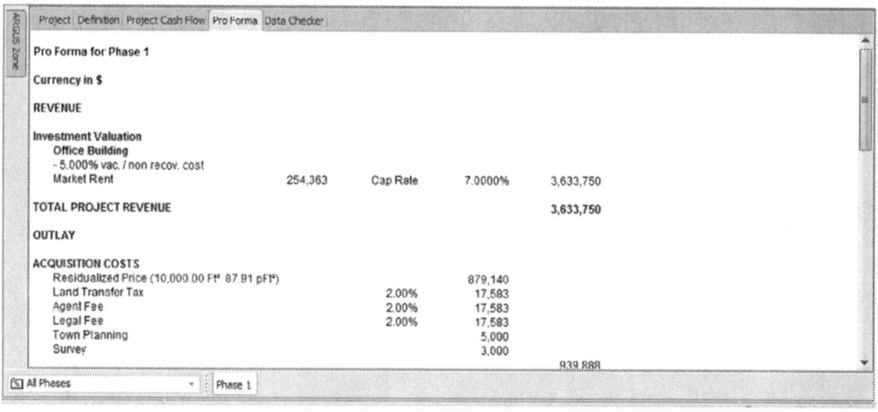

Figure 4-45. Screen shot of top part of Pro Forma sheet

Figure 4-46. Accessing Pro Forma print preview from menu

Licensed Copy

Development Pro Forma

Book Example

Suburban Centre
1234 Any Street

Bigsville

Report Date: July 03, 2013

Prepared by TMH|

Pro Forma for Phase 1

Currency in $

REVENUE

Investment Valuation
  Office Building
  - 5.000% vac. / non recov. cost

Market Rent	254,363	Cap Rate	7.0000%	3,633,750

TOTAL PROJECT REVENUE 3,633,750

OUTLAY

ACQUISITION COSTS

Residualized Price (10,000.00 Ft² 87.91 pFt²)			879,140
Land Transfer Tax		2.00%	17,583
Agent Fee		2.00%	17,583
Legal Fee		2.00%	17,583
Town Planning			5,000
Survey			3,000
			939,888

CONSTRUCTION COSTS

Construction	ft²	Rate ft²	Cost	
Office Building	9,000 ft²	140 pf²	1,260,000	1,260,000
Contingency		5.00%	63,000	
Hard and Soft Landscaping	7,000 ft²	25.00 pf²	175,000	
Statutory/Municipal			50,000	
				288,000

Figure 4-47. (continued)

PROFESSIONAL FEES			
Architect	4.00%	50,400	
Quantity Surveyor	2.00%	25,200	
Structural Engineer	1.00%	12,600	
Mech./Elec.Engineer.	1.00%	12,600	
Project Manager	1.00%	12,600	
			113,400
MARKETING & LEASING			
Marketing		80,000	
Leasing Agent Fee	10.00%	25,436	
Leasing Legal Fee	5.00%	12,718	
			118,154
DISPOSAL FEES			
Sales Agent Fee	2.00%	72,675	
Sales Legal Fee	1.50%	54,506	
			127,181
FINANCE			
Debit Rate 7.00% Credit Rate 3.00% (Nominal)			
Total Finance Cost			181,501
TOTAL COSTS			**3,028,125**
PROFIT			
			605,625

Performance Measures	
Profit on Cost%	20.00%
Profit on GDV%	16.67%
Profit on NDV%	16.67%
Development Yield% (on Rent)	8.40%
IRR	23.35%
Rent Cover	2 yrs 5 mths
Profit Erosion (finance rate 7.000%)	2 yrs 7 mths

Figure 4-47. The Pro Forma printed out

It is somewhat difficult to see the goal of our calculation, namely the residualized land value, but it is under the section headed Acquisition Costs showing a value of $879,140. This is the maximum sum that should be paid for the land to achieve the target figure of 20 percent profit on cost.

We will assume that this is the end of the appraisal and no other calculation is required.

Profitability Calculation

As noted earlier, development appraisals are most commonly done for one of two main reasons. The first reason is to calculate the amount the developers can bid for the site and still meet their target profit figure (assuming that their assumptions are valid). To do this, the appraiser has to fix the profit percentage, and it becomes the known in the equation. The alternative calculation is to calculate the profitability of a scheme. To do this, the land value, or rather price, has to be known, and the unknown variable, the residual sum of the calculation, is the profit figure.

With Developer, this calculation is simple. Essentially, the data entered is the same; it just requires the setup of the program to be slightly different.

Let us assume that the developer can purchase the land for the development at $1,000,000.

The first change is to switch the program into Fixed Land Value mode in the assumptions for calculation. As noted earlier, this is the default setting for the program. Accessing the assumptions through the shortcut on the ribbon bar allows you to access the Residual assumptions tab (Figure 4-48). If it has not defaulted to Fixed Land Cost, click into this mode. The land value on the Definition tab will be zeroed (unless a previous sum or calculation has been made) and the program will now expect you to insert a sum into the appropriate place. The program will now be running in order to calculate development profitability. A warning box will be displayed as soon as these assumption changes have been saved, as these changes will have a significant result on the appraisal outcome. However, since these changes were intended, we can ignore this.

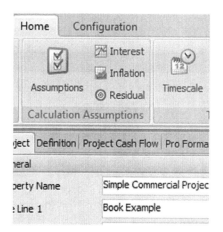

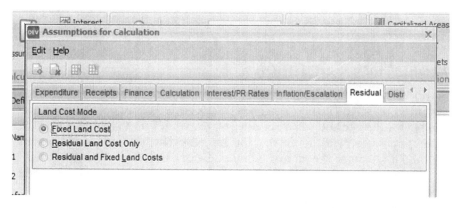

Figure 4-48. Shortcut to, and the assumptions made for calculation setup, for profit calculation

Figure 4-49. Warning that calculation mode has been changed; this can be ignored

The second change required is to enter the land purchase price into the now open box in the Definition tab (Figure 4-50).

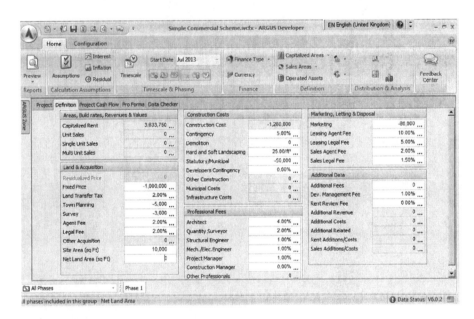

Figure 4-50. Land value entered into Definition tab

All other entries in the program are as per the previously discussed calculation.

The summary/pro forma for this appraisal is similar to what we have seen earlier, so this gives us the opportunity to look at the other way of looking at the performance data from the property—the Key Performance Indicators (KPI) that are accessed from the Configuration tab (Figure 4-51).

Figure 4-51. *Accessing the Configuration tab*

Clicking on the KPI Dashboard Template brings up both the KPI ribbon bar at the bottom of the screen (which is actually the program's default view—I have turned it off to give more screen space) and an analysis of the returns from the project using a wide series of measures (Figure 4-52).

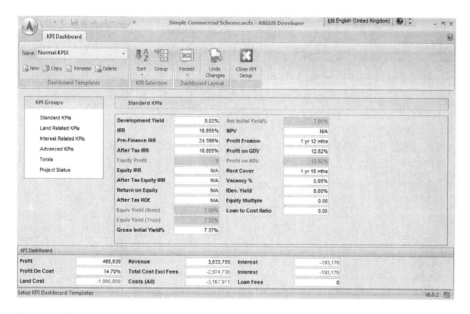

Figure 4-52. *Standard KPIs for our project*

These are the performance measures that are the vitally important outcomes for the developer. The KPI dashboard, which is a relatively new addition to the software, puts a whole series of alternative measures instantly in front of the developer/appraiser. These measures represent the key performance benchmarks that developers and financiers use to assess whether a project is viable. The normal benchmark for a commercial scheme is 20 percent. So this scheme, at 14.7 percent profit on cost, is probably not viable at this land cost. The developer would have to negotiate the bid downward, buy in the anticipation that the market would improve, or walk away from the bidding process.

More Complex Projects: Introduction

Argus Developer is ideally suited to complexity. Indeed, this is one of the program's key advantages over self-constructed Excel models, which often struggle to adapt to increasing complexity and, in particular, scheme alterations.

This section looks at examples of more complex (and thus often more realistic projects for the real world, where complexity is the norm rather than the exception) projects that are often encountered in practice, illustrating in each one how Developer can solve the problems faced in appraisal.

Because the setup, data entry, and output are essentially the same as those covered in our simple commercial project, this section will concentrate on the specific items of variance required for the topic.

Multiple Buildings and Types

Often, a development involves the construction of more than one type of building at a time. This is often the case in larger sites and also in mixed-used developments. These often mix commercial and residential uses together. Residential development appraisal has its own section in this book because of its special characteristics. However, it seems appropriate to include a residential element in one of the examples, as this will be a common component of a multiple-type scenario in practice.

The first example we will look at will be a mixed commercial scheme that has two 10,000ft^2 and three 7,500ft^2 office buildings, plus 50,000ft^2 of retail warehousing in four buildings, two of 15,000ft^2 and two of 10,000ft^2.

This development will also form the basis of the multiple timings/single phase development below, but for this initial development, we will assume that they will occur in the same time frame and not attempt to fine-tune the timings.

This initial appraisal will be run as a land residual.

As noted above, the basic procedure for setting up the project is identical for that which was followed for the simple scheme (Figure 4-53). However, for the record, the interest rate used here is a flat rate of 6 percent in a single interest set, and the target profit figure for the land residual is 20 percent profit on cost.

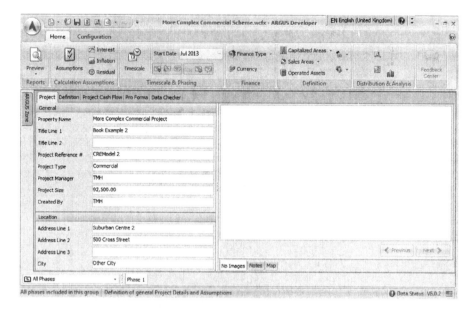

Figure 4-53. Project tab for multi-building scheme

No timescales were defined in the project brief, but here I have assumed an immediate purchase of the site, six months of planning and pre-construction, followed by a 12-month build period and a 12-month leasing period before the development is sold (Figure 4-54).

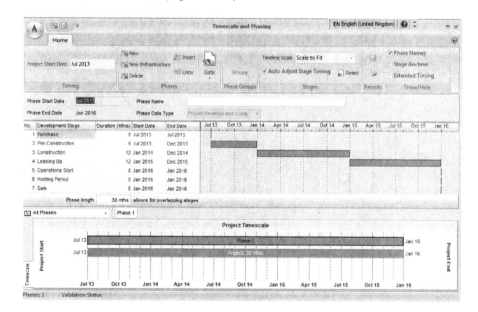

Figure 4-54. Timescales for the multi-building project

Once we have entered these parameters into the program, we can move to the Definition tab. The way that we can deal with the problem of multiple buildings is very simple; we must create multiple tabs in the commercial area drill-down screen.

We have a total of nine buildings—five offices and four retail warehouses. We could create a separate area record for each building—and there are great advantages in doing this regarding the flexibility this gives in terms of timing. But for speed (and assuming this is an initial feasibility study), we will group together the buildings of the same size and use giving us four separate area records (Figures 4-55 to 4-58).

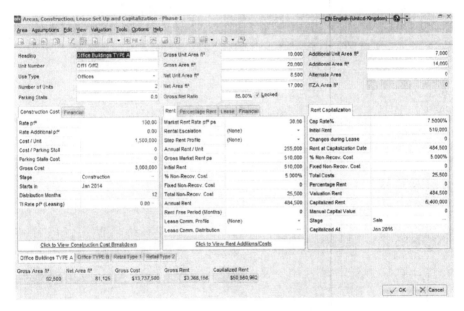

Figure 4-55. Office Type A Area record

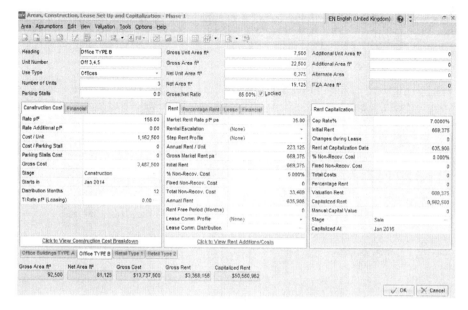

Figure 4-56. Office Type B Area record

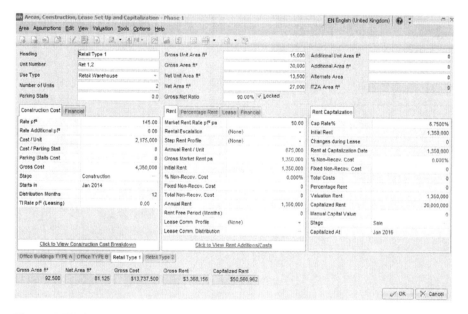

Figure 4-57. Retail Warehouse Type 1 Area record

Areas, Construction, Lease Set Up and Capitalization - Phase 1   EN English (United Kingdom)

Area Assumptions Edit View Valuation Tools Options Help

Heading	Retail Type 2		Gross Unit Area ft²	10,000	Additional Unit Area ft²	0
Unit Number	Ret3,4		Gross Area ft²	20,000	Additional Area ft²	0
Use Type	Retail Warehouse		Net Unit Area ft²	9,000	Alternate Area	0
Number of Units	2		Net Area ft²	18,000	ITZA Area ft²	0
Parking Stalls	0.0		Gross:Net Ratio	90.00% ☑ Locked		

Construction Cost / Financial

Rate pf²	145.00
Rate Additional pf²	0.00
Cost / Unit	1,450,000
Cost / Parking Stall	0
Parking Stalls Cost	0
Gross Cost	2,900,000
Stage	Construction
Starts in	Jan 2014
Distribution Months	12
TI Rate pf² (Leasing)	0.00

Rent / Percentage Rent / Lease / Financial

Market Rent Rate pf² pa	52.50
Rental Escalation	(None)
Step Rent Profile	(None)
Annual Rent / Unit	472,500
Gross Market Rent pa	945,000
Initial Rent	945,000
% Non-Recov. Cost	5.000%
Fixed Non-Recov. Cost	0
Total Non-Recov. Cost	47,250
Annual Rent	897,750
Rent Free Period (Months)	0
Lease Comm. Profile	(None)
Lease Comm. Distribution	

Rent Capitalization

Cap Rate%	6.5000%
Initial Rent	945,000
Changes during Lease	0
Rent at Capitalization Date	897,750
% Non-Recov. Cost	0.000%
Fixed Non-Recov. Cost	0
Total Costs	0
Percentage Rent	0
Valuation Rent	945,000
Capitalized Rent	14,538,462
Manual Capital Value	0
Stage	Sale
Capitalized At	Jan 2016

Click to View Construction Cost Breakdown | Click to View Rent Additions/Costs

Office Buildings TYPE A | Office TYPE B | Retail Type 1 | Retail Type 2

Gross Area ft²	Net Area ft²	Gross Cost	Gross Rent	Capitalized Rent
92,500	81,125	$13,737,500	$3,368,156	$50,560,962

✓ OK   ✗ Cancel

Figure 4-58. Retail Warehouse Type 2 Area record

This subdivision, although preventing the individual timing of each building in the subclass (see below), does allow minor variations in cost, rental, and capital value items that would probably occur in practice. Smaller buildings often cost more per square foot to build because the ratio of expensive items—walls, cladding, windows, and doors—to floor area is greater than in larger buildings, and working space is reduced. That leads to inefficiencies in on-site activities. Conversely, there is sometimes a discount for size in rents paid per square foot for larger buildings (or a premium for smaller; the effect is the same). Larger buildings often attract bigger companies, usually with greater financial stability, than those that occupy smaller premises. Therefore, the yield is often bid down for larger buildings, which causes the values to rise. These considerations have been factored into the area records.

All other assumptions that have been made for this appraisal are as per Developer's template.

Returning to the Definition tab, it can be observed that the total sum of the values of the four area records containing the detail of the nine properties are amalgamated in the Capitalized Rent box. Similarly, the total construction cost is displayed in the Construction Cost box (Figure 4-59).

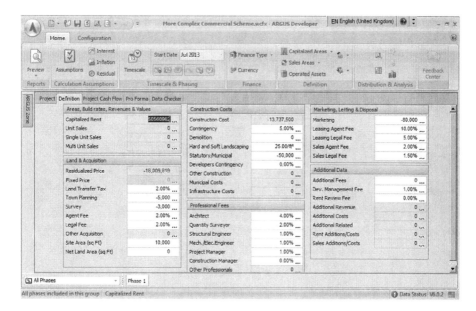

Figure 4-59. The completed Definitions Tab for the multi-building scheme

The remainder of the Definition tab has been filled in with appropriate values for this type of development. These will, of course, vary from scheme to scheme, and the reader should view these values as being for illustrative purposes only. I have made no variation to the standard template used by Developer. Note that Developer calculates the residualized price for the land in the mode that it is running in.

All the data that was created in the Areas records and entered into the Definition tab are, as always, automatically used to create the cash flow (Figure 4-60).

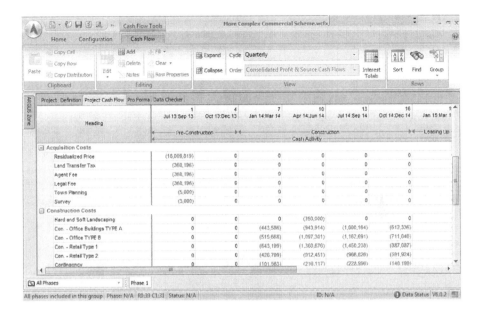

Figure 4-60. Cash flow for the multi-building scheme

As you can see from the extract from the cash flow, the template builds all the buildings together side by side. This probably would not occur in practice but is sufficiently accurate for an initial feasibility study to let it ride. Similarly, all of the buildings are assumed to be sold and leased at the same time, namely at the end of the leasing period. This is also rather unrealistic, but it would also be a normal assumption for an initial, rough appraisal done to test the basic feasibility of the scheme. We will soon address the question of timings.

The appraisal summary/pro forma for this scheme is laid out in Figure 4-61.

Pro Forma for Phase 1

Currency in $

REVENUE

Investment Valuation
Office Buildings TYPE A
- 5.000% vac. / non recov. cost

Market Rent	484,500	Cap Rate	7.5000%	6,460,000
Office TYPE B				
Market Rent	669,375	Cap Rate	7.0000%	9,562,500
Retail Type 1				
Market Rent	1,350,000	Cap Rate	6.7500%	20,000,000
Retail Type 2				
Market Rent	945,000	Cap Rate	6.5000%	14,538,462
				50,560,962

TOTAL PROJECT REVENUE   **50,560,962**

OUTLAY

ACQUISITION COSTS

Residualized Price (10,000.00 Ft² 1,800.98 pFt²)		18,009,819	
Land Transfer Tax	2.00%	360,196	
Agent Fee	2.00%	360,196	
Legal Fee	2.00%	360,196	
Town Planning		5,000	
Survey		3,000	
			19,098,409

CONSTRUCTION COSTS

Construction	ft²	Rate ft²	Cost	
Office Buildings TYPE A	20,000 ft²	150 pf²	3,000,000	
Office TYPE B	22,500 ft²	155 pf²	3,487,500	
Retail Type 1	30,000 ft²	145 pf²	4,350,000	
Retail Type 2	20,000 ft²	145 pf²	2,900,000	
Totals	**92,500 ft²**		**13,737,500**	**13,737,500**
Contingency		5.00%	686,875	
Hard and Soft Landscaping	14,000 ft²	25.00 pf²	350,000	
Statutory/Municipal			50,000	
				1,086,875

PROFESSIONAL FEES

Architect	4.00%	549,500	
Quantity Surveyor	2.00%	274,750	
Structural Engineer	1.00%	137,375	
Mech./Elec.Engineer	1.00%	137,375	
Project Manager	1.00%	137,375	
			1,236,375

MARKETING & LEASING

Marketing		80,000	
Leasing Agent Fee	10.00%	336,816	
Leasing Legal Fee	5.00%	168,408	
			585,223

DISPOSAL FEES

Sales Agent Fee	2.00%	1,011,219	
Sales Legal Fee	1.50%	758,414	
			1,769,634

Figure 4-61. (continued)

FINANCE
  Debit Rate 6.00% Credit Rate 3.00% (Nominal)
  Total Finance Cost   4,620,116

TOTAL COSTS   42,134,131

PROFIT
                                                                        8,426,830

Performance Measures
  Profit on Cost%   20.00%
  Profit on GDV%   16.67%
  Profit on NDV%   16.67%
  Development Yield% (on Rent)   7.99%
  Equivalent Yield% (Nominal)   6.82%
  Equivalent Yield% (True)   7.13%

  IRR   10.33%

  Rent Cover   2 yrs 6 mths
      Profit Erosion (finance rate 6.000%)   3 yrs 1 mth

Figure 4-61. Pro forma for multiple building type development

We can see that Developer copes with multiple building types very easily. The program is highly flexible and well thought-out, which is not surprising after over 20 years of development and feedback from the many thousands of Developer users. It also allows easy alteration of these details without issue.

Mixed-Use Buildings

Still under the heading of multiple buildings, let us examine the case of a mixed-use building, (in other words, different uses within the same building.) As noted in the introduction to this section, the most common type of mixed-use building involves residential property. In city centers, for example, you often have residential apartments over a commercial ground floor.

The reason I wanted to specifically cover this type of development here, even though there is a separate section for residential development (and there will be some inevitable repetition, for which I apologize), is that there are very specific timing issues that we must address to produce a more accurate appraisal when mixing commercial and residential properties in the same appraisal.

The program is basically set up in the same way as for the previous developments (Figure 4-62), so I will not go through this process for this scheme, other than to say the interest rate assumed is 6 percent and the total development period is 20 months, which includes a three-month pre-construction period and a nine-month construction phase. We will discuss the remaining details. Also, you will note that rather than go through the steps of the buildup for the appraisal, we are analyzing the makeup of a completed appraisal.

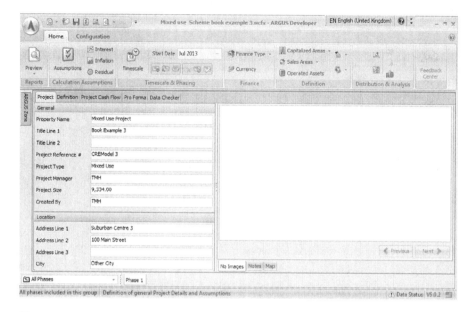

Figure 4-62. Project tab for the mixed-use development example

Reference to the completed Definition tab (Figure 4-63) illustrates that both the Capitalized Rent field, used primarily for commercial property, and the Unit Sales field, used mainly for residential units sold on, have been used in this appraisal.

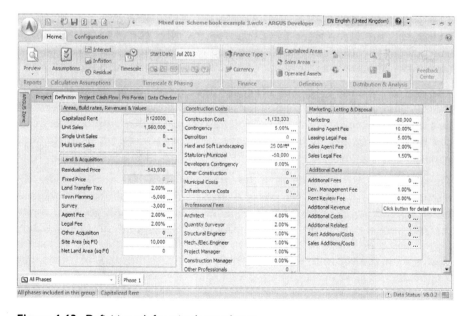

Figure 4-63. Definition tab for mixed-use scheme

It is necessary to fill in the gross (built) area so that the construction cost can be calculated (Figure 4-64). All other elements remain the same.

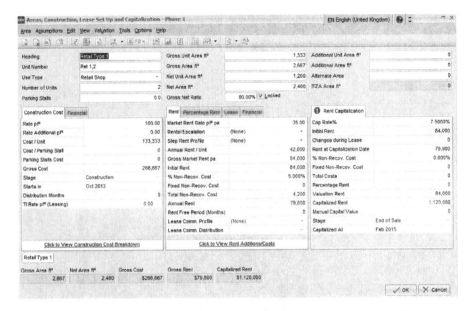

Figure 4-64. The completed Commercial Area screen for the retail part of the development

The Unit Sales screen is the basic data entry point for residential development. It used to be the only area where residential developments were modeled until the more sophisticated Area sheets were added in Version 4 of Developer. (These will be covered in the specific section on residential development.) The Unit Sales screen can be used to adequately model most residential development, as is the case here (Figure 4-65).

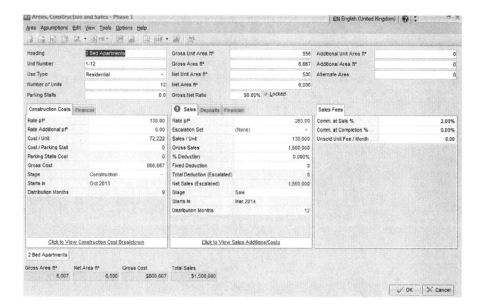

Figure 4-65. Unit Sales Area screen for the residential part of the scheme

The data entry here is relatively self-evident. The development produces 12 apartments with a net area of 500 square feet each. These are expected to sell for $130,000 each. Developer allows you to enter this sum as a unit value, calculating the value per unit of area as a function of this data. The gross area of the apartment block, including circulation space, is calculated for use in the determination of the total built area of the residential element (shown in the lower left of the screen).

What is less evident is the timing issues. In the earlier developments we have looked at so far, the timings of the stages have been linear; one has followed the next without overlap. Developer does, however, allow overlapping stages. Indeed, it is essential for the accurate modeling of many schemes. Overlapping is achieved in the timing screen by dragging and dropping the requisite bar, holding the left mouse button down while hovering the curser over the timing bar, and dragging it to the required place.

With the mixed-use development, I have done this with the sales period (Figure 4-66).

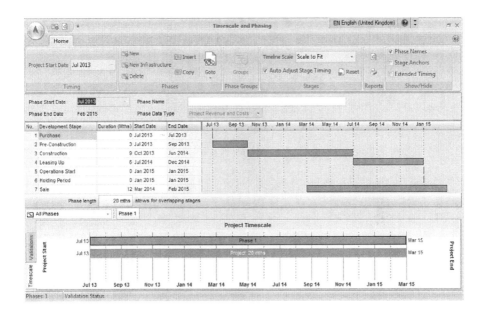

Figure 4-66. The timing for the mixed-use development with overlapping timings for the sales period

I have done this because of the nature of residential sales. Where residential units are developed, they are unlikely to be sold at once, but instead sales will be made over an extended period of time. This may well be, in many projects, before the end of the construction period. It will almost always occur in the development of housing projects and often in the development of blocks such as this one. To model this needs a longer sale period and the ability to distribute sales along it. This demand, from residential developers, led to the feature being included in Developer from Version 3 onward.

Take care with this function, however. The sales are not automatically distributed along the length of the extended sale period. Indeed, in the template, they are timed to occur at the beginning of the sales period. Without intervention, the site value or profitability would be overstated, as all the sales would occur well before the end of the development. Note that in a single-phase scheme like this one, this would also apply to the commercial element of the project as well.

To correct this, you must override the timing of the sales of both the capitalized rent (commercial) and unit sales (residential) components. You can achieve this by clicking on the three dots next to the Sale Stage box in each of the respective Area screens. For the residential element, the Custom Timing box is checked, as well as Whole Units (Figure 4-67). (If you don't check these boxes, then an unrealistic distribution based on a percentage of values will be used.) You can then choose the desired distribution; in this case, I have chosen to distribute evenly over the stage, which gives the distribution of sales as illustrated in 4-68.

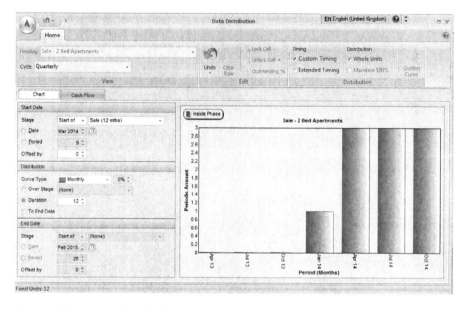

Figure 4-67. Overridden distribution of residential sales

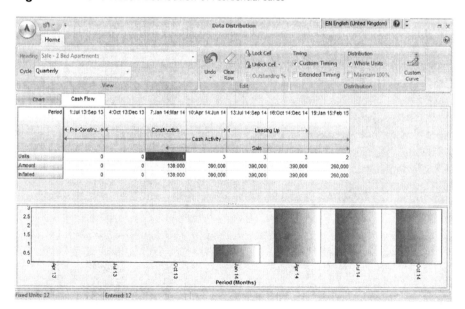

Figure 4-68. Second screen of custom timing showing how a mini-cash flow specific to the item is displayed and can be adjusted as required

The correction of the distribution of the commercial element is simpler. Again, the template distribution must be adjusted. The simplest way of achieving this is to again check the Custom Timing box and then, on the drop-down box immediately below, change from "start of" to "end of." This will move the assumed sale from the beginning to the end of the sale (Figure 4-69).

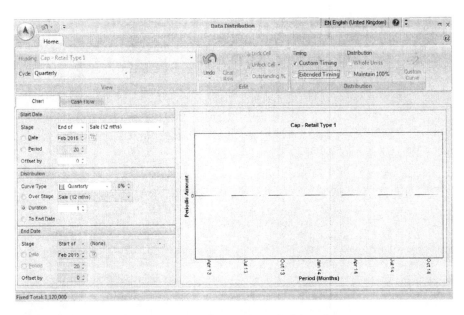

Figure 4-69. Commercial sale timing moved to the end of the sale stage

The results of the change in timing can be observed (and checked) using the cash flow (see Figure 4-70). This illustrates the desired distribution with the sales agent's fees from the disposal of the unit's building to the final sale of the freehold of the retail unit. Note that this ability to control and distribute expenditure allows for multiple timings of individual buildings and any other expenditure or receipt items within a single phase. This gives the appraiser a very powerful fine-tuning tool for development appraisals, and it underlines the characteristics of Developer. Its automatic functions allow for a quick yet reasonably accurate initial calculation, while its ability for every item to be specifically adjusted allows for a detailed and accurate final calculation as more information becomes available.

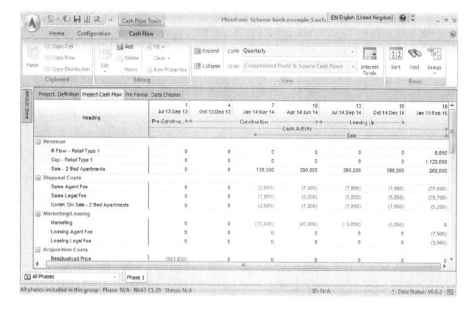

Figure 4-70. Cash flow extract from mixed-use scheme

The KPIs for the project are presented in Figure 4-71.

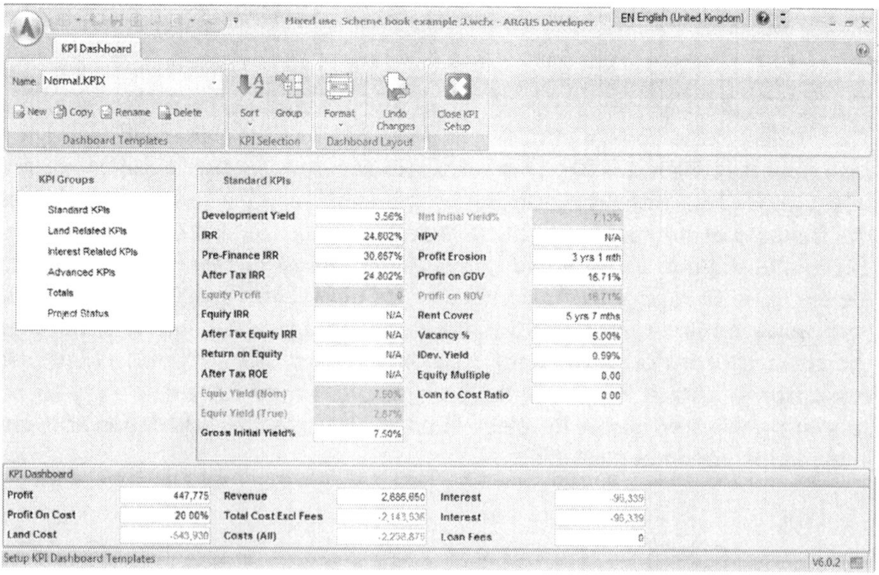

Figure 4-71. KPIs for mixed-use project

Multiple Phasing

Multiple phases are common in development. Often, developers will not want to build out a complete development scheme on a large site. The reasons are legion; overproduction can swamp a marketplace, driving down values and increasing vacancy rates. There are huge resource implications, too. Development is capital intensive as well as requiring the use of physical assets such as plant, labor, materials, and management to complete, and a developer may not have sufficient resources to complete the whole project at once. There are advantages in splitting a development up into packages; a developer may choose not to build out a stage themselves but sell the site onto another developer and take the short-term value increase in the site value rather than the longer-term returns they might achieve from the development itself. Whatever the reason, phasing is very common in all types of development and a development appraisal tool must be able to cope with this aspect.

Argus Developer was designed from the outset to deal with phasing. The program can deal with unlimited phases. These phases can be parallel (that is, the timing of each phase can be the same), consecutive, overlapping, or with gaps between them. In a phased appraisal, the appraiser must carefully consider some factors when setting up the program so as to achieve the outcome they desire. These issues will be outlined below.

When a project is multi-phased, Developer creates a tab for each phase as well as also a Merged Phase tab that amalgamates the results from all the phases together.

The main issue (and potential pitfall) is in regards to land value/cost. As noted several times, Developer has two basic modes of calculation: profitability and land residual calculation. If the profitability calculation is chosen, the appraiser/developer will have to decide whether and how to apportion the land cost between each phase or whether to put the land cost into only one of the phases. In the latter case, only the Merged Phase tab will provide an accurate assessment of the return from the project. If, however, the land cost is apportioned, there will be issues with the assumed timing of the purchase for the second and subsequent phases if they are timed to occur later. One issue is that with the land purchase, setting up the timescales in the most obviously intuitive way will assume that the land purchase for the later phases occurs in the future.

A similar problem exists with the land residual calculation. Again, you have the option (this time prompted by the program) to calculate a single land residual or a separate land residual for each phase. Essentially, the same timing issues and lack of analytical power issues occur.

This may seem to be a trivial issue, but it is, in fact, very serious. It can lead to either overstating the expected returns from a multi-phase scheme or else overstating the values or the bid price of the land.

These issues can best be illustrated in an example. The development being appraised is an Industrial/Distribution Warehouse scheme (Figure 4-72). The industrial part will be developed first, followed 12 months later by the distribution warehouse.

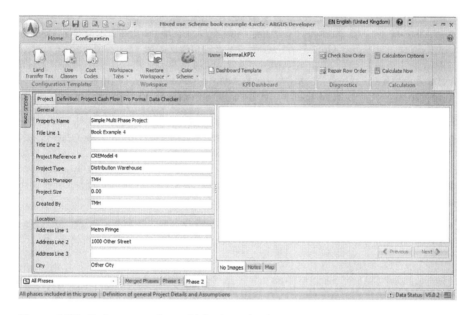

Figure 4-72. Project screen for multiple phase development

The land has cost the developer $9,000,000. This has been apportioned $4,000,000 for the industrial phase and $5,000,000 for the more valuable (and larger) distribution warehouses.

The basic setup of the program is the same as we have covered previously. The first difference that we will come across is with the Timing screen (Figure 4-73).

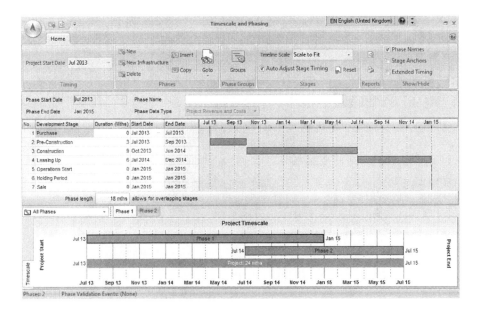

Figure 4-73. Timing screen

The first phase is created as we have seen previously. The second phase is created by clicking on the green plus symbol (Figure 4-74). Figure 4-75 shows a box that allows the definition of a phase start date. The natural inclination, given that we are told that Phase 2 starts 12 months after the project commencement, is to set the phase start date as July 2014. Figure 4-76 shows a window that pops up giving you options to let the program adjust timing or to do it yourself.

Figure 4-74. Clicking the New icon creates the new phase

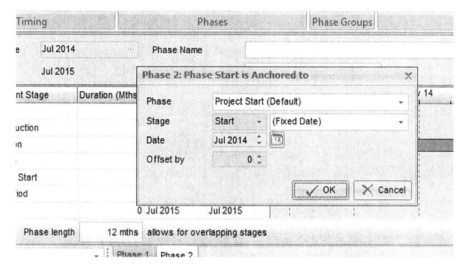

Figure 4-75. Setting the phase start dates

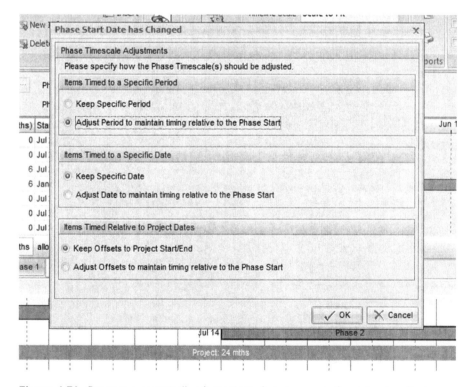

Figure 4-76. Program automatically adjusts timing but gives users the option to adjust timing as well

The creation of a second phase means that three tabs are created on the control panel, with both Active Phases and a Merged Phases tab, as discussed above (Figure 4-77).

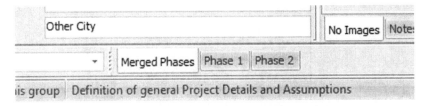

Figure 4-77. Results summary ribbon illustrating the creation of three tabs when a two-phase project is created; note that the highlighted tab is the active screen

---

Caution Be sure you enter data into the correct phase. It is not possible to enter data via the Definitions tab of the Merged Phases tab.

The completed Definition tabs for Phase 1 and Phase 2 are illustrated in Figures 4-78 and 4-79. For details of data entry, see the earlier parts of this section.

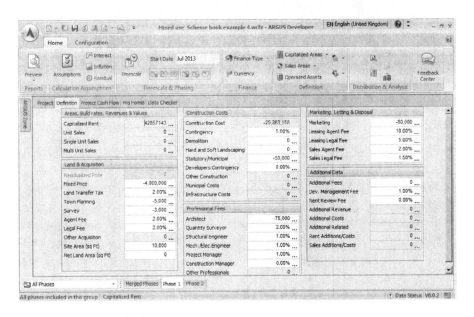

Figure 4-78. Phase 1 Definition tab

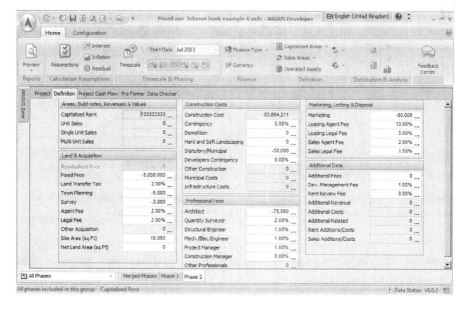

Figure 4-79. Phase 2 Definition tab

As noted, the Definition tab combines the data entered into each of the other phases and provides a consolidated result (Figure 4-80). Alterations must be made in the respective phase Definition tab. It is possible, however, to make amendments to the merged phases cash flow. This is because each line in the cash flow is associated with its individual phase, so any alteration made in the merged phases cash flow can automatically carry through to the phase cash flow. This is a very useful project management tool.

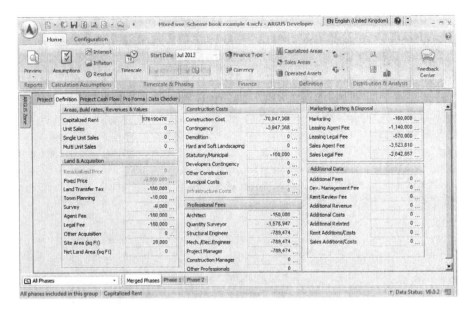

Figure 4-80. Merged Phases tab

This produces an apparently viable appraisal, and, if the cash flow were not scrutinized and the appraisal summary used as the appraisal output, the error in the appraisal would be missed. The error becomes apparent only when the merged phase cash flow is viewed (Figure 4-81).

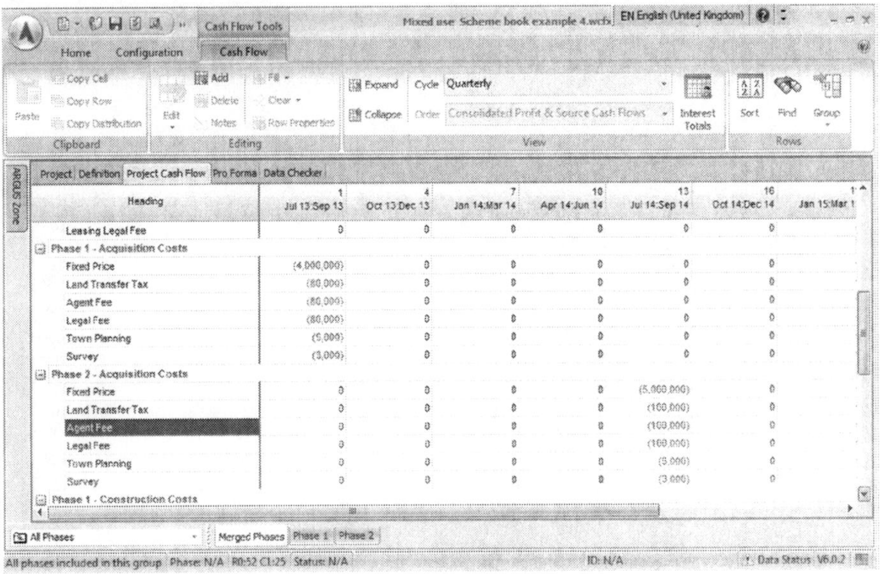

Figure 4-81. Merged cash flow for the uncorrected scheme, concentrating on the timing of land acquisition (quarterly view cycle)

As you can see, the program has split the land purchase, assuming that the land expenditure for Phase 2 occurs in Month 12, which is clearly incorrect.

It is obvious that this could have been avoided by not apportioning the land but lumping all of the purchase into Phase 1. Then the choice of the phase start date would have had no effect. The downside to this is that it would then be impossible to determine the performance of each phase accurately; only the Merged Phases sheet would show the true project returns.

You can avoid this problem by using the purchase stage of the Timing screen. The phase start date for Phase 2 must be returned back to the same as the main project. Then the value of the purchase months can set to the correct 12-month gap (Figure 4-82).

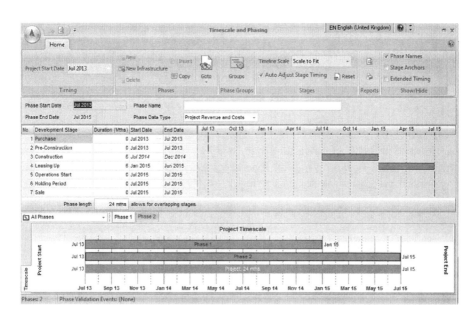

Figure 4-82. Corrected timescale

Reference to the merged cash flow shows that this corrects the land purchase, bringing both to the same point in time (Figure 4-83).

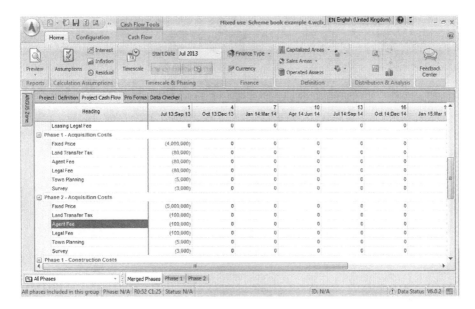

Figure 4-83. Merged phases cash flow of the corrected project

Again, we will review the outcome of the project using the KPI dashboard (Figure 4-84). Because of the multiple phasing, it is important to look at the performance of the project on an overall basis and also at the phase level. Developer allows you to do this. It is also possible to prepare reports on an overall basis and for each of the phases (Figures 4-85 to 4-88).

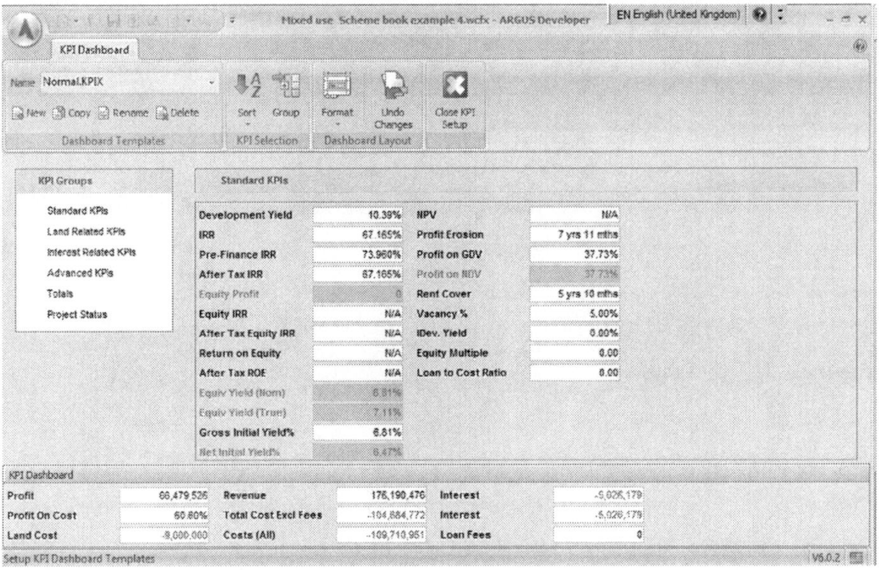

Figure 4-84. KPI dashboard setup

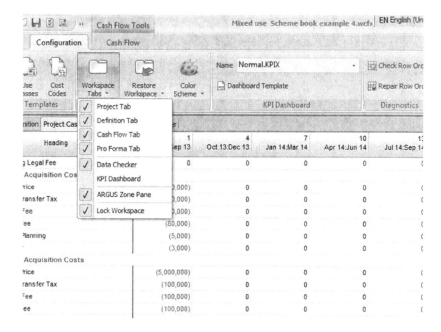

Figure 4-85. KPI ribbon bar setup

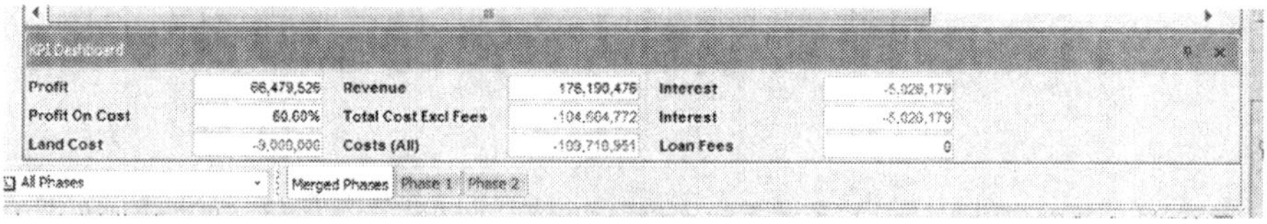

Figure 4-86. KPI merged project

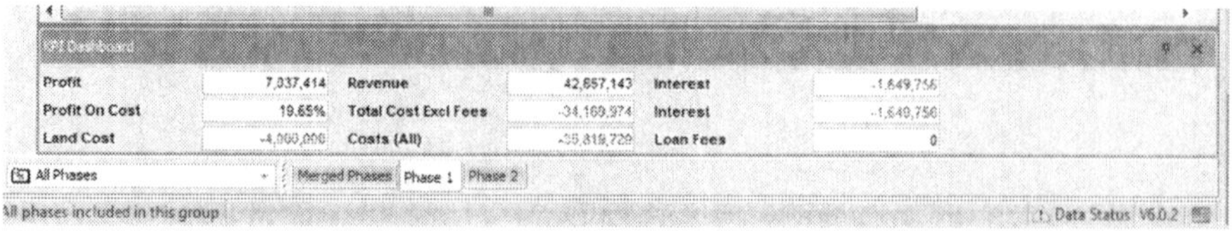

Figure 4-87. KPI Phase 1

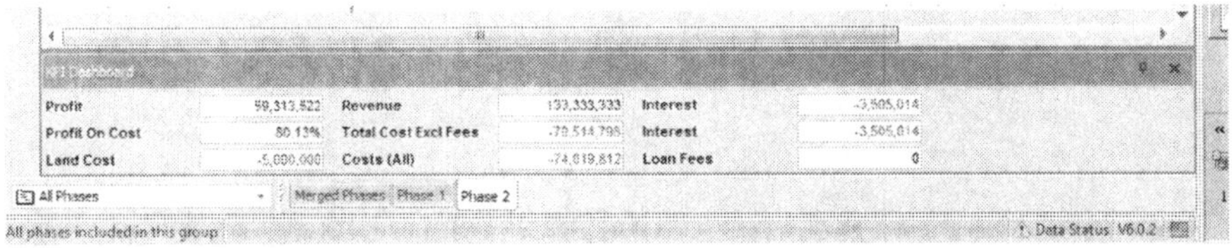

Figure 4-88. KPI Phase 2

The same issues apply when the program is run in land residual mode. You have the choice to calculate a single land residual or a land residual for each phase. Unless the land is to be sold/purchased at the beginning of each phase rather than at the project start, the same correction is required to produce an accurate appraisal.

Please note that this is not an error in the program; it is simply a common error that can be made with multiple-phased projects and an illustration that care must be taken when such projects are being constructed. In fact, the multiple phasing mode of Developer is very well thought-out and works extremely well.

Appraisal Using Multiple Interest Sets

The structured finance allows very sophisticated modeling of the financial makeup of a project. We will be looking at this module later. However, you can still do fairly sophisticated financial modeling with the basic version of Developer. One of the elements that can be modeled is the use of multiple interest sets in the program. These sets can be run consecutively or simultaneously.

The former is not really multiple interest sets. It is instead a single, variable rate loan, used either where the loan is scheduled to periodically change by fixed steps, or where the loan is on a variable rate and it is expected that the rate will fluctuate. To model this, all that needs to change is the rates in the interest set (see Figure 4-89).

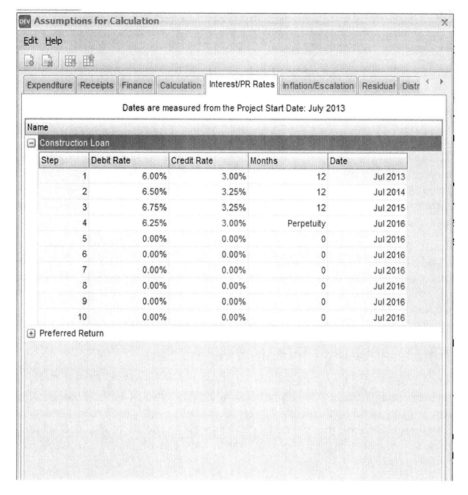

Figure 4-89. Multiple interest rates to model market interest rates movements

Note that I have made two changes. I have introduced a credit rate, the rate of interest that will accrue on any sums if the project goes into surplus. The second is to schedule the differing rates of interest. Note that you have to specify the amount of time (in months) that the rate is expected to continue Also, the last rate in the schedule should have a 0 against it to avoid the interest schedule running out and a zero percentage being charged against the development costs.

The resulting interest rates will then appear in the finance cash flow (Figure 4-90).

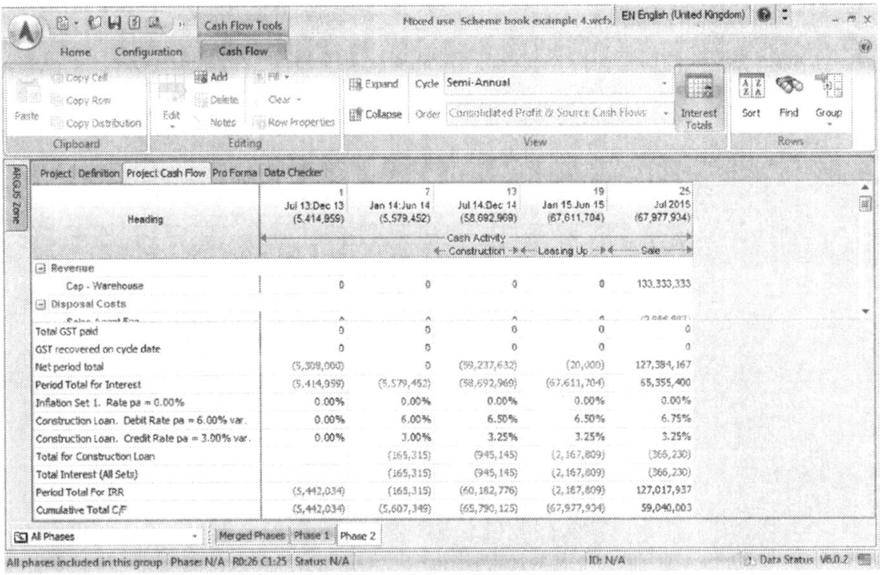

Figure 4-90. Resultant cash flow (semi-annual view and with results bar in alternative position)

The creation of multiple interest sets for a project also requires changes to be made to the interest rate sets, but in this case using the green plus button to add new sets. You can then rename them to suit the requirement of the user. Here I have created two new sets while deleting the empty loan set. I have maintained the rates used in the multiple rate example used above but renamed this set as the Main Construction Loan (Figure 4-91). The two additional sets created are a land loan (Figure 4-92), which is at a single flat, lower rate, something that often can be achieved against land purchase given the lower risks involved, and a mezzanine loan at a typically higher rate (Figure 4-93). (Mezzanine finance is usually arranged to top up existing finance. It is usually short-term, high-risk lending on the margins of a scheme.)

Step	Debit Rate	Credit Rate	Months	Date
1	6.00%	3.00%	12	Jul 2013
2	6.50%	3.25%	12	Jul 2014
3	6.75%	3.25%	12	Jul 2015
4	6.25%	3.00%	Perpetuity	Jul 2016
5	0.00%	0.00%	0	Jul 2016
6	0.00%	0.00%	0	Jul 2016
7	0.00%	0.00%	0	Jul 2016
8	0.00%	0.00%	0	Jul 2016
9	0.00%	0.00%	0	Jul 2016
10	0.00%	0.00%	0	Jul 2016

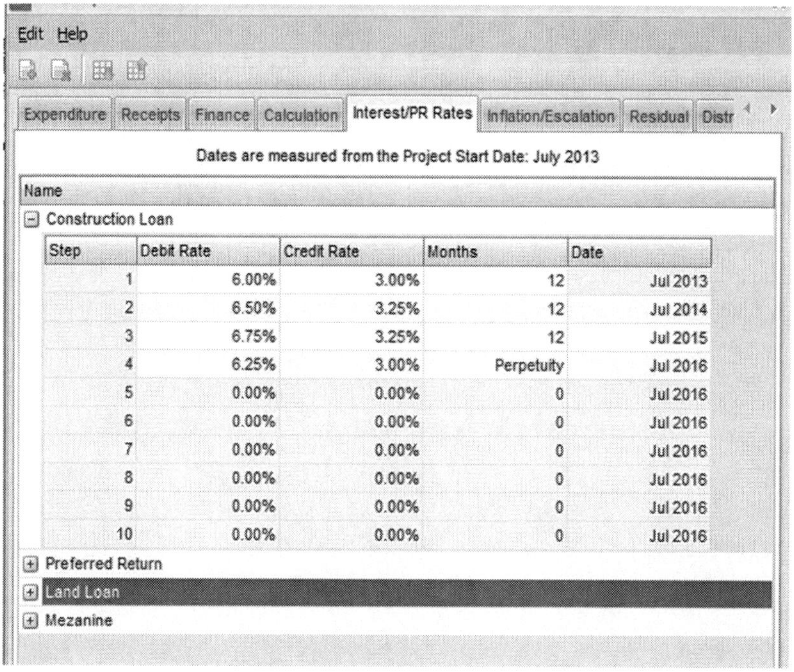

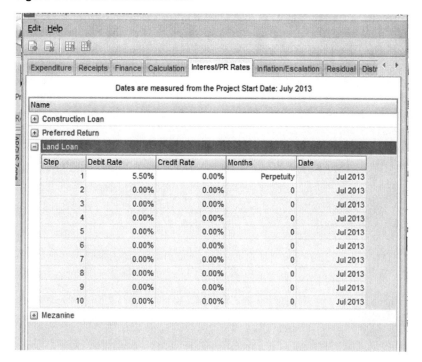

Figure 4-91. Main construction loan

Step	Debit Rate	Credit Rate	Months	Date
1	5.50%	0.00%	Perpetuity	Jul 2013
2	0.00%	0.00%	0	Jul 2013
3	0.00%	0.00%	0	Jul 2013
4	0.00%	0.00%	0	Jul 2013
5	0.00%	0.00%	0	Jul 2013
6	0.00%	0.00%	0	Jul 2013
7	0.00%	0.00%	0	Jul 2013
8	0.00%	0.00%	0	Jul 2013
9	0.00%	0.00%	0	Jul 2013
10	0.00%	0.00%	0	Jul 2013

Figure 4-92. Land loan

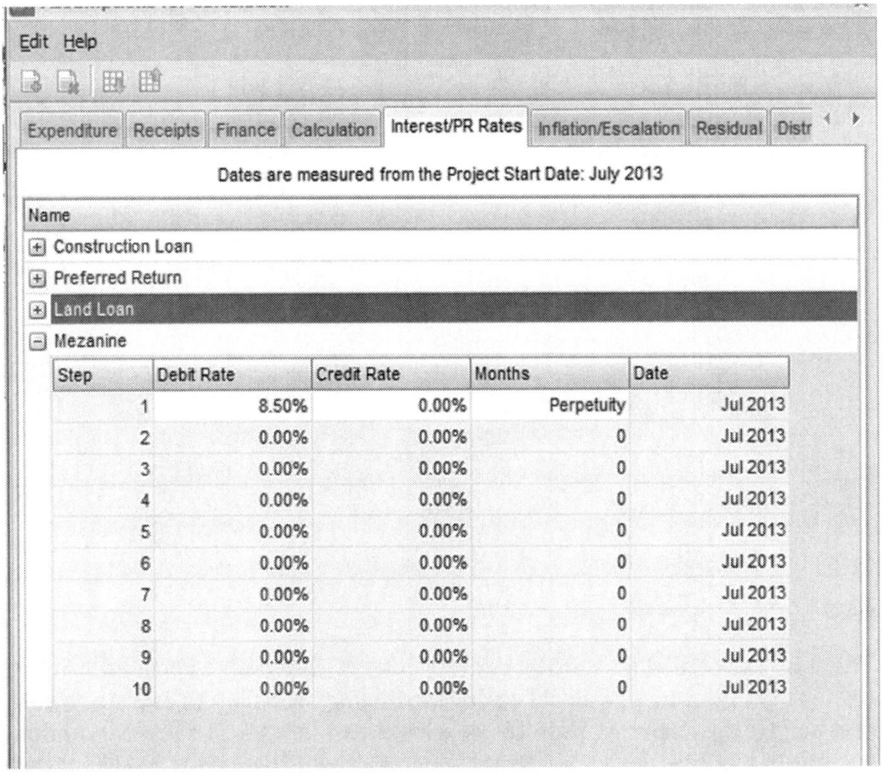

Figure 4-93. Mezzanine loan

Note that with no other changes, Developer would only use the first set of interest rates it finds in this section, in this case the main construction loan. The appraiser has to manually intervene to change the assumptions made.

Most of the schemes use the main construction loan. However, the construction in Phase 2 (warehousing) is financed via the mezzanine loan, while the land is purchased using the separate (and lower) land loan.

As noted above, by default the program already uses the main construction loan, so the only changes we need to make are to associate the correct loans with the construction of Phase 2 and the land purchase against the land loan. There are two separate techniques involved.

With the construction loan, any items that need to be changed are normally done via the appropriate place on the Definitions tab or on the Area screen. This latter procedure is illustrated with the main construction activity (Figure 4-94).

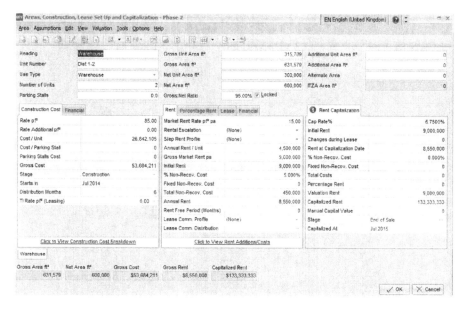

Figure 4-94. Area screen

There is a tab behind the construction calculation tab headed Financial. Clicking on this tab opens up a series of options, including the ability to ascribe an inflation set to this element (also by reference to a library in the Assumptions screen). In this case, we want the second box down. This opens up the interest sets, and we can select any that we have previously created (Figure 4-95).

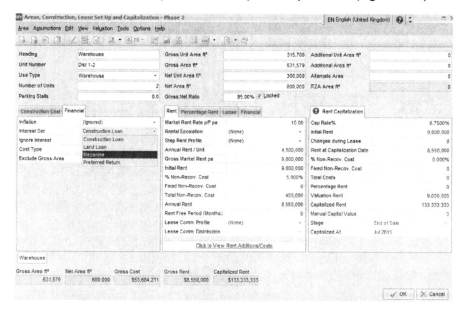

Figure 4-95. Changing the interest set in the Financial tab

The process needed to change items such as the interest set against the land purchase is more involved. Most items in the Definition tab have a financial screen when a drill down into the cell detail is made. That for the Statutory/Municipal expenditure in Phase 2 is illustrated (Figures 4-96 and 4-97). (Note that the icon View Financial Data has to be pressed to make active.)

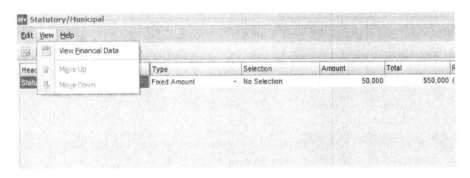

Figure 4-96. Allowing financial information to be viewed and edited for specific items

Figure 4-97. Financial detail of demolition item Phase 2

This option is not available for the two items of land cost. Association with an alternative interest set has to be done via the cash flow. (Indeed, you can make all changes using the method we are about to present.) As there are land purchase items in both phases, it is easiest to make the changes in the merged phases cash flow (Figure 4-98).

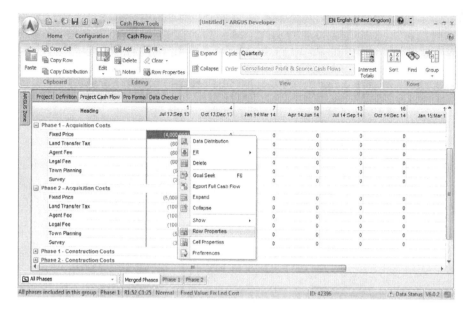

Figure 4-98. Merged phases cash flow with the Row Properties dialog box highlighted

To access the area that needs to be changed, the user has to click into the appropriate row and then right-click to bring up the dialog box (Figure 4-99).

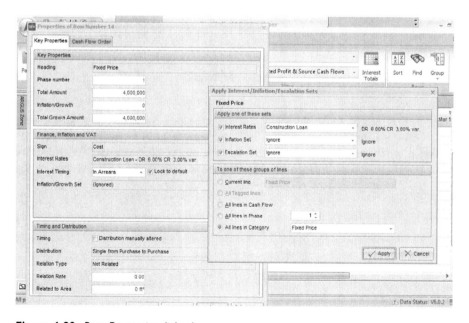

Figure 4-99. Row Properties dialog box

As you can observe, any item that is not grayed out can be changed. In this case, we need to click on Interest and change the interest set to the land loan. Clicking the Interest button opens up another dialog box (Figure 4-100). Once you close this box, the changes will be made and the appraisal total will adjust.

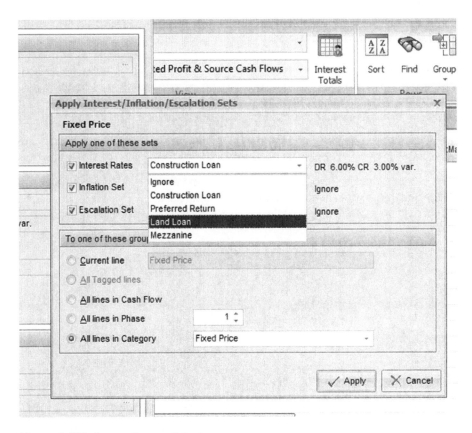

Figure 4-100. Interest button dialog box

Developer does acknowledge when multiple interest sets are used, but it is not particularly informative as to the detail in the summary outcome and reports.

Summary

This chapter has covered the bulk of the functionality of the "core" Developer program. It has shown how the software deals with simple and complex situations, how it can model the development of different types of real estate, and how the user can either accept the default settings in the program's template to do a quick and reasonably accurate appraisal or step in and override the settings to set specific assumptions or timings. I often use a sophisticated camera as an analogy for this characteristic; a good DSLR or high-end compact will always have a fully auto setting that will give reasonable results in most circumstances. However, say in low light or where the photographer wants a specific result, the user can always manually set the camera up. Developer works in just the same way.

We have also looked at more complex developments with different real estate types and timings, including multiple phasing.

You will see that Developer has the scope and flexibility to deal with all of these situations. Over the next few chapters, therefore, we will look at the more sophisticated features of the program, particularly the structured finance module—essential in many circumstances.

Residential Feasibility Studies

Simple to Complex

The split between residential and commercial development appraisals is somewhat artificial. Essentially, all development appraisals are the same, regardless if they are residential or commercial; an appraisal is done to test viability, or to calculate the value of the land for development purposes or for a bid price.

In reality, though, developers often make a distinction between the two types of appraisals. This is due partly to the fact that, in many countries, the types of developers who carried out residential development in the past were different from those who pursued commercial schemes. Although the division in the industry is now often blurred, if not entirely gone, some of the tradition of distinguishing the two has carried through to the conduct of appraisal.

What is more important, however, is the difference in the nature of the product of the residential development process. While the commercial process tends to produce a small number of buildings that are frequently disposed of in a single sale or over a fairly narrow time frame, residential development produces multiple buildings (or disposable elements in the case of apartment blocks) that have both multiple starts and longer, multiple disposal points.

This second distinction produces quite disparate cash flows, and it is this difference that distinguishes residential appraisals from commercial appraisals. I will be examining these different characteristics in this section of the book. As an aside, it is perhaps instructive to note that many of the principal changes made to Argus Developer over recent years have been to make the program more attuned to producing residential development appraisals. This reflects the fact that the program was originally designed to reflect the needs of the market in the late 1980s and early 1990s, when the demand for the software primarily came from commercial developers, and residential property development was the preserve of the major house builders. As the market moved toward more mixed use and residential development and away from the big house builders, the program changed.

Simple Residential Project: Single Building Type/Single Phase Project

The initial appraisal will be undertaken on the simplest of projects—the development of detached dwellings on a vacant residential plot in an established residential area (Figure 5-1). This immediately moves us away from one of the characteristics just discussed—the need to model multiple unit sales over overlapping development and sale periods. However, some of the distinctive characteristics of development appraisal will be clear from the feasibility model.

Figure 5-1. Developer opening screen

Land Bid Calculation

The feasibility study is being done on a residential development plot that was advertised for sale on an Internet brokerage site.

The main setup assumptions are identical to those used for the commercial and mixed-use projects reviewed earlier in the book (Figures 5-2, 5-3, 5-4, and 5-5). The template Developer uses is flexible enough for both residential and commercial projects.

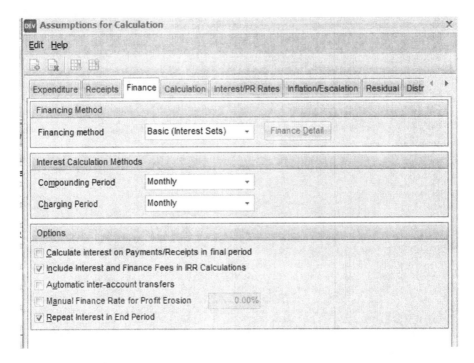

Figure 5-2. The finance assumptions

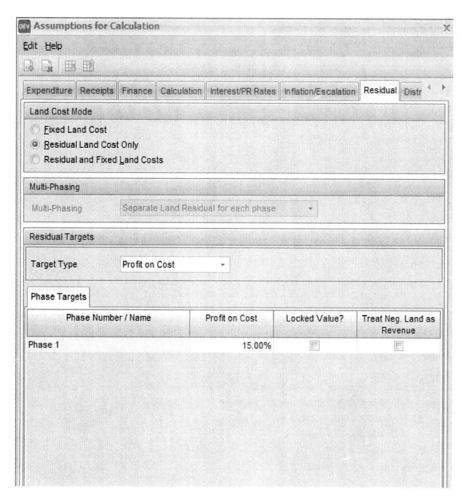

Figure 5-3. The residual assumptions

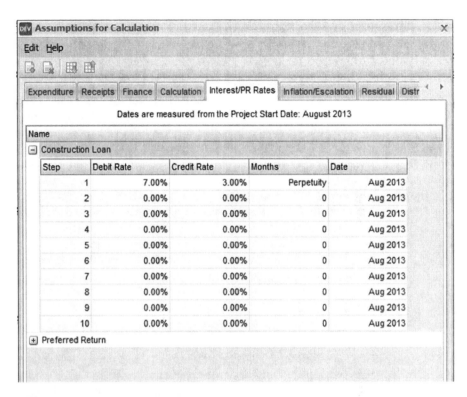

Figure 5-4. Interest sets assumptions

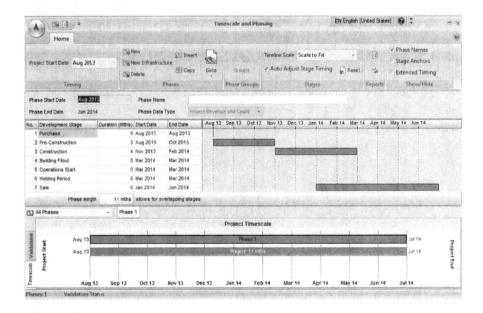

Figure 5-5. Project timescale assumptions

One value difference is in regard to the target profit figure used when a residual land value is calculated (Figure 5-3). The required profit figure for residential developments tends to be lower than for commercial schemes. Essentially, this stems from the belief that the risk for residential projects is lower.

We can attribute the lower risk to the fact that the market for the end product of the development process in residential schemes is wider than for any commercial project. With any commercial project—offices, retail spaces, industrial buildings, or leisure areas—the number of potential end users (occupiers and owners) will naturally be more restricted because there are simply fewer businesses than households in any market. One feature of successful speculative development (in other words, development projects that do not have a specific end user in mind at inception) of any type is to ensure that the end product is not so specialized that it excludes all but a very few buyers/occupiers from considering it. This is particularly true of commercial projects. One of the criticisms often leveled at developers is that their output is bland and unadventurous. But, sadly, bold and innovative designs limit the market appeal and raise development risks to a level that is unacceptable to both developers and their funders alike.

Note Experienced developers keep their offerings on the generic side for a good reason: If you get too specialized with built space, you limit the market for it.

The interest rate used in this appraisal is indicative of the rates that a residential developer with a good track would probably obtain at the time of writing (mid-2013, Figure 5-4). Note that a credit rate has been allowed so that you can accrue interest if the project goes into surplus. This is not something that is likely to happen with this single-building project, but it is something that can occur in multiple unit projects where sales take place over an extended time period and where the crossover between deficit and surplus almost certainly will occur before the final unit is sold and the development project has ended.

As noted, this is a simple project that is assumed to start three months after land purchase and have a four-month construction period (Figure 5-5). I have, however, assumed that there could be a full six months after the end of completion for the developer to find a buyer and agree to a sale. This reflects the uncertainty of the market at the time of writing; however, you should make some allowance for this in most appraisals as an extra protection against risk.

There is an issue with the assumed timing of the sale in Argus Developer's default template.

As previously noted, Developer has three Area sheets that cover different types of residential development. For this, we will use the Single Unit Sales sheet, the one that has been included in the program since the inception of the Windows-based version of the program (Figure 5-6). As you can see, this is a simplified version of the commercial Area sheets, lacking the capitalization of income area—because a sale of the house or flat is assumed to be the disposal method. (Note that even with investment residential property, it is rare that the investment method is used to determine the value.)

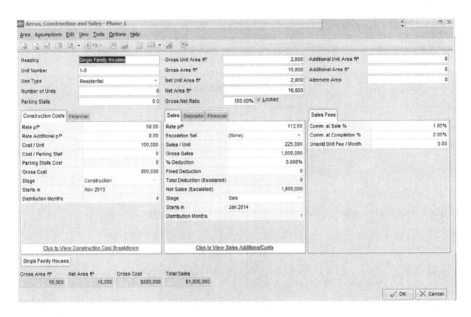

Figure 5-6. The single unit sales area

Note that it is normal to enter sale values (and often construction costs) as a "per unit" rate rather than an area rate.

As previously noted, there is a need to amend the timing from the default that exists in the template when an extended time period is used in Argus Developer. The template defaults the timing of the sale to the beginning rather than to the end of the period (Figure 5-7). I believe that this is the case because the programmers thought that if an extended time period were selected, the sales would be multiple and need to be distributed across the full time range. You can also avoid it if you choose one of the post construction times. However, I believe that most users prefer to use the option that I have chosen. This timing issue is a potentially dangerous trap for the unwary; it will inflate the value/development profitability if you do not spot it. You can correct it by clicking into the sales timing link on the Area Sales sheet, checking Custom Timing and Whole Units—the Whole Units selection will stop the impossible reality of a fraction of a house being sold—and changing the timing to be distributed monthly over the entire sales period (Figure 5-8).

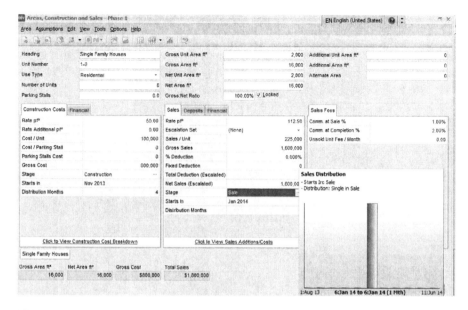

Figure 5-7. Sales construction timing: initial setup from template

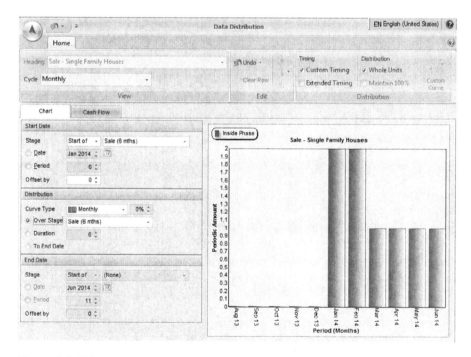

Figure 5-8. Sales construction timing corrected

The Definitions tab for a residential scheme is largely similar to those we have seen previously (Figure 5-9). Quite often, there are fewer members of the professional team than for a large commercial development. Indeed, some projects may have only an architect and project manager, or, often, just a project manager where the design has been brought in. Similarly, there is no need for a rental agent or rental legal fees unless you are creating an investment vehicle. In our scenario, the only disposal fees are those for the sale agent.

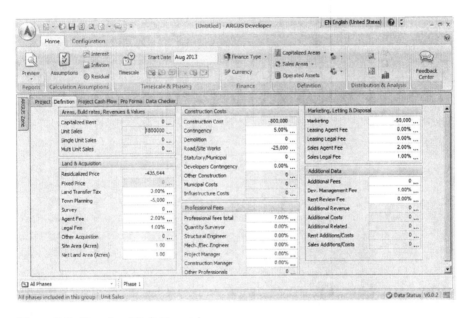

Figure 5-9. Completed Definitions tab

The cash flow (Figure 5-10) is relatively simple but provides a useful visual tool for assessing whether the key assumptions have been timed to occur as anticipated (Figure 5-11).

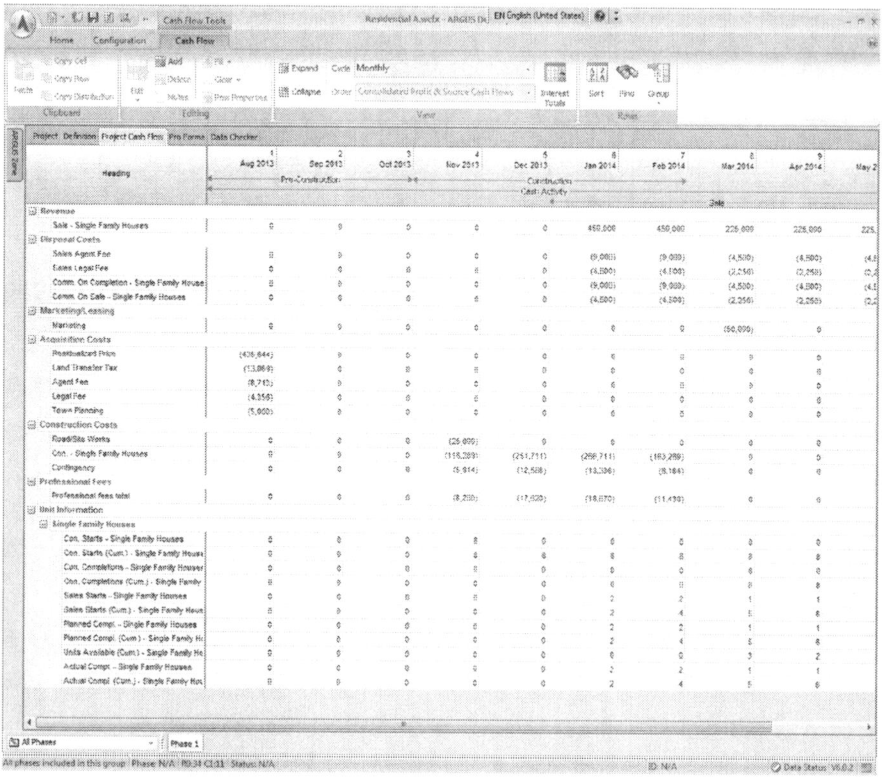

Figure 5-10. Project cash flow

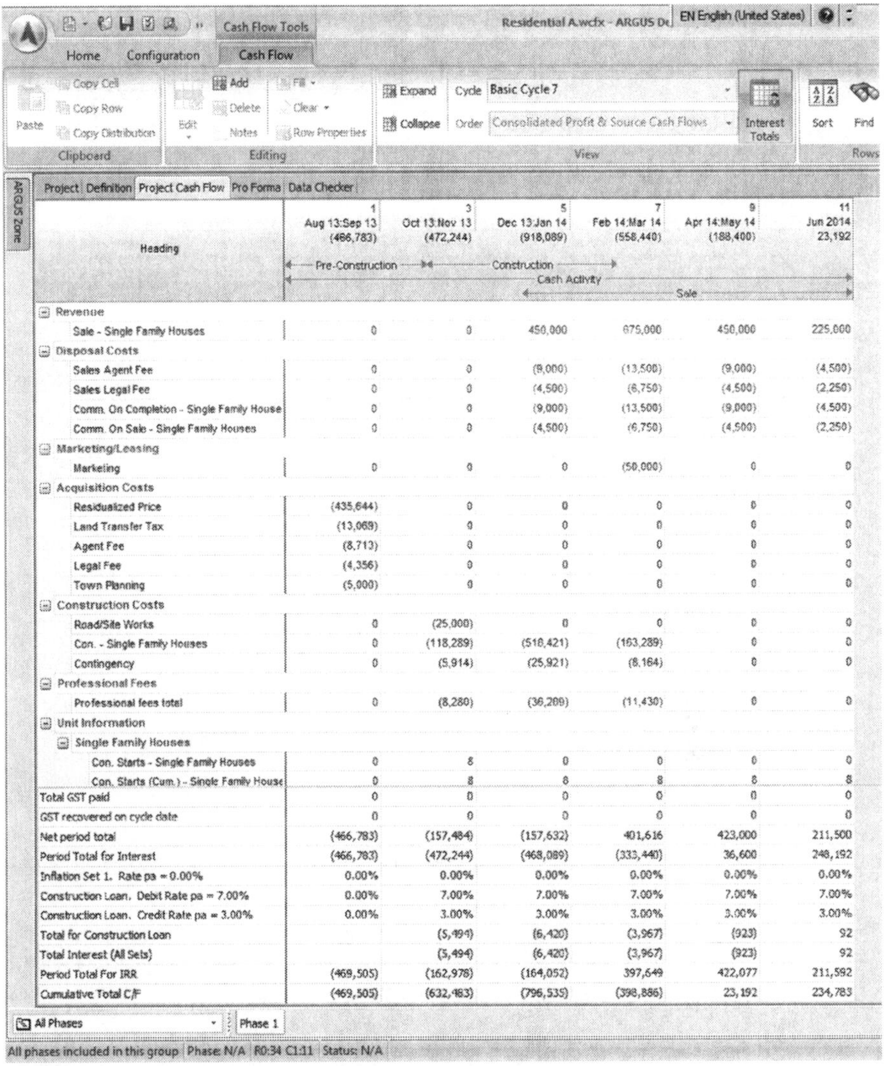

Heading	1 Aug 13:Sep 13 (466,783)	3 Oct 13:Nov 13 (472,244)	5 Dec 13:Jan 14 (918,089)	7 Feb 14:Mar 14 (558,440)	9 Apr 14:May 14 (188,400)	11 Jun 2014 23,192
Revenue						
Sale - Single Family Houses	0	0	450,000	675,000	450,000	225,000
Disposal Costs						
Sales Agent Fee	0	0	(9,000)	(13,500)	(9,000)	(4,500)
Sales Legal Fee	0	0	(4,500)	(6,750)	(4,500)	(2,250)
Comm. On Completion - Single Family House	0	0	(9,000)	(13,500)	(9,000)	(4,500)
Comm. On Sale - Single Family Houses	0	0	(4,500)	(6,750)	(4,500)	(2,250)
Marketing/Leasing						
Marketing	0	0	0	(50,000)	0	0
Acquisition Costs						
Residualized Price	(435,644)	0	0	0	0	0
Land Transfer Tax	(13,069)	0	0	0	0	0
Agent Fee	(8,713)	0	0	0	0	0
Legal Fee	(4,356)	0	0	0	0	0
Town Planning	(5,000)	0	0	0	0	0
Construction Costs						
Road/Site Works	0	(25,000)	0	0	0	0
Con. - Single Family Houses	0	(118,289)	(518,421)	(163,289)	0	0
Contingency	0	(5,914)	(25,921)	(8,164)	0	0
Professional Fees						
Professional fees total	0	(8,280)	(36,289)	(11,430)	0	0
Unit Information						
Single Family Houses						
Con. Starts - Single Family Houses	0	8	0	0	0	0
Con. Starts (Cum.) - Single Family House	0	8	8	8	8	8
Total GST paid	0	0	0	0	0	0
GST recovered on cycle date	0	0	0	0	0	0
Net period total	(466,783)	(157,484)	(157,632)	401,616	423,000	211,500
Period Total for Interest	(466,783)	(472,244)	(468,089)	(333,440)	36,600	248,192
Inflation Set 1. Rate pa = 0.00%	0.00%	0.00%	0.00%	0.00%	0.00%	0.00%
Construction Loan. Debit Rate pa = 7.00%	0.00%	7.00%	7.00%	7.00%	7.00%	7.00%
Construction Loan. Credit Rate pa = 3.00%	0.00%	3.00%	3.00%	3.00%	3.00%	3.00%
Total for Construction Loan		(5,494)	(6,420)	(3,967)	(923)	92
Total Interest (All Sets)		(5,494)	(6,420)	(3,967)	(923)	92
Period Total For IRR	(469,505)	(162,978)	(164,052)	397,649	422,077	211,592
Cumulative Total C/F	(469,505)	(632,483)	(796,535)	(398,886)	23,192	234,783

Figure 5-11. Finance cash flow (custom view showing a two-month cycle)

The project's pro forma and KPI summary are presented in Figures 5-12, 5-13, and 5-14.

Project	Definition	Project Cash Flow	Pro Forma	Data Checker

REVENUE

Sales Valuation	Units	ft²	Rate ft²	Unit Price	Gross Sales
Single Family Houses	8	16,000	112.50	225,000	1,800,000

| TOTAL PROJECT REVENUE | | | | 1,800,000 | |

OUTLAY

ACQUISITION COSTS

Residualized Price (1.00 Acres 435,643.96 pAcre)			435,644		
Land Transfer Tax		3.00%	13,069		
Agent Fee		2.00%	8,713		
Legal Fee		1.00%	4,356		
Town Planning			5,000		
				466,783	

CONSTRUCTION COSTS

Construction	ft²	Rate ft²	Cost	
Single Family Houses	16,000 ft²	50 pf²	800,000	800,000
Contingency		5.00%	40,000	
Road/Site Works			25,000	
				65,000

PROFESSIONAL FEES

Professional fees total	7.00%	56,000	
			56,000

MARKETING & LEASING

Marketing	50,000	
		50,000

DISPOSAL FEES

Sales Agent Fee	2.00%	36,000	
Sales Legal Fee	1.00%	18,000	
Single Family Houses		18,000	
Single Family Houses		36,000	
			108,000

FINANCE

Debit Rate 7.00% Credit Rate 3.00% (Nominal)	
Total Finance Cost	19,434

TOTAL COSTS	1,565,217

PROFIT

	234,783

Performance Measures

Profit on Cost%	15.00%
Profit on GDV%	13.04%
Profit on NDV%	13.04%
IRR	58.68%

All Phases ▾	Phase 1

Figure 5-12. Pro forma

Standard KPIs	
Development Yield	0.00%
IRR	58.676%
Pre-Finance IRR	65.068%
After Tax IRR	58.676%
Equity Profit	0
Equity IRR	N/A
After Tax Equity IRR	N/A
Return on Equity	N/A
After Tax ROE	N/A
Equiv Yield (Nom)	0.00%
Equiv Yield (True)	0.00%
Gross Initial Yield%	0.00%
Net Initial Yield%	0.00%
NPV	N/A
Profit Erosion	2 yrs
Profit on GDV	13.04%
Profit on NDV	13.04%
Rent Cover	0 yrs 0 mths
Vacancy %	0.00%
IDev. Yield	0.00%
Equity Multiple	0.00
Loan to Cost Ratio	0.00

Figure 5-13. Key Performance Indicators (KPIs) dashboard

KPI Dashboard					
Profit	234,783	Revenue	1,800,000	Interest	-19,434
Profit On Cost	15.00%	Total Cost Excl Fees	-1,545,783	Interest	-19,434
Land Cost	-435,644	Costs (All)	-1,565,217	Loan Fees	0

Figure 5-14. KPI dashboard summary

This calculation suggests that the developer can pay up to $435,644 for the site and still meet the profit target.

View Cycle

Sometimes it is useful or necessary to view more of the project than you can see in a single screen on your desktop. Developer has a few options (monthly, quarterly, semi-annually, and so on), but what if you want a different cycle, such as two or four months at a time? Developer can accommodate this.

To change the view cycles in the cash flow, select the Cash Flow sub-tab in the Cash Flow Tools screen. At the bottom of the Cycle drop-down box, there is an Edit View Cycles option (Figure 5-15).

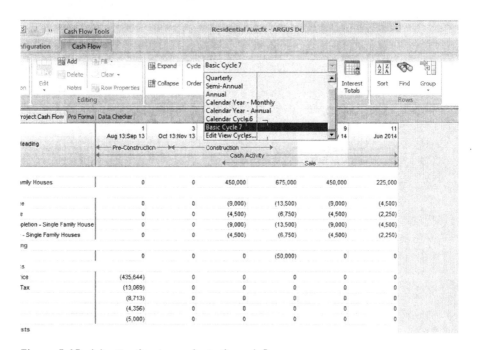

Figure 5-15. Adjusting the view cycles in the cash flow

Once the Edit screen has been brought up, you can use the green Plus and red Delete box to create or remove different view cycles (Figure 5-16, 5-17, and 5-18).

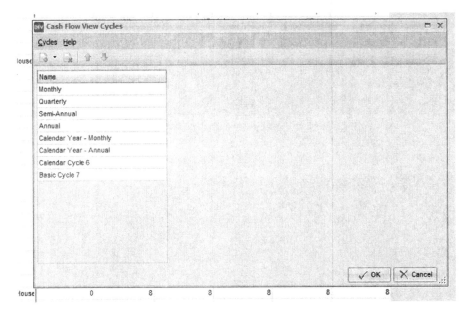

Figure 5-16. Cash Flow View Cycles editing screen

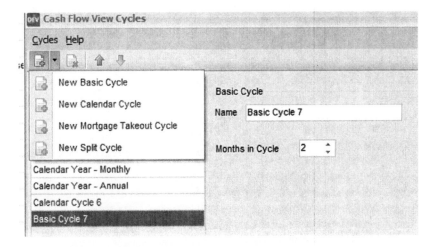

Figure 5-17. Types of cash flow views that can be created

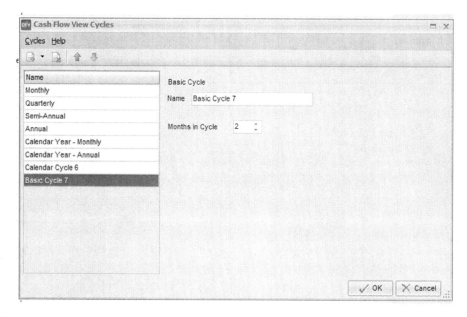

Figure 5-18. Creating the two-month view (you can rename this, but I have kept the default title)

You can use this feature for any project, not just residential ones.

More Complex Residential Projects

The second case study considers a more complex project that better illustrates the characteristics of residential development and its associated modeling issues. It is, indeed, these characteristics that the traditional residual models struggle to cope with, so it is instructive to examine these in more detail.

Many residential developments are multi-phased, something common to the commercial projects we have already looked at. However, the fact that residential units can be developed and sold in smaller, discrete parcels (in other words, individual houses and flat units) means that each phase can comprise a series of starts and completions.

The problems that this poses for the traditional model should become apparent. Residual appraisals struggle to model multi-phased schemes adequately; as tools, their scope is too broad to deal with this additional complexity. Adopting a cash-flow approach is really the only solution, and, although time-consuming, you can develop an Excel model relatively easily to deal with these issues. Surprisingly, however, the older versions of Developer also had issues with dealing with this specific problem, which perhaps reflects its roots in commercial development appraisal. This was corrected from Version 4 of the program onward (released in mid-2008). It should be noted that you can model developments with these characteristics in the older versions of the program, but there is more work involved.

The project modeled over the next pages is a two-phase residential development project (Figure 5-19). There are two elements to the project: first, the conversion of existing industrial buildings into loft apartments, and, second, a new build phase of detached houses. These two individual elements form the individual phases but both have "mini-phases"—staged starts and completions within the phases.

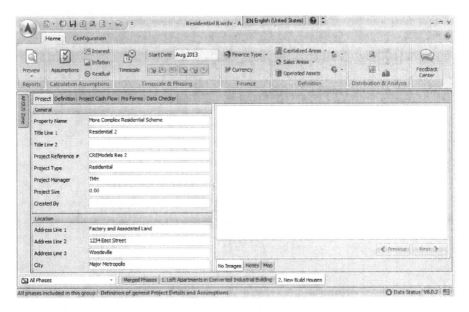

Figure 5-19. Project screen for a more complex project

The basic setup and assumptions are the same as for the simple residential project. I have applied a loan rate that is relevant to market conditions at the time of writing (mid-2013).

The timescale and phasing section (Figure 5-20) is worth commenting on. First, it is intended that Phase 2 (building new houses) will start ten months after the project's commencement (renovating lofts for living space). This has been achieved by using an extended preconstruction stage for Phase 2 (Figure 5-21) with both stages' start dates being simultaneous. This covers the issue discussed in the multi-phased commercial section above, namely, to achieve an accurate project return/land valuation assessment by ensuring that the land purchase for each phase occurs in the correct time frame.

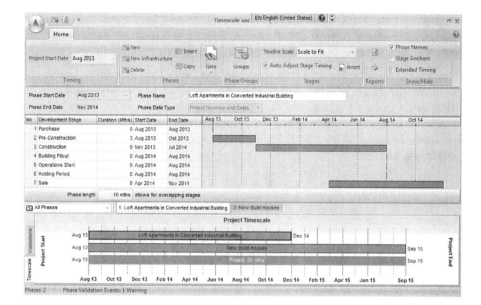

Figure 5-20. Stage 1 timescale

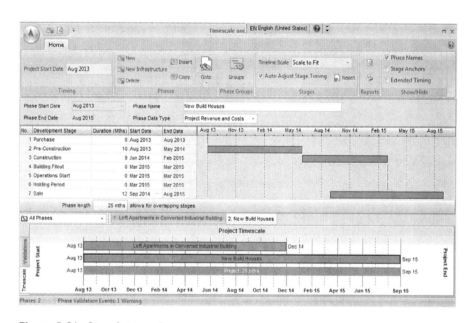

Figure 5-21. Stage 2 timescale

The second thing to say about the timescale and phasing definition is that, unlike what we have seen previously, the timing for key elements in the project (the construction and sale of the units) is not actually determined here. Note, however, that all other timings of the other elements of the project are set here, so the timescale still needs to be defined.

Definitions Tab

The big difference in the appraisal is found in the Definitions tab. Instead of using the first or second (Capitalized Rent or Unit Sales) of the four buttons in the upper left-hand part of the Definitions screen, you use the third, the Single Unit Sales option (Figure 5-22).

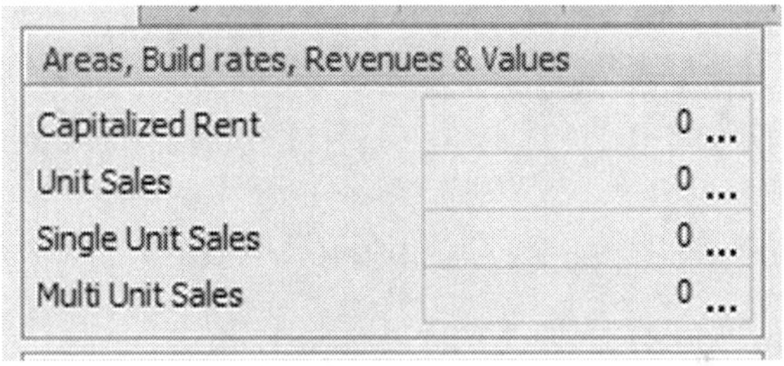

Areas, Build rates, Revenues & Values	
Capitalized Rent	0 ...
Unit Sales	0 ...
Single Unit Sales	0 ...
Multi Unit Sales	0 ...

Figure 5-22. The Area screen in the Distribution screen

Note   Prior to Version 4 of the program, only the first two buttons on the Definitions screen were available. Readers with older versions of Developer will find that they do not have the Single Unit Sales and Multi Unit Sales options.

For this feasibility study, I have assumed that the developer does not yet know the exact areas of the apartments/houses being developed. This is not critical for residential type schemes because we can use whole units to calculate both construction costs and sales.

Pressing the Single Unit Sales button opens up a dialog box that invites the user to create a new Area screen (Figure 5-23), and this itself is an indication that a new area of the program is being opened up. And, indeed, we need to stress the importance of redefining elements of the timescale in this screen (Figure 5-24). This *must* be done because selecting this option means that the construction costs and sales data will not be distributed as per the underlying template but instead will default to single month expenditure and receipts, which will greatly distort the outcome of the appraisal. I am stressing this point because regular users of Developer will be used to its largely foolproof and transparent characteristics and may be lulled into a false sense of security.

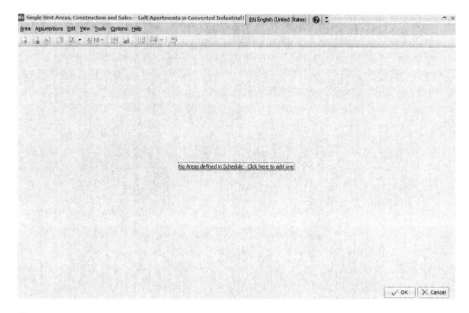

Figure 5-23. Initial screen when you select Single Unit Areas

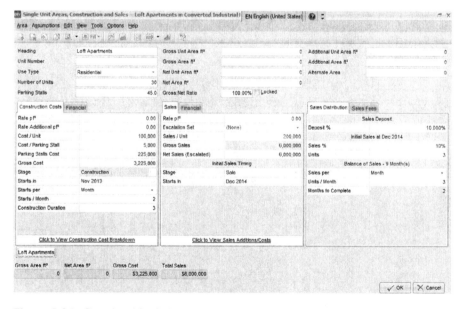

Figure 5-24. Completed Single Unit Area sales sheet

What makes this worse is that the Single Unit Sales Area is quite similar in appearance to the Unit Area sales sheets and a user in a hurry could confuse the two. The mistake would become obvious if the user examined the cash flow, but the user could rather easily overlook it as well.

Where the differences come in between the two sheets are found in the data entry boxes for Construction Costs and Sales.

For the former, at the bottom of the Construction Cost area are two boxes— Starts/Month and Construction Duration (Figure 5-25). These boxes must be filled in to model the construction expenditure correctly. This function creates a nested series of S-curved expenditure profiles. Here I have assumed that two loft apartments are started every month and that the construction work on each takes three months.

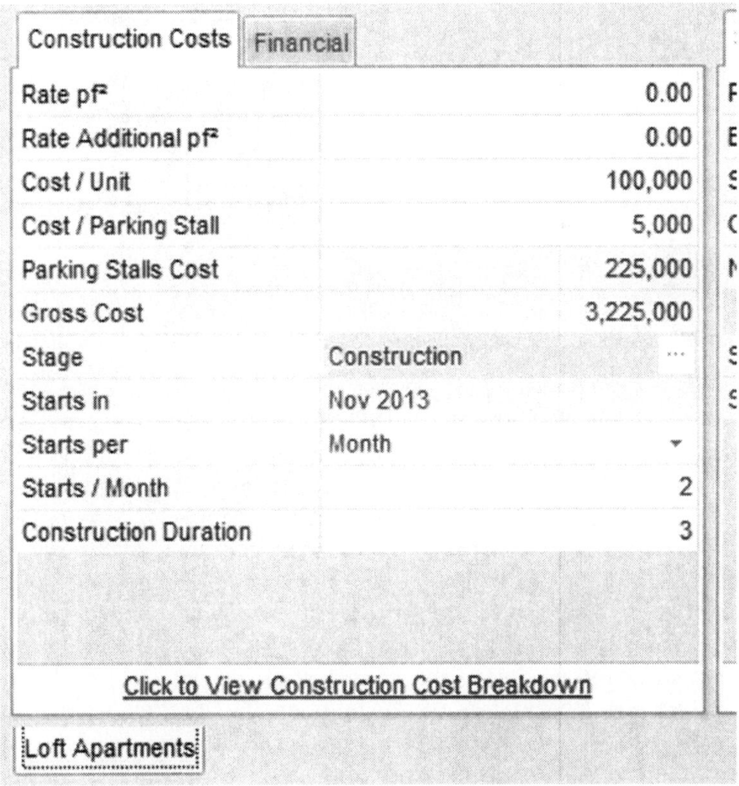

Construction Costs	Financial	
Rate pf²		0.00
Rate Additional pf²		0.00
Cost / Unit		100,000
Cost / Parking Stall		5,000
Parking Stalls Cost		225,000
Gross Cost		3,225,000
Stage	Construction	...
Starts in	Nov 2013	
Starts per	Month	▼
Starts / Month		2
Construction Duration		3

Click to View Construction Cost Breakdown

Loft Apartments

Figure 5-25. The Construction Cost data entry area showing the two additional boxes at the bottom of the list

The distribution of the construction costs generated by what are effectively 30 mini-projects can be seen in Figure 5-26.

Figure 5-26. Construction cost distribution generated

A similar procedure is followed for the sales of the completed units. Again, if the Single Unit Sales option is chosen, these entries must be made. There are five input areas that are unique to this section, and entry into four of them are mandatory (Figure 5-27). The first mandatory entry is to define when the sales are to start, although this will default to the start of the sales period defined in the timescale and phasing assumptions. The second area that needs to be defined is the number of units that the developer expects to sell at the commencement of the sales period. This allows for units sold "off-plan" or otherwise disposed of during the construction or pre-construction period. The final two mandatory areas are the number of units the developer expects to sell each month and the length of time each sale will take to complete. The optional entry is in regards to the deposit. If an assumption is made, the program will model the deposit being made when the sale is made and the balance being paid on the expected completion.

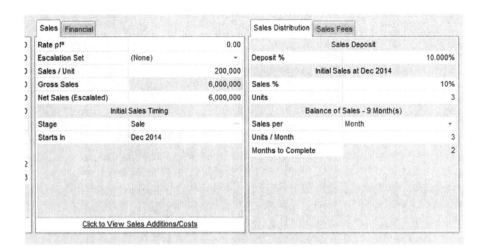

Figure 5-27. Sales structure assumptions

The distribution of these individual sales can be examined using the graphical function that was developed for this module (Figures 5-28 and 5-29).

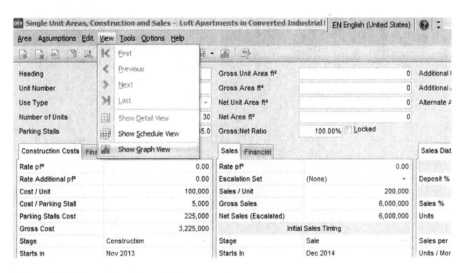

Figure 5-28. Accessing the graph view

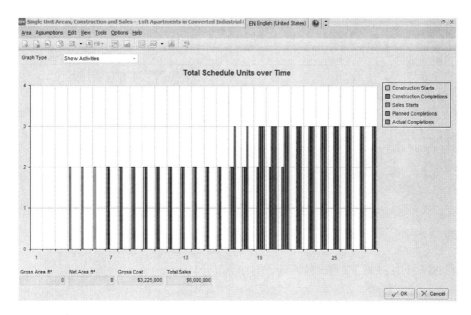

Figure 5-29. The graph view here shows sales distribution for Phase 1, which results from the assumptions made within the Single Unit Sales Area screen

As noted, it is possible to achieve virtually the same results with the Unit Area Sales and with older versions of the program. To do this, you would create a separate Area screen for each individual unit (apartment or house) and define the timing for each one individually. While this is possible with small developments, it becomes onerous for larger projects.

The results of the assumptions made are best seen in the cash flow screens (Figures 5-30, 5-31, and 5-32). You can amend the data distribution directly within these screens if required.

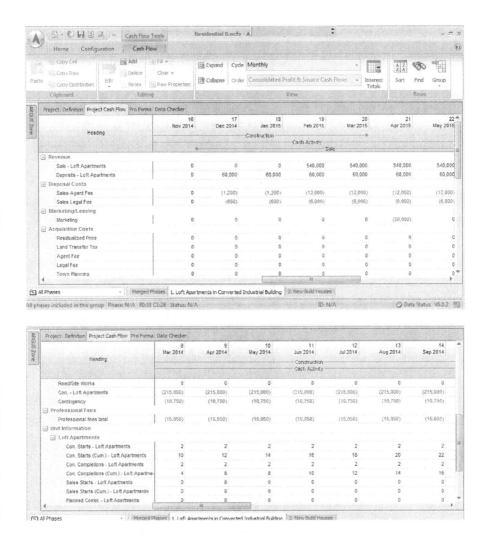

Figure 5-30. Phase 1 cash flow (two screen shots, with the lower showing how information on construction starts, completions, and sales are displayed for the user)

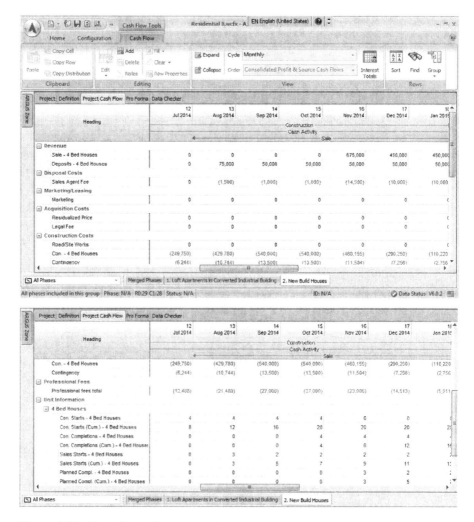

Figure 5-31. Phase 2 cash flow, again with two screenshots illustrating detail

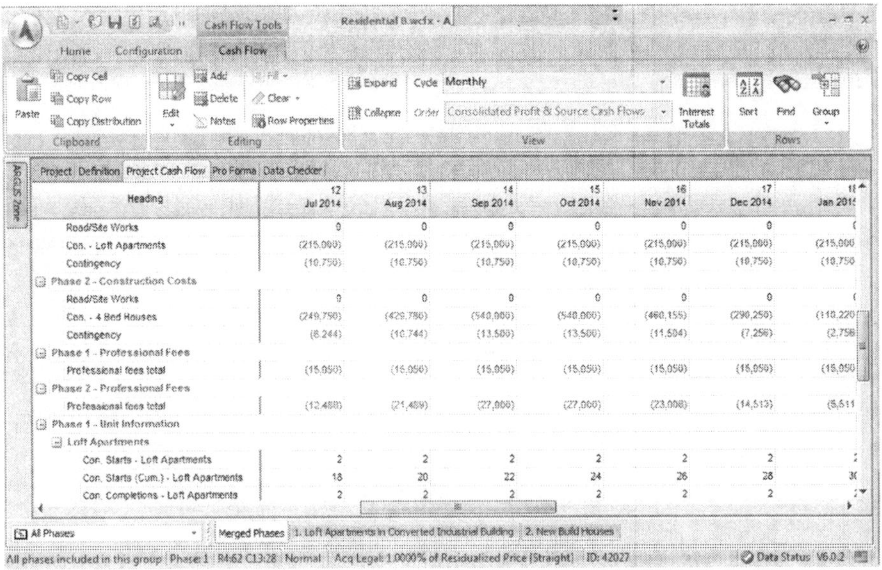

Figure 5-32. Merged phases cash flow

The development can then be summarized via the Pro Forma screen and print output, which lays out the project in the traditional residual (pro forma) format, and in the KPI dashboard.

Pro Forma for Merged Phases 1 2

Currency in $

REVENUE

Sales Valuation	Units	Unit Price	Gross Sales	
Loft Apartments	30	200,000	6,000,000	
4 Bed Houses	20	250,000	5,000,000	
Totals	50		11,000,000	

TOTAL PROJECT REVENUE   11,000,000

OUTLAY

ACQUISITION COSTS

Residualized Price (3.00 Acres 645,196.40 pAcre)			1,935,589	
Land Transfer Tax		3.00%	28,541	
Agent Fee		2.00%	19,028	
Legal Fee		1.00%	9,514	
Legal Fee		2.00%	19,684	
Town Planning			5,000	
				2,017,356

Construction	Units	Unit Amount	Cost	
Loft Apartments	30 un	100,000	3,000,000	
Loft Apartments (Parking Stalls)	45	5,000.00	225,000	
4 Bed Houses	20 un	125,000	2,500,000	
4 Bed Houses (Parking Stalls)	40	5,000.00	200,000	
Totals			5,925,000	5,925,000

Contingency		5.00%	161,250	
Contingency		2.50%	67,500	
Road/Site Works			175,000	
				403,750

PROFESSIONAL FEES

Professional fees total		7.00%	225,750	
Professional fees total		5.00%	135,000	
				360,750

MARKETING & LEASING

Marketing			80,000	
				80,000

DISPOSAL FEES

Sales Agent Fee		2.00%	220,000	
Sales Legal Fee		1.00%	60,000	
				280,000

FINANCE

Debit Rate 7.00% Credit Rate 3.00% (Nominal)

Total Finance Cost   493,887

TOTAL COSTS   9,560,743

PROFIT

                                                                                          1,439,257

Performance Measures

Profit on Cost%	15.05%
Profit on GDV%	13.08%
Profit on NDV%	13.08%
IRR	16.61%
Profit Erosion (finance rate 7.000%)	2 yrs

As noted, while it is possible to model these types of projects in the older versions of Developer (and in Excel), the Single Unit Sales module makes the process of modeling complex residential projects with quite detailed and sophisticated assumptions relatively easy.

Note that the fourth option for project schemes within the program, Multiple Unit Sales, allows the modeling of the construction and sales of blocks of residential units, something that is rarely encountered in the UK and US markets. Essentially, though, the procedures followed are similar to those outlined in this section.

Summary

The changes made to Developer from Version 4 onward greatly increased the usability of the program for residential developers. The move reflects the increasing internationalization of the software; prior to this version, the program was optimized for users in the UK market even though, increasingly, the software was being used globally. The ability of the software to model blocks of residential units being developed throughout a phase using an automatic function was a huge step forward—as is the topic covered in the next chapter: Operated Assets. It underlines Developer's position as the world's leading development feasibility modeling tool.

More Complex Projects

Using the Operated Assets Module

Operated assets are specialized kinds of commercial property that include hotels, golf courses, marinas, and care homes. Although these are diverse property types, they have one thing in common: The properties and the businesses that operate them are closely interlinked, and the value of these interests is less determined by market rent than the value of the net income stream an efficiently run business can generate. In many markets, these properties tend to be valued using their own method, sometimes called the Profits Method, and development appraisal has been very difficult to conduct on these properties because of their specialist nature. Even though this is still the case in terms of obtaining market evidence, Developer has offered a module that makes the physical act of calculating the appraisal of such assets relatively simple.

Operated Assets: Golf Course Development

I am going to run through an example appraisal for the development of a pay-and-play golf course. Please note that the values used are just for illustrative purposes for the module only and should not be used as an accurate guide. The appraisal has been completed so you will see an analysis of how the values were created in the following pages.

Setting up the appraisal is similar to previous appraisals (Figure 6-1). Therefore, we will skip this detail. The first change to what is probably the norm in setting up Developer is in regards to the timescale and phasing (Figure 6-2).

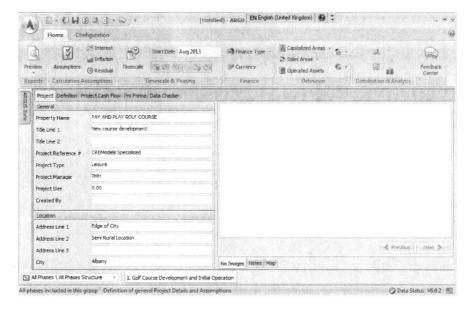

Figure 6-1. Appraisal of the pay-and-play golf course: initial Project screen

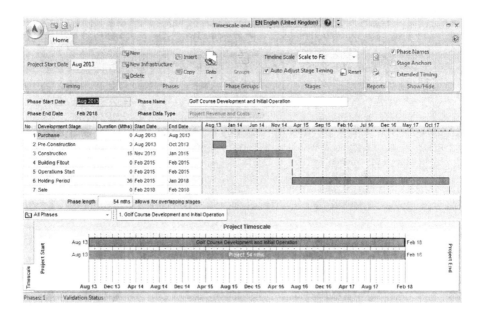

Figure 6-2. Timescale and phasing setup for golf course development appraisal

We find the first clue to the assumptions required in the phrase "operated asset" itself. This type of property creates its value through operations and the generated net income after deducting running costs. It will probably take time for this business to become established. Consequently, we must model the income and expenditure over a period of time. Essentially, what we are working toward is a "stabilized net operating income" a phrase that will be very familiar to US appraisers but perhaps less so to UK and European appraisers. In any case, we need to have a period where the operation of the business can be modeled. We can do this via development stage 6 of the timescale and phasing sheet, nominally labeled as Holding Period. I have allowed a 36-month period.

Figure 6-3 shows the complete Definitions screen. Perhaps the only difference from the norm is that the architect's fee is not a percentage but a grayed out box with a sum in it. I have done this to allow for the fees for a separate golf course designer to be included. I have also made certain that the architect's fees are associated only with the buildings constructed on the site rather than the whole design (Figure 6-4). This may or may not be appropriate to other schemes.

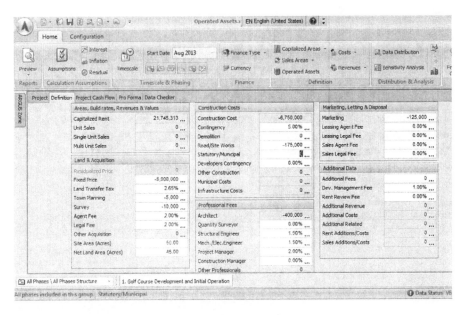

Figure 6-3. Definition screen for golf course development

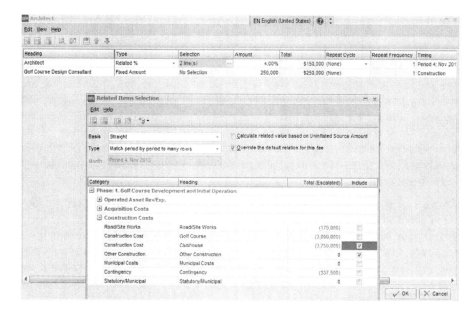

Figure 6-4. Details (top) of architect's fees

We find the main changes when we click into the Capitalized Rent section. When we select certain use types from the drop-down menu (such as Amusement Park, Golf Course, New Hotel, Marina, and other operated assets—Figure 6-5), the center part of the screen—as before, the part that deals with income flow—changes. It now has only two boxes (partially showing): Occupancy/Rates Profile and Income Start Timing. Additionally, at the bottom of this section is a blue link to "View Operated Assets"(not shown.) Clicking on this link opens up the screens to create the operated assets detail.

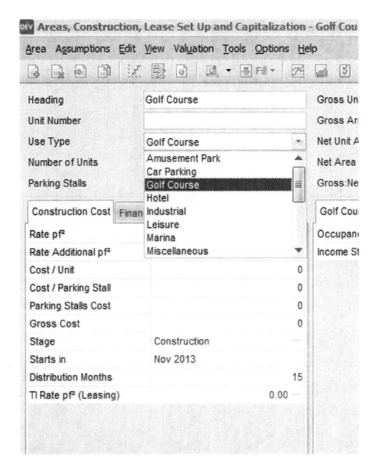

Figure 6-5. The Area screen with an operated asset selected

The Operated Assets Editor screen is largely empty when a new asset is first created (Figure 6-6). On the top left of the screen is a part called "Asset Profile." In this context, a profile is a set of calculation assumptions related to an element of the asset. For this example, I have chosen to separate the income of the course itself from that earned from the clubhouse and professional's shop.

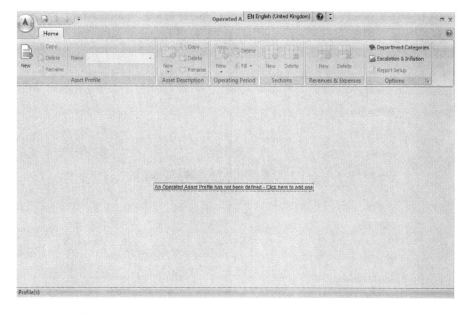

Figure 6-6. The operated assets editor

The main calculation that produces the income forecast from the two profiles uses figures from the Occupancy and Rates and Operating Revenue/Expenses tabs (Figure 6-7).

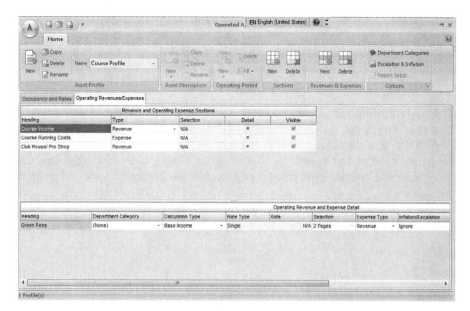

Figure 6-7. Course income calculation

The Occupancy and Rates section is where reference sections on data related to income is created. For a hotel, you would probably use at least three sub-tabs—for the number of rooms available in each period, the rates for each room, and the expected occupancy levels in each period. You would create each of these sub-tabs using the first of the plus signs in the tool ribbon above the section. You can create additional years of projection using the second plus sign to the right. You can delete unwanted sections using the appropriate minus buttons.

For the golf course, you can create several sub-tabs. For example, you might create tabs for green fees, the number of rounds sold each month, membership fees (although I am modeling a pay-and-play course, memberships will still exist for priority and discounted booking at key times, as well as for handicaps and competitions), and the number of memberships sold and renewed each month. In this case, I have kept it simple, just creating green fee costs over the year and the expected number of rounds per month. (See Figures 6-8 and 6-9.)

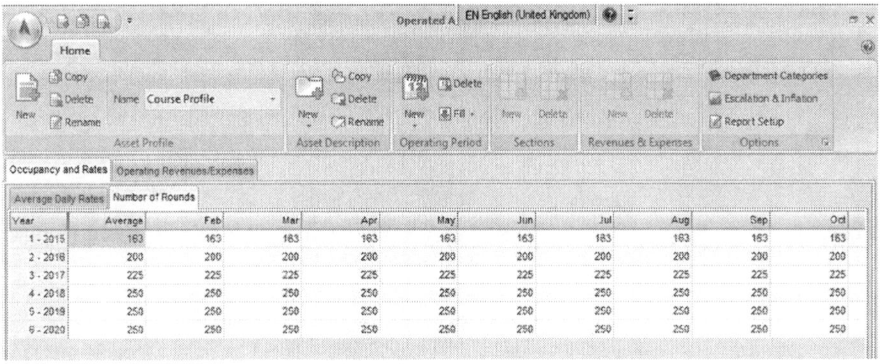

Figure 6-8. Greens fees

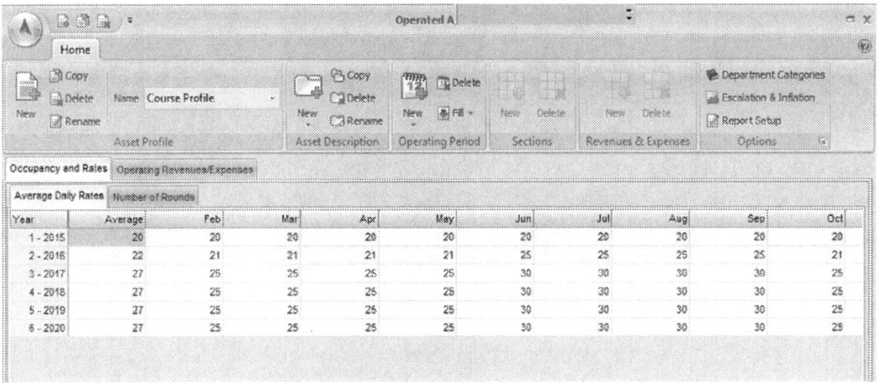

Figure 6-9. Number of rounds per month projections

The flexibility of the Rates tab allows you to create any combination of occupancy percentages, rates, and other assumptions.

Now let's turn to the Operating Revenues/Expenses tab, where this data is used. On the Operating Revenues/Expenses tab, you must create and calculate the income and the expenditure for each element. The income side tends to use the income information I just defined, but it does not have to.

In this case, we have two revenue elements: the greens fees and the clubhouse/pro shop income. Each one is calculated by relating the appropriate quantity schedule with the cost schedule. In our scenario, the cost of each greens fee is associated with the expected number of greens fees sold using the selection column and checking the appropriate boxes (Figure 6-10). Both are classified as course income in this case, and both are base income items.

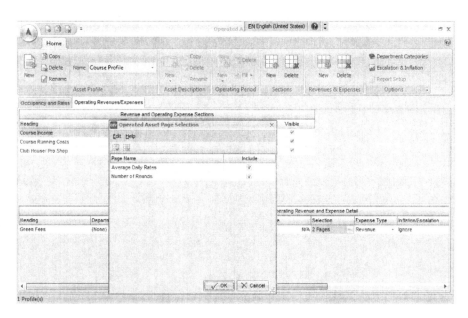

Figure 6-10. Detail of course income calculation showing reference back to Occupancy and Rates tab

For the course expenditure, (in other words, the running costs associated with operating the course itself), I have made a simplifying assumption, taking costs as a percentage of total income and adding on an allowance for fixed costs. In practice, you would probably make a more sophisticated calculation. Developer allows a range of calculation techniques, but I have chosen to calculate them as monthly, stand-alone items (Figure 6-11). Arguably, you could also allocate an overall management/head office cost.

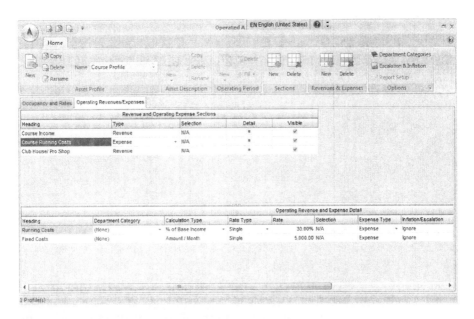

Figure 6-11. Course expenses (running cost) calculation

I have followed a similar calculation process for the clubhouse (Figure 6-12). In this case, I have projected simple monthly income streams for the bar and food receipts and for the rent for the professional's shop. I have chosen to calculate expenses as a percentage of the base income figures, in this case 60 percent. Calculating expenses in this manner is a rather crude rule of thumb and is perhaps not advisable in a real project, but it is sufficient here to illustrate the principles of calculation.

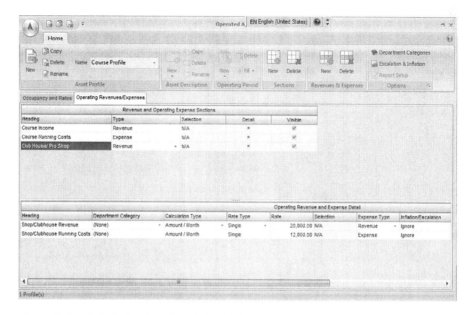

Figure 6-12. Calculating the value of the clubhouse element

You can associate each profile you have created—and there are no limits to the number of profiles—with the appropriate development element using the top drop-down box in the center area of the Area screen (Figure 6-13). The income is displayed as the NOI at sale in the right-hand section and can be capitalized using an appropriate yield as per a normal investment (Figure 6-14).

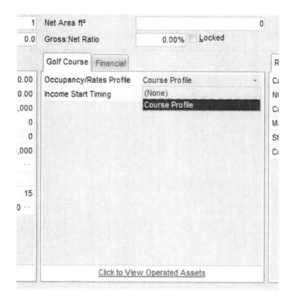

Figure 6-13. Selecting the Operated Assets profile in the Area tab

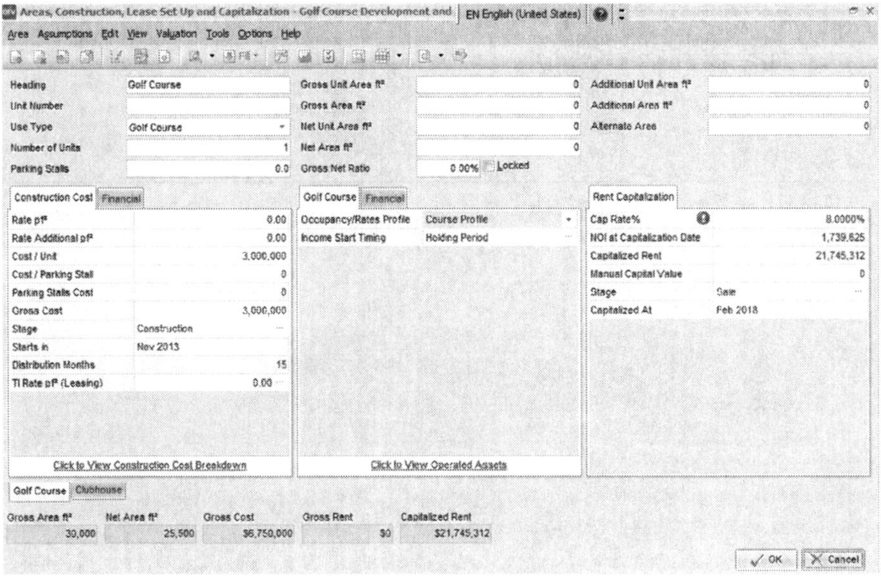

Figure 6-14. Completed Area tab

The results of the assumptions made in the operated assets sections can be examined and adjusted in the cash flow, as has been the case with previous examples. (See Figures 6-15 and 6-16.) With this powerful took, you can ensure that you have appraised the asset using the correct assumptions.

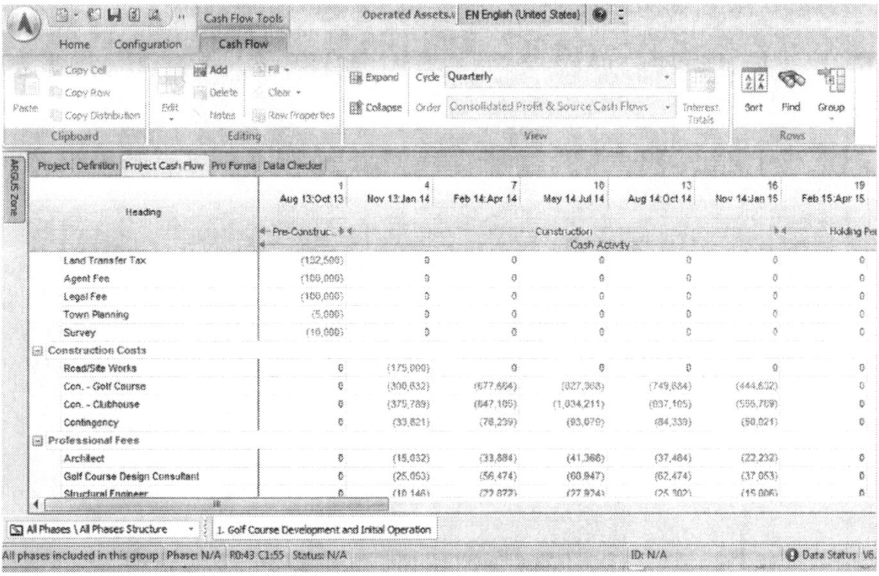

Figure 6-15. Cash flow for golf course development (construction)

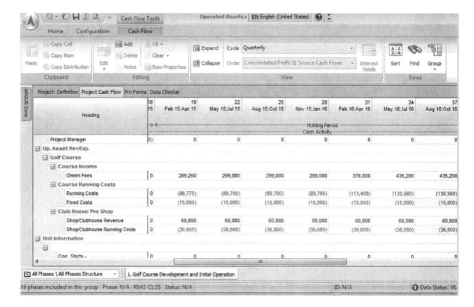

Figure 6-16. Cash flow for golf course development (income/running costs)

■ **Note** The cash flow statement may be imported into Excel; sometimes an Excel view is easier to interpret than the cash flow view in the program.

The Pro Forma lays out the calculation in a traditional fashion:

| Project | Definition | Project Cash Flow | Pro Forma | Data Checker |

Pro Forma for Phase 1 Golf Course Development and Initial Operation

Currency in $

REVENUE

Investment Valuation
Golf Course
Course Income

Green Fees	2,433,750	Cap Rate	8.0000%	30,421,875
Course Running Costs				
Running Costs	(730,125)	Cap Rate	8.0000%	(9,126,563)
Fixed Costs	(60,000)	Cap Rate	8.0000%	(750,000)
				(9,876,563)
Club House/ Pro Shop				
Shop/Clubhouse Revenue	240,000	Cap Rate	8.0000%	3,000,000
Shop/Clubhouse Running Costs	(144,000)	Cap Rate	8.0000%	(1,800,000)
				1,200,000
				<u>21,745,313</u>
				21,745,313

Operated Assets
Golf Course
Course Income

Green Fees	5,011,425	
		5,011,425

Course Running Costs

Running Costs	(1,503,428)	
Fixed Costs	(180,000)	
		(1,683,428)

Club House/ Pro Shop

Shop/Clubhouse Revenue	720,000	
Shop/Clubhouse Running Costs	(432,000)	
		288,000
		3,615,998

TOTAL PROJECT REVENUE	25,361,310

OUTLAY

ACQUISITION COSTS

Fixed Price (50.00 Acres 100,000.00 pAcre)		5,000,000	
Land Transfer Tax	2.65%	132,500	
Agent Fee	2.00%	100,000	
Legal Fee	2.00%	100,000	
Town Planning		5,000	
Survey		10,000	
			5,347,500

CONSTRUCTION COSTS

Construction	Units	Unit Amount	Cost	
Golf Course	1 un	3,000,000	3,000,000	
	ft²	**Rate ft²**	**Cost**	
Clubhouse	30,000 ft²	125 pf²	3,750,000	6,750,000
Contingency		5.00%	337,500	
Road/Site Works			175,000	
				512,500

PROFESSIONAL FEES

Architect	4.00%	150,000	
Golf Course Design Consultant		250,000	
Structural Engineer	1.50%	101,250	
Mech./Elec.Engineer	1.50%	101,250	
Project Manager	2.00%	135,000	
			737,500

MARKETING & LEASING

Marketing	125,000	
		125,000

TOTAL COSTS	13,472,500

PROFIT

Balancing Account	11,888,810	
		11,888,810

Performance Measures

Profit on Cost%	88.25%
Profit on GDV%	54.67%
Profit on NDV%	54.67%
Development Yield% (on Rent)	12.91%
Equivalent Yield% (Nominal)	8.00%
Equivalent Yield% (True)	8.42%
Pre-Finance IRR%	18.22%
Project IRR% (with Interest)	18.22%
Equity IRR% (with Interest)	N/A
Return on Equity%	N/A

After Tax Performance Measures

Project IRR% (with Interest)	18.22%
Equity IRR% (with Interest)	0.00%
Return on Equity%	N/A

Summary

In summary, the Operated Assets module extends the already extensive range that Developer offers the appraiser. It is true that most mainstream users of the program will not need to appraise such specialized projects, but the ability to do so exists, making the appraisal of assets such as hotels, marinas, leisure facilities, and care homesfar easier.

Modeling Project Finance

Using the Structured Finance Module in Developer

All of the appraisals/feasibility studies that I have used in the book so far have been done using the simple financial module that is built into Developer. I did this for a number of reasons.

First, keeping the finance simple meant that we could concentrate on building the underlying development model. Second, in many countries, Developer is supplied in this base format, while the Structured Finance module is an add-on that costs more. However, this book is primarily focused on the North American market, where development is as much about the financing deal as it is about the real estate fundamentals. The Structured Finance module is fundamental to this market. For this reason, I am going to devote a chapter to looking at its use and characteristics.

To do this, I am going to turn back to one of the feasibility studies I completed earlier in the book (Chapter 4). I modeled it originally using the simple finance module, but here I will build a new set of financial assumptions using the Structured Finance module. This is actually my preferred way of working in practice; I like to model a project using simple finance assumptions first in order to test its underlying viability, and then add in more realistic financing. As an appraiser, I feel this method gives me a better "feel" for the basic viability of the project. Thirty years of experience in construction and development has also told me that it is usually the financing that makes or breaks a project. Having a powerful and flexible financial modeling tool is therefore absolutely essential, and Argus Developer provides this.

One final introductory observation has to be made: There is, perhaps, an infinite variety of ways of financing a project. Developer's Structured Finance module reflects this in its span and scope. This chapter tries to cover the most salient features of this module, giving the reader guidance on how to work it. However, this chapter cannot cover every feature and every financing variant.

The Base Project

As you will see from the Project screen (Figure 7-1), I will be illustrating this section with the second commercial example I used earlier in Chapter 4. I will be making one significant change to the assumptions regarding the timescale of the scheme in that, previously, I assumed a sale at the end of the leasing-up period. I have added a holding period of 60 months (five years), during which time rents will be received. I have done this so I can illustrate the use of the mortgage finance section of the module, which requires an income stream to be in place. This is, after all, what would occur in practice where a developer sought to "develop and hold," and needed to switch from short-term project finance to longer-term finance.

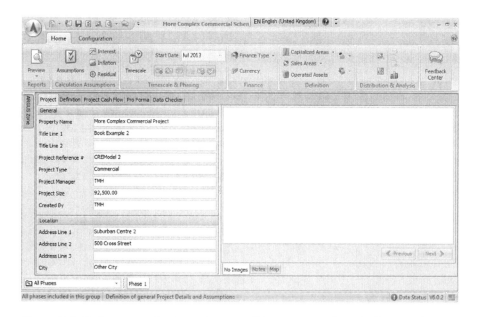

Figure 7-1. Project screen for the project we will be using to explore the Structured Finance module

The timing change is illustrated in Figure 7-2.

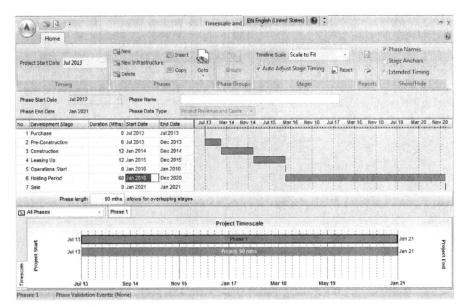

Figure 7-2. Timescale adjustments

Using the Structured Finance Module

To access the setup screens for the Structured Finance module, you need to click on the Finance Type icon on the ribbon bar (Figure 7-3), and select the Structured Finance option.

Figure 7-3. Accessing the finance module

The opening screen for the Structured Finance module (Figure 7-4) always has two structures, an All Phases structure and a Default structure. We will be working in the All Phases structure since we only have a single-phase project and a single finance structure. However, keep in mind that this feature does allow you to create different financial assumptions for different phases or sections of a project. Make sure that the correct financial structure is applied to the desired section of the project.

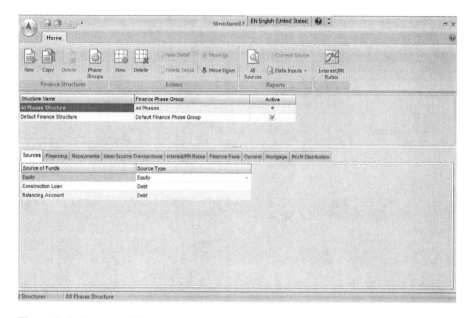

Figure 7-4. Structured Finance opening screen

Underneath the Finance structure are nine sub-tabs that work together to construct each aspect of the financial structure. We will be dealing with each in turn.

You can adjust new phase structures and the partners within the structures using the specific finance ribbon bar tools. This is how we create and edit finance sources (Figure 7-5). For our initial run-through, we will assume that there is a single equity source, the developer's own funds, but that the developer will be using two sources of debt funding—the main project loan and mezzanine, or gap, financing to cover the shortfall between the equity funds available and what the main lender is willing to lend.

Figure 7-5. Structured Finance ribbon bar—icons in the Finance Structures section allow you to create and delete new financial phase structures, while the Editors section adds and deletes funding sources within each of the structures

The new financing source is created by clicking the New icon in the Editors section on the ribbon bar. This creates a new line in the Sources sub-tab, which is initially blank and classified as Equity (Figure 7-6). You can use the drop-down menu in the appropriate box to rename it and switch to listing it as a debt source (Figure 7-7).

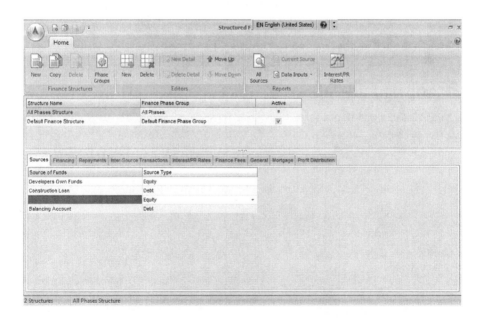

Figure 7-6. Creating a new finance source in the Structured Finance Sources screen

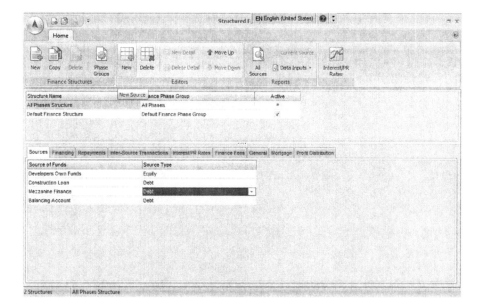

Figure 7-7. Editing the new finance source in the Structured Finance Sources screen

Note that each of the Source of Funds entries is user-editable.

Financing Sub-Tab

Once all the potential sources of funds have been listed, the user then turns to the Financing sub-tab (Figure 7-8). In this screen, you define the amount of money pledged to the project (with the exception of mortgage finance).

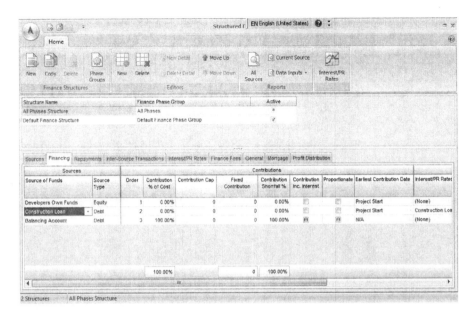

Figure 7-8. The Financing sub-tab

By default, only a single equity and a single debt source of finance are included. Additional debt sources have to be added (using the New icon in the Editors section) and their characteristics then defined. Note that there is always a line for a balancing account. This is a technical requirement of the software. It will identify where there is a project-funding shortfall or where surplus funds have not been distributed. The aim is for the balance in this account to always be zero. This account cannot be deleted.

When you add a new finance source, the program creates a blank line in the Financing screen (Figure 7-9). Once this is in place, a drop-down menu in the Source of Funds list allows the required source to be identified (Figure 7-10). Essentially, this is a lookup to the Sources tab, so it is important to set up that list before proceeding to the Financing sub-tab.

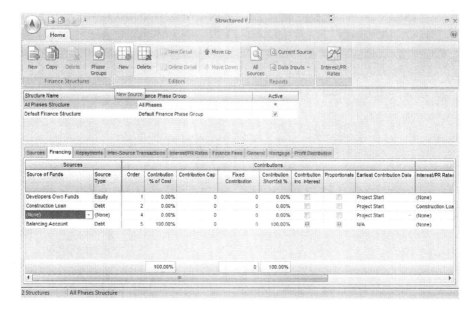

Figure 7-9. Adding a finance source to the Financing sub-tab, initial step

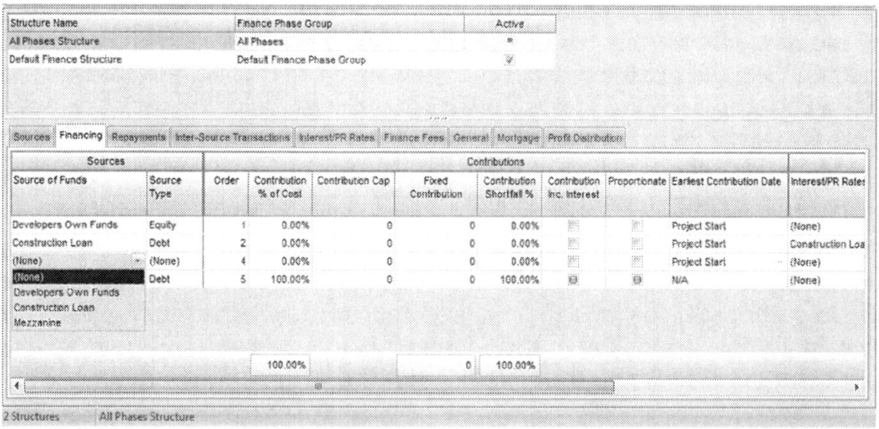

Figure 7-10. Adding a finance source to the Financing sub-tab, second step

Once all the required sources are in place, the characteristics of the finance—the amount, the order of drawdown, any fixed limits on its extent, and so on—can be defined using this screen. As can be seen from the screenshots (Figures 7-11 and 7-12), a high degree of control and definition is possible.

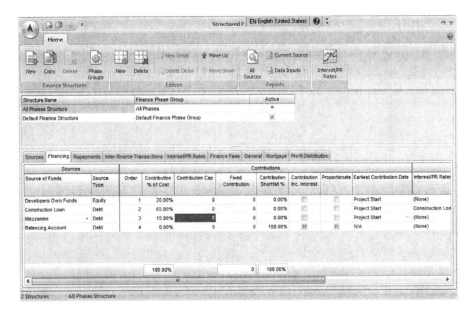

Figure 7-11. Setting the financial structure of the project—left side of Financing sub-tab

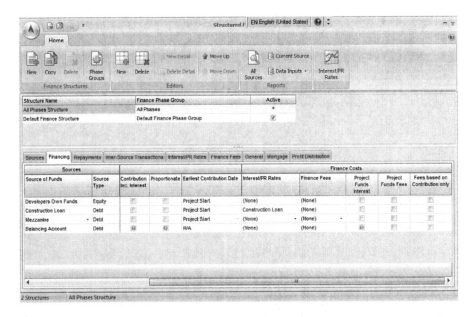

Figure 7-12. Setting the financial structure of the project—right side of Financing sub-tab

In this case, I have left many of the default assumptions in place. What I have defined are the percentage limits of each financing source and the order of drawdown, which, for this project, is the equity first, then the main construction loan, with the more expensive mezzanine drawdown last, to minimize its cost to the project.

■ **Note** Side-by-side drawdowns are permissible in Developer and are modeled by giving each source the same drawdown order.

Let's turn now to how the cost is defined for each funding source. It is, in fact, quite a convoluted process. With interest on equity, you will normally do this as a profit distribution using a preference return. I will return to this later in the chapter. As for the debt sources, you will need to follow a number of steps.

The first step is to define a set of interest rates that are applicable to each source. This is done using the Interest/PR (Preferred Rate) sets just as we did with the simple finance projects, though there is a shortcut within the finance module (Figures 7-13, 7-14, and 7-15).

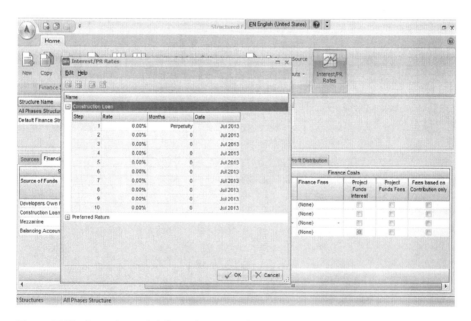

Figure 7-13. Accessing and defining the various Interest and Profit Rate/PR sets

Figure 7-14. Adding a new Interest set—click on the green plus sign

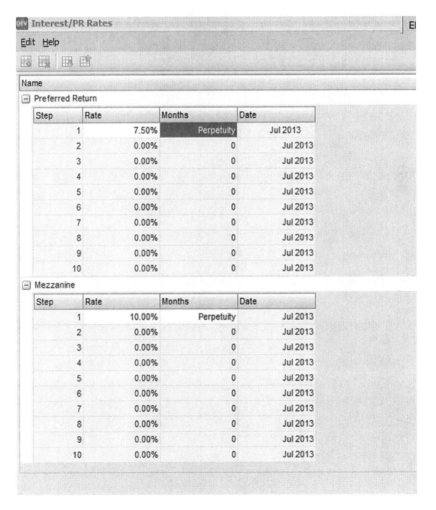

Figure 7-15. Creating the Mezzanine Rate and a Preferred Return Rate

Interest/PR Rates

Once these interest sets have been created, we can then return to the Structured Finance module and click on the Interest/PR Rates tab (Figure 7-16). The sets we have just created are not on the list in this section—this is often confusing for new users of Developer—because the Structured Finance module is a self-contained calculation engine. We need to define what finance sources are active and available to this financial structure. Once this is done, the links to the details of the set will be made.

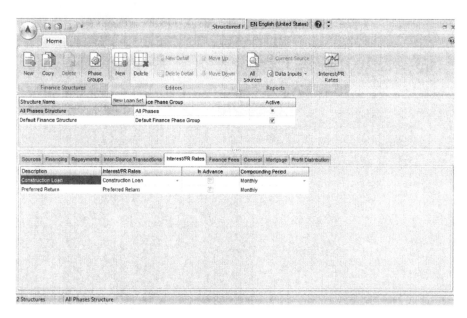

Figure 7-16. Creating the list of active finance accounts in Structured Finance module

The sequence of linking and naming these sets is shown in Figures 7-17 and 7-18.

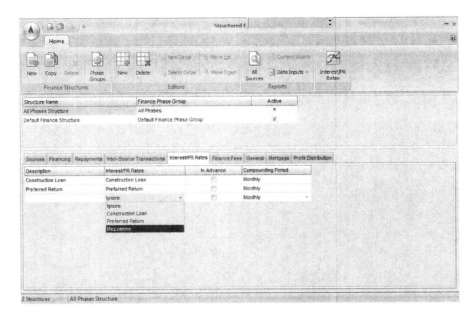

Figure 7-17. Adding the reference to the Interest/PR set to the Structured Finance module

Sources	Financing	Repayments	Inter-Source Transactions	Interest/PR Rates	Finance Fees	General	Mortgage	Profit Distribution

Description	Interest/PR Rates		In Advance	Compounding Period	
Construction Loan	Construction Loan		☐	Monthly	
Preferred Return	Preferred Return		☐	Monthly	
Mezzanine	Mezzanine	▾	☐	Monthly	▾

Figure 7-18. The completed list for our project

Once the required list of Interest/PR sets has been made within the Structured Finance module, we can then return to the Financing sub-tab to allocate the costs to each finance source (Figure 7-19).

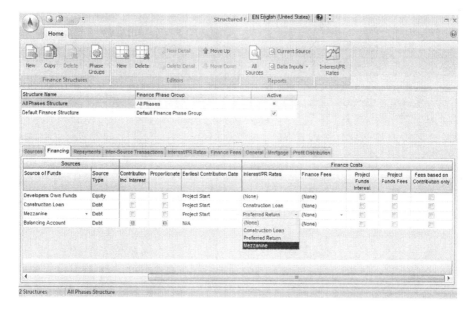

Figure 7-19. Allocating the correct rate back on the Financing sub-tab

Finance Fees

To the right of the Interest/PR Rates column is a Finance Fees column. This again links to another sub-tab where these costs are defined. The process of creating these fee sets is shown in Figures 7-20, 7-21, and 7-22. Again, a great deal of flexibility in the definition is possible allowing the user to model virtually all fee variations.

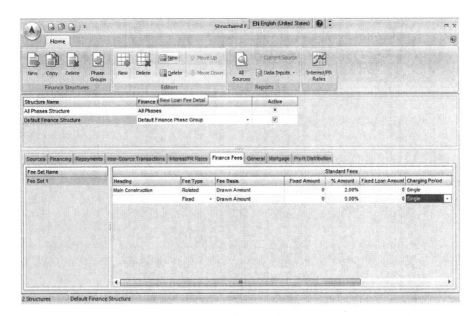

Figure 7-20. Details of Finance Fees sub-tab (note that new fee sets are created with the first of the Editors New buttons while editing within the fee set is done with the smaller New and Delete buttons to the right of these)

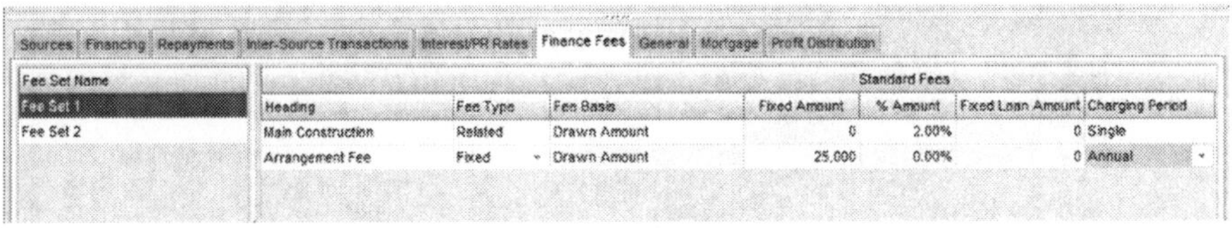

Figure 7-21. Details of Fee Set I (construction loan)

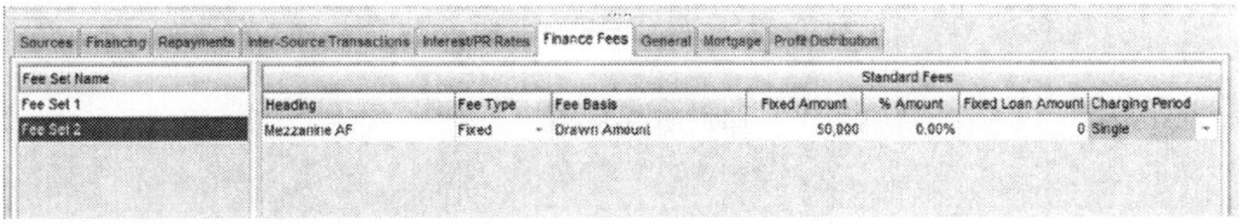

Figure 7-22. Details of Fee Set 2 (mezzanine)

Once we have created the fee sets, we return to the Financing sub-tab, where we can now allocate the appropriate cost to each financing source (Figure 7-23).

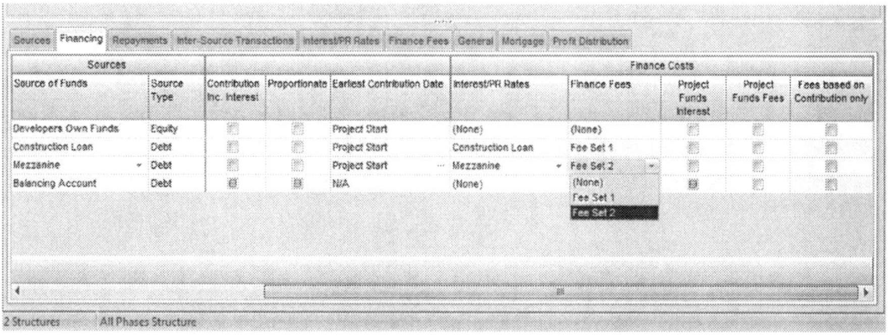

Figure 7-23. Allocating the fee sets in the Financing sub-tab

Although this may appear to be complex, finance for development projects comes in a huge variety of forms and sources, so a finance module must be comprehensive enough to deal with as many eventualities as possible while still maintaining usability. Developer's finance module is complex, but it stays—just—on the right side of usability.

Repayments

We now need to look at how the money is repaid or returned to the financing sources. Note that this section excludes the profit distribution, which is dealt with separately. The Repayments sub-tab is shown in Figures 7-24 and 7-25.

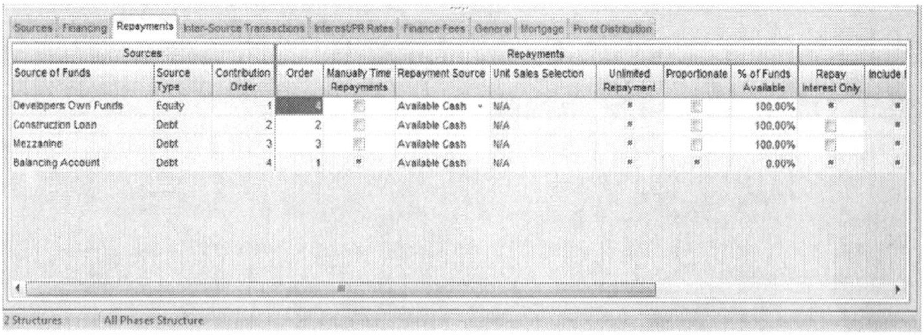

Figure 7-24. Repayments sub-tab—left side of screen

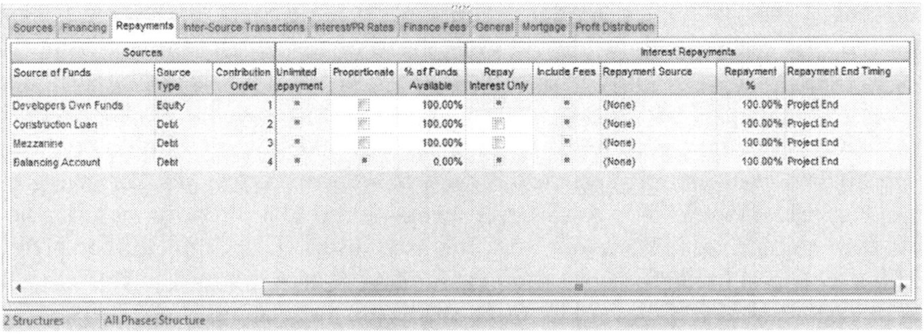

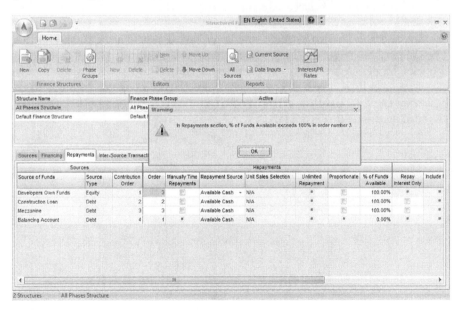

Figure 7-25. Repayments sub-tab—right side of screen

The Repayments sub-tab is rather less complex than the Financing sub-tab, but it is, nonetheless, comprehensive and gives you considerable control in your ability to define exactly how the monies are returned to the equity and debt parties. These include key factors such as timing, the order of debt repayment, and the sources of the funds for repayment.

One minor issue to note is that when we add a funding source, like the mezzanine, the program defaults to ranking the repayment order as equal with the equity sources. In this case, it gives both the equity and mezzanine a repayment order of 3 (Figure 7-26), the main construction loan naturally having the first call while, for technical reasons, the balancing account always has to be repaid first. (Because the goal is to have a zero balance in this account, this has no effect.)

Figure 7-26. Repayments sub-tab—error message when working with default ordering of repayment

In reality, the mezzanine lenders would normally expect to have a higher priority for repayment and should rank ahead of any repayment of the developer's equity at least, if not all equity partners. There is also another technical issue regarding the percentage of funds available to repay the funding source. In most circumstances, all funds (in other words, 100 percent) should be made available to repay funding parties. However, where there is equal ranking of funding repayment, it is up to the user to define the split of the funds available. As the program cannot assume what the user wants to do, it defaults to giving 100 percent of funds to repay the first funding source created. In this case, it is the equity, which leaves no funds to repay the mezzanine.

This obviously must be corrected. One solution is to split the funds fifty-fifty between the two sources. However, as noted, debt normally ranks above equity in priority of repayment, so a better solution would be to rank the mezzanine finance as 3 and the equity as 4 in order of repayment, adjusting the percentage of funds available to 100 percent. Note that if the latter is adjusted *without* changing the funding order, the program stops you from proceeding and produces the warning box, as illustrated in Figure 7-26.

The Inter-Source Transactions and General Tabs

Working along the sub-tabs from left to right, the next two (not including Interest/PR and Finance Fees, which I've covered) are necessary but often less frequently used. Inter-Source Transactions (Figure 7-27) allows funds to pass between funding sources outside of the normal funding/repayment flows. Obviously, contractual and other reasons might cause this to occur in a project, and the finance module needs to have a mechanism to model this. The General tab (Figure 7-28) contains some setup options as well as allowing the user to define a project cash reserve, a ring-fenced source of funds that can ease cash flow issues primarily on multi-phased projects. In these cases, if parties are fully paid off at the end of one phase, there may be a funding shortfall as the next phase starts.

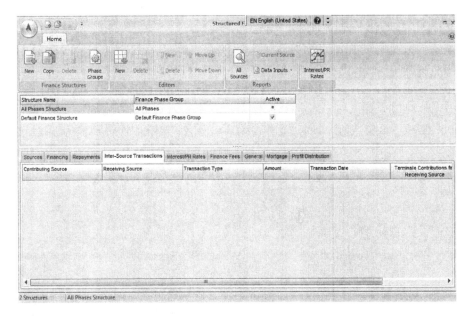

Figure 7-27. Inter-Source Transactions tab

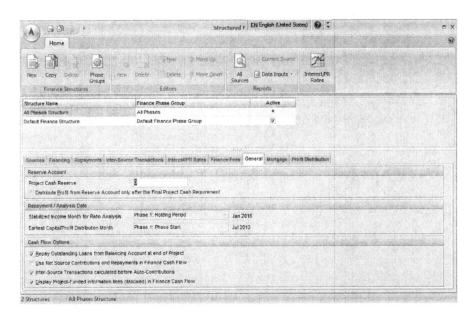

Figure 7-28. General tab with general setup assumptions and project cash reserve definition

Mortgages

The next sub-tab deals with mortgages (Figure 7-29).

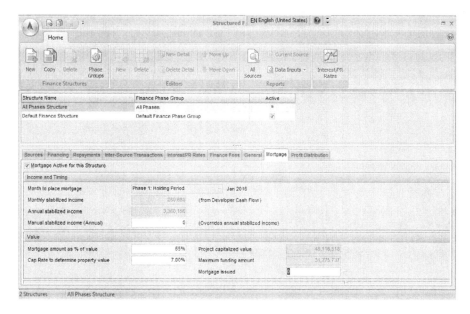

Figure 7-29. Mortgage sub-tab

By default, the mortgage funding is inactive in the financing assumptions. If, however, the developer intends to hold the real estate created, the user should check the box entitled Mortgage Active for this structure.

Normally, the program will then import the cash flow data from the income producing real estate defined in the Definition tab. It will, however, only do this if there is a period within the development time frame when income is actually received. This is the reason why I amended the timing assumptions to allow a 5-year/60-month holding period. If you do not wish to do this, or if only part of the scheme is to be funded by mortgage, it is possible to manually override the inputs and insert a manual stabilized income. The user also sets the remaining mortgage parameters such as loan to value (LTV), cap rate, mortgage interest rate, and duration.

Profit Distribution

Once this tab has been completed, you can, if required, turn to the final sub-tab in the Structured Finance screen, Profit Distribution (Figure 7-30).

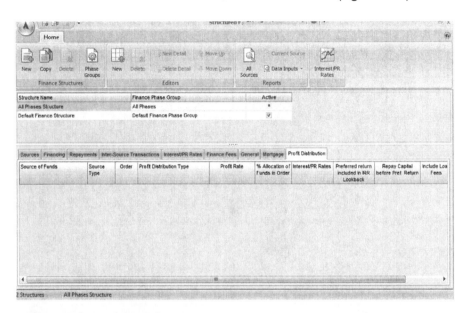

Figure 7-30. Profit Distribution initial screen

In the next example, we will look at more complex profit distributions with multiple parties. However, even when a single equity source is involved, it is important to deal with the profit distribution.

Again, use the New button on the Editors ribbon to populate the list with funding sources you want to distribute the profit to. In this case, I've selected the Developers Own Funds source.

When you are dealing with a single equity source, the program offers you limited choices for profit distribution: Promote, essentially a guaranteed interest return on funds invested that utilizes the Interest/PR sets; and Residual Percentage, basically the funds left over after all the parties and interest have been repaid. We will naturally assume that all residual funds are the developers', so 100 percent of the residual funds are distributed to them (Figures 7-31 and 7-32).

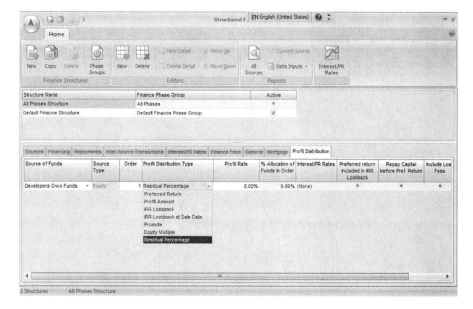

Figure 7-31. Profit Distribution Type options

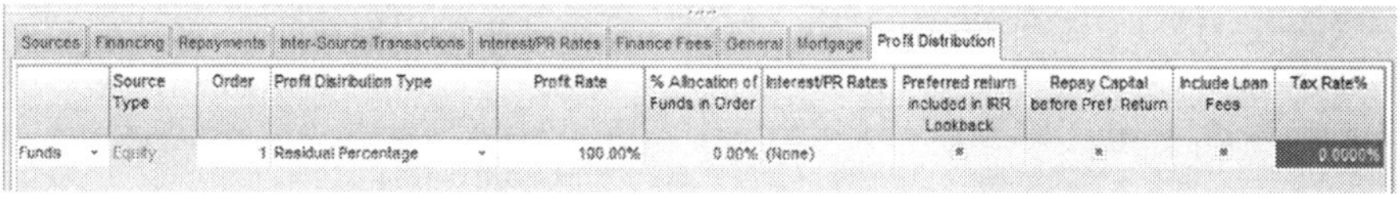

Figure 7-32. Profit distribution for this project

Once you have decided on the profit distribution, you can return to the main program or print a report from within the finance module (Figure 7-33).

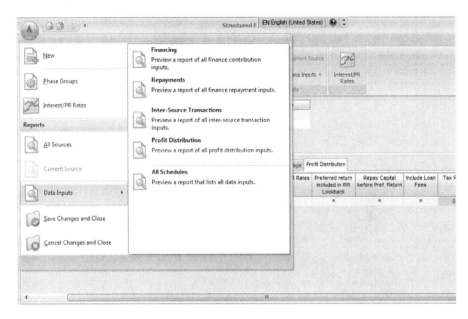

Figure 7-33. Financing reports available within the Structured Finance module

Returning to the main program, you can review the impact the new financial assumptions have had on the KPIs (Figure 7-34). You will see that the analysis includes the key return on equity measures.

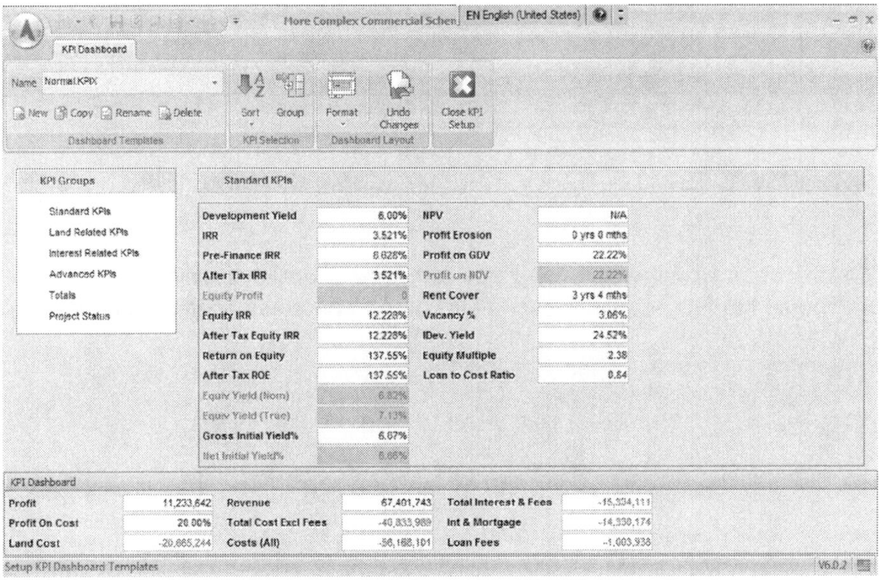

Figure 7-34. KPI dashboard after Structured Finance assumptions are entered

The Structured Finance module also creates a detailed finance-sources cash flow statement. If you have been working in the simple finance mode initially, it is likely that this Cash Flow tab will have been turned off and will need to be turned back on. This is done via the Configuration tab by selecting the appropriate check box on the drop-down menu (Figure 7-35).

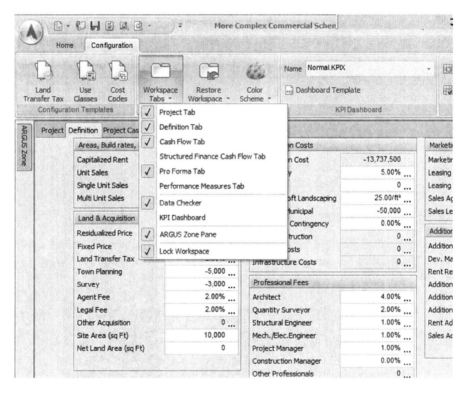

Figure 7-35. Turning on the Structured Finance Cash Flow tab from the Configuration tab

The Structured Finance Cash Flow tab gives a detailed cash flow for each individual funding source (Figure 7-36) plus a combined finance cash flow.

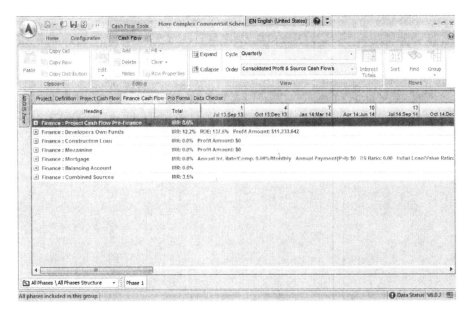

Figure 7-36. Collapsed view of cash flow showing all of the finance sources

This affords you deep insight into the predicted financing characteristics of the project, enabling you to identify potential problem areas and to explore ways of reducing the financing costs. The individual cash flows also have override lines (in dark blue) that allow you to enter manually timed payments in, and repayments outside of, the defined project finance structure (Figure 7-37).

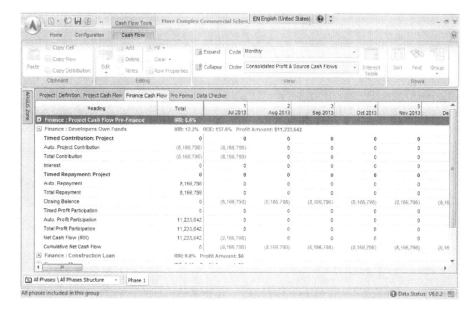

Figure 7-37. Detail of the Structured Finance Cash Flow screen showing the timed override lines (Timed Contribution: Project and Timed Repayment: Project)

▓ **Note** This review should give both an outline of how the Structured Finance module works and also insight into its power. I was working for the company at the time of its launch of Version 3 of the program in 2006; its introduction transformed the way it worked and greatly extended the software's ability from that point onward.

More Complex Financial Arrangements: Waterfall Profit Distributions

The previous project has illustrated most of the functions of the finance module in which a single developer/equity source of finance is involved. Like many aspects of Developer, the program really comes into its own when the situations get more complex—for example, where there are multiple development and/or equity partners. Some of the issues that this raises have already been dealt with in the simple example, such as the drawdown and repayment of finance—although, of course, the more partners involved, the more complex this will be. However, one area, the distribution of profits, is infinitely more complex. Often this involves something called a *waterfall*, a tiered hierarchy of tranches of profit distribution.

For this example, I will dispense with looking at the project itself and concentrate completely on the financial setup.

In the project, we have two potential debt sources, one for the purchase of the land and one for the construction. (These are often at different rates, as the two loans have very different risk profiles.) The project also has three equity sources: the developer, an actively involved equity partner, and a further equity investor who tops up the funds.

As before, the first step is to identify the source of funds (Figure 7-38). This makes them available for inclusion in the financing structure.

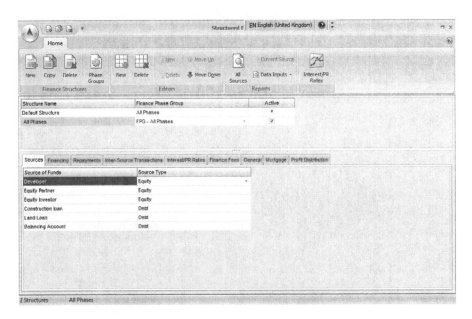

Figure 7-38. Detail of the structured finance arrangement for a project with three equity partners (including the developer)

The next step is to define the financing of the project, that is, how the monies are coming in. This is shown in Figures 7-39 and 7-40. In this situation, the developer is not going to make a percentage contribution but will put in $1.5 million up front. This is the limit of the developer's liability. The equity partner is to provide 20 percent of the total costs with the equity investor putting in 10 percent. They are to do this on a side-by-side basis before the construction loan is drawn down.

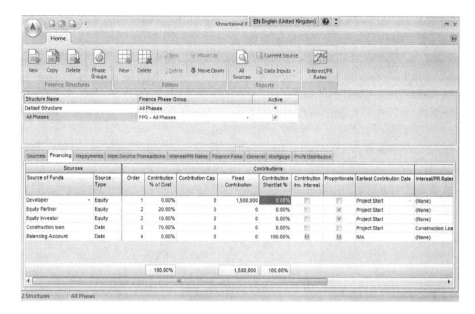

Figure 7-39. Financing screen of the structured finance arrangement for a project with three equity partners (left side)

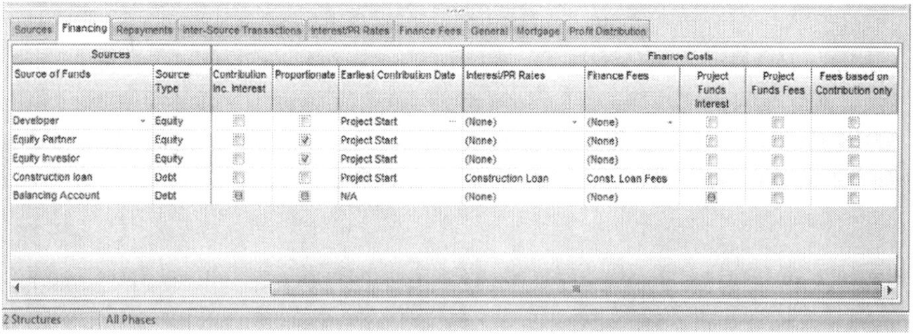

Figure 7-40. Financing screen of the structured finance arrangement for a project with three equity partners (right side)

Note the land loan is not active in this scenario.

Note that the construction loan references the Construction Loan Interest set (Figures 7-41 and 7-42) and has arrangement fees and costs that are defined under the Finance Fees sub-tab (Figure 7-43). Note also that two preference returns have been defined in the Interest/PR sets for later use in the waterfall.

Description	Interest/PR Rates	Nominal Rates	In Advance	Compounding Period
Construction Loan	Constr Loan	✓		None
12% Preferred Return	12% Pref Return	✓		Monthly
10% Preferred Return	10% Pref Return	✓		Monthly

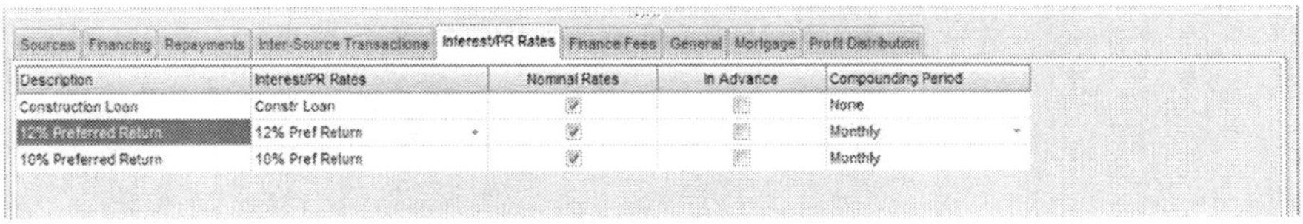

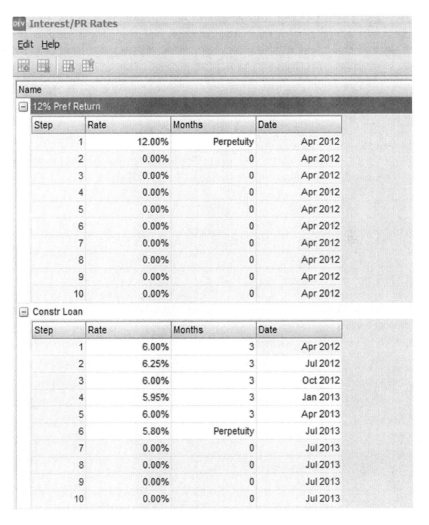

Figure 7-41. Interest/PR sets used in the structured finance arrangement for a project with three equity partners

12% Pref Return

Step	Rate	Months	Date
1	12.00%	Perpetuity	Apr 2012
2	0.00%	0	Apr 2012
3	0.00%	0	Apr 2012
4	0.00%	0	Apr 2012
5	0.00%	0	Apr 2012
6	0.00%	0	Apr 2012
7	0.00%	0	Apr 2012
8	0.00%	0	Apr 2012
9	0.00%	0	Apr 2012
10	0.00%	0	Apr 2012

Constr Loan

Step	Rate	Months	Date
1	6.00%	3	Apr 2012
2	6.25%	3	Jul 2012
3	6.00%	3	Oct 2012
4	5.95%	3	Jan 2013
5	6.00%	3	Apr 2013
6	5.80%	Perpetuity	Jul 2013
7	0.00%	0	Jul 2013
8	0.00%	0	Jul 2013
9	0.00%	0	Jul 2013
10	0.00%	0	Jul 2013

Figure 7-42. Details of two of the Interest/PR sets used

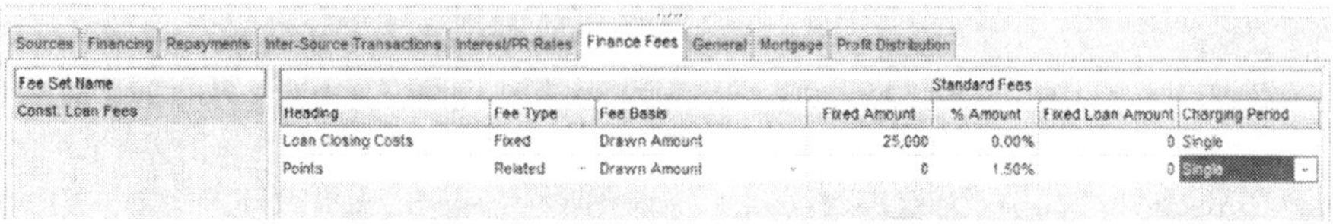

Figure 7-43. Details of the finance fees on the construction loan

Once the financing has been structured to suit the requirements of the project, you can construct the Repayment sub-tab. Note that this is the return of the funds actually invested in the scheme, not the profits/surplus that is dealt with in the profit distribution. The order mirrors the Financing screen albeit in reverse, with the debt having the highest priority and the two equity partners having a side-by-side repayment with the developer being repaid last (Figures 7-44 and 7-45).

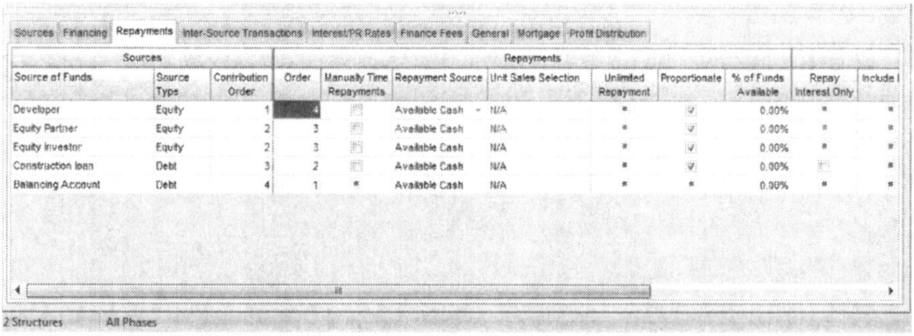

Figure 7-44. Repayments screen of the structured finance arrangement for a project with three equity partners (left side)

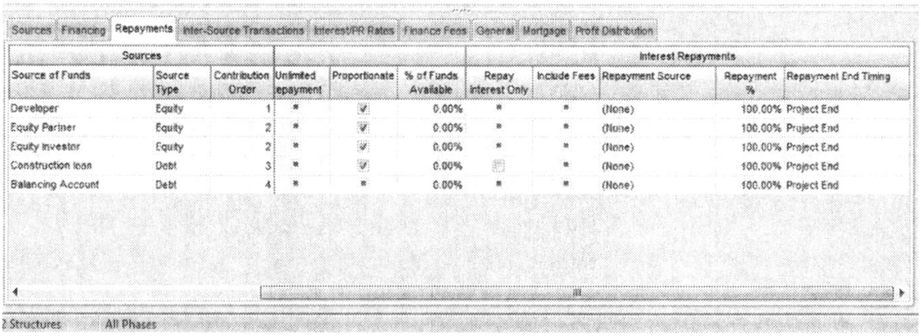

Figure 7-45. Repayments screen of the structured finance arrangement for a project with three equity partners (right side)

There is a mortgage active for this scheme. The details are shown in Figure 7-46. There are no specific project entries in the Inter-Source Transactions and General sub-tabs, so these are, therefore, not shown.

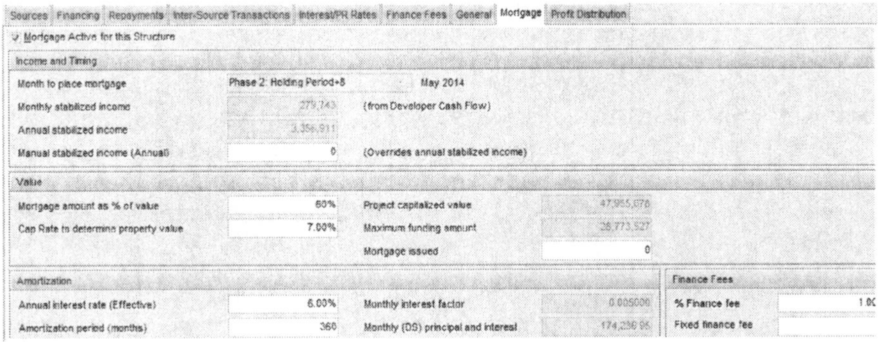

Figure 7-46. The Mortgage setup screen

What we are interested in is the profit distribution. (See Figure 7-47.)

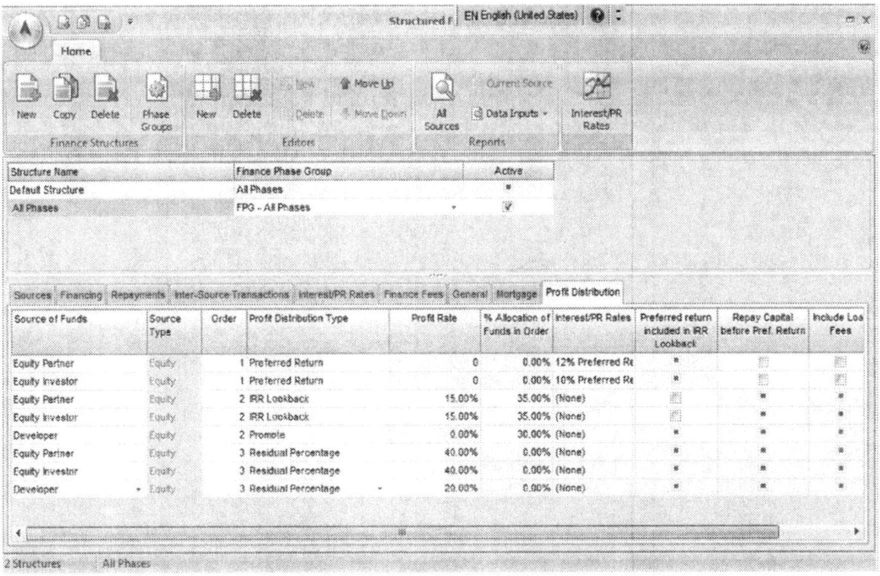

Figure 7-47. The waterfall distribution showing the three tranches of profit distribution

The distribution can look daunting for the inexperienced. However, if examined carefully, the structure is logical. As per the example illustrated at the beginning of this chapter, each new profit distribution line is created in this schedule using the New button in the Editors section on the ribbon bar.

Here the waterfall has three tranches of distribution. The first is what is termed a "preferred return for the equity partner and the equity investor." A preferred return is essentially a guaranteed interest rate to the investor on the funds they invest—like a coupon rate on a bond. The partner expects a 12-percent return, and the investor, a ten-percent return. You can calculate this by linking this tranche to the appropriate Interest/PR set. (See Figure 7-47.) In this tranche, both have first order distributions; in other words, they are paid first.

The second tranche of distribution is called an "IRR lookback." This requires the definition of a particular target IRR—in this case 15 percent—and an instruction as to how profits are distributed up to this point. Here the equity partner and investor share 70 percent of the profits up to this point while the developer gets its first profit share. The partner to an IRR lookback is called a "promote," and this is what is defined here. All three distributions are second-order distributions.

Finally, any other profit left over after the first two tranches must be divided. This is done via a residual distribution. As you can see, this is done on a forty-forty-twenty basis.

Once the distribution has been constructed, the partners will want to check the returns that the project is projected to produce. This can be done via a number of routes including the reports, the finance cash flow, and the pro forma. But there is also a specific Performance Measures tab, which we have not yet looked at. This is turned on via the Configuration tab using the Workspace tab drop-down tool to check the appropriate box (Figure 7-48).

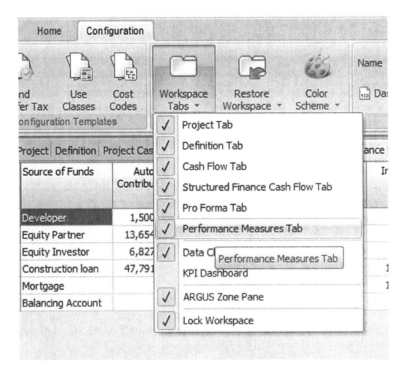

Figure 7-48. Viewing the Performance Measures tab by turning it on in the Workspace tabs' part of the Configuration tab

This produces the Performance Measures analysis shown in Figures 7-49 and 7-50.

Source of Funds	Auto Contribution	Timed Contribution	Total Contribution	Balance Outstanding at Project End	Interest	Fees	Preferred Return Paid	Profit	Total Interest, Fees, Preferred Return
Developer	1,500,000	0	1,500,000	0	0	0	0	3,051,200	3,051,200
Equity Partner	13,654,622	0	13,654,622	0	0	0	3,629,533	6,865,926	10,495,459
Equity Investor	6,827,311	0	6,827,311	0	0	0	1,461,733	4,390,450	5,852,183
Construction loan	47,791,177	0	47,791,177	0	1,591,014	765,733	0	0	2,356,746
Mortgage	0	0	29,061,262	0	1,446,466	287,735	0	0	1,734,201
Balancing Account	0	0	0	0	0	0	0	0	0

Figure 7-49. The Performance Measures tab for the project with three equity partners—left side

Project | Definition | Project Cash Flow | Finance Cash Flow | Pro Forma | Performance Measures | Data Checker

Source of Funds	Auto Contribution	Timed Contribution	Total Contribution	Balance	Interest	Fees	Preferr	Profit	Total Interest, Fees, Preferred Return	Peak Financing	IRR%	ROE%	Tax on Profit	After Tax IRR%	After Tax ROE%
Developer	1,500,000	0	1,500,000	0	0	0	0	3,0	3,051,200	1,500,000	46.308%	203.413%	0	46.308%	203.413%
Equity Partner	13,654,622	0	13,654,622	0	0	0	3,6	6,8	10,495,459	13,654,622	30.449%	76.864%	0	30.449%	76.864%
Equity Investor	6,827,311	0	6,827,311	0	0	0	1,4	4,3	5,852,183	6,827,311	33.089%	85.717%	0	33.089%	85.717%
Construction loan	47,791,177	0	47,791,177	0	1,591	76!	0	0	2,356,746	36,723,260	0.000%	N/A	0	0.000%	N/A
Mortgage	0	0	29,061,262	0	1,446	28:	0	0	1,734,201	0	7.478%	N/A	0	N/A	N/A
Balancing Account	0	0	0	0	0	0	0	0	0	0	0.000%	N/A	0	N/A	N/A

Figure 7-50. The Performance Measures tab for the project with three equity partners—right side

These screens provide a wealth of key information—for example, the peak financing projection, the IRRs, and return-on-investment (ROI) percentage. These are valuable planning and development management tools for developers and investors. It shows here, for example, that although the developer seems to be getting a raw deal in terms of the profit distribution, the developer actually does very well, in fact, better than any of the other equity partners. If you look closely you will see that although developers get the smallest slice of the profit, their project returns dwarf their contribution. But remember, however, that their return is at the greatest risk because they are the last to be repaid and the last to receive a profit distribution. Any deterioration in market conditions will mean that the developers' profit will disappear first.

Summary

As noted in the introduction, the complexity of financing in development projects means that it is impossible to cover all financing arrangements in this chapter. What we have covered, however, should illustrate the capabilities of Developer to model a range of financing from the simple to the very complex in a transparent, powerful, and flexible way to give users what they need most: the ability to model the financing flows into and out of a project in such a way that the most efficient use is made of this precious resource and that all parties reach their investment targets.

The Structured Finance module is perhaps the most valuable modeling component available to the developer within the program.

Understanding and Modeling Risk in Feasibility Studies

Using the Sensitivity Analysis Module

Property development is a risky activity. We know this from the level of return that is assumed in land appraisal calculations—witness the "standard" 20-percent profit margin used in commercial project appraisal. These returns can be obtained and, indeed, returns in excess of 20 percent are quite possible. But it is almost equally possible to experience heavy losses in development projects.

Why is this the case? Well, to start with, development projects tend to be completed over relatively long timescales. As a result, developers need to make judgments about cost and values that are going to occur in the future (frequently from two to five years) before they go ahead with a project and decide how much to bid for the development site. Factors affecting profitability are very hard to predict over such long time frames.

A second problem arises from the fact that the development appraisal itself is highly sensitive to the key input data, which may be derived from assumptions that are themselves based on uncertainty. The reason for such sensitivity is that the outcome of the development appraisal is actually the marginal difference of the ratio between costs and value. A slight change in this ratio can cause a major percentage difference in the marginal outcome.

The key variables are anything to do with value—rents, yields, and sale prices. A fairly small reduction in value (say 5 percent) has a disproportionate effect on land value or development profitability—sometimes 50 percent or more.

It is, therefore, worth examining risk closely. Risk has two aspects. Something can have a low risk of happening (such as being involved in an aircraft crash) but severe consequences (death, serious injury, or long-term trauma). Other things can have a high risk of occurrence (for example, catching a cold) but insignificant consequences (minor discomfort). Real estate development is subject to factors that have a high risk of variance. (Rents, cap rates, and sale values are rarely static.) The stakes and potential consequences are huge because of the large capital sums involved.

Successful developers have to be risk takers. They also have to be optimists. If you are overly pessimistic and extremely cautious, you will never have a scheme projected to make a profit nor will you be able to outbid the market for a piece of land due to the nature of the development appraisal. This does not mean, however, that developers and developer advisers should blindly ignore risk; risk needs to be identified and managed right from the start.

Tip   Plan to identify and manage risk right from the start of a project.

I believe that there are three components to managing risk in the appraisal process.

First, we must accept that the outcome of a single development appraisal is just one possible answer. It is up to the person or body constructing it to test and retest the assumptions made for soundness and reasonableness wherever possible. The sounder the underlying assumptions are, the more reliable the outcome will be.

Second, the tools used to carry out the development appraisal should have mechanisms to test the sensitivity of the appraisal to variations in the input variables.

Finally, the person carrying out the feasibility study should have the skills and knowledge to use this sensitivity analysis properly. All too often, there is a temptation to simply carry out a "standard" sensitivity analysis—varying the rent and yield by 10 percent and recording the results. I would argue that this is just going through the motions—it is not truly "analysis." The key skill in sensitivity analysis is knowing what questions to ask to fully appreciate and explore the risk to the development (and the developer).

The first of these components—testing assumptions and adjusting them as necessary—comes down to developer/appraiser in an individual project. Developers must understand the market, understand the forces that act on it, and understand the product they are intending to produce. This understanding can only come from experience and good research.

The latter two components are different because they are concerned with the tools and methodology—in other words, how the tools are used. Fortunately, Argus Developer has a good sensitivity analysis module (though it is not without its drawbacks), and this section will look at how to use it.

Sensitivity analysis can be carried out in a number of different ways with each method having different utilities and uses. Consider these forms:

- **Simple sensitivity:** Single variable analysis is done by changing variables one-by-one by fixed, similar amounts. This allows you to determine which variables you should pay the most attention to in your project.

  There's also single variable analysis for the break-even point. Here, the object is to discover the value of the variable that will reduce the profitability of the scheme to zero. Although this is not that far removed from the basic simple sensitivity approach, it is sometimes more informative for the developer.

- **Scenario-based sensitivity analysis:** You examine basic scenarios by determining which groups of variables might move together and by exploring the effect that this has on the development's profitability or land value compared with the base assumptions.
  Probability-linked scenario analysis is basically an extension of the above analysis but with an attempt made to ascribe the probability of the scenarios occurring. Although this in itself can be subjective, it can really inform the development decision process.

- **Simulation:** You can do this by running a Monte Carlo–type analysis on the development variables.

Now let's look at the sensitivity analysis modules within the software and then at how you can undertake the different types of sensitivity analysis.

The Sensitivity Analysis Module in Argus Developer

To explore how basic sensitivity analysis is done in Argus Developer, we will return to one of the projects we examined earlier in Chapter 4 (Figure 8-1). We have switched the mode of calculation from Land Residual to Fixed Land Value, but everything else remains the same. This provides an assessment of development profits, giving us a wider range of options in the results.

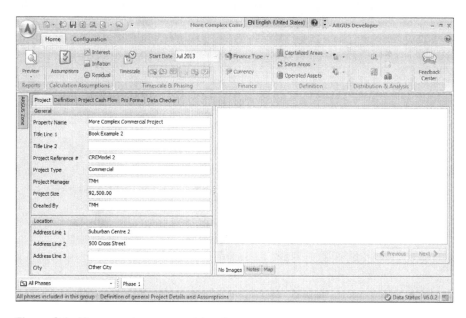

Figure 8-1. More complex commercial project

The Sensitivity Analysis module is accessed via the dedicated button on the toolbar (Figure 8-2).

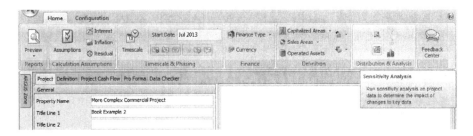

Figure 8-2. Accessing the Sensitivity Analysis module in Argus Developer

If a sensitivity analysis has not previously been done, the user can create sensitivity fields (Figure 8-3). It is obvious, therefore, that sensitivity analysis is not an automatic feature in Developer; the user has to select the fields to be tested and then define the values of the parameters. Developer allows three variables to be tested together at any one time, or four if the fourth variable selected is time.

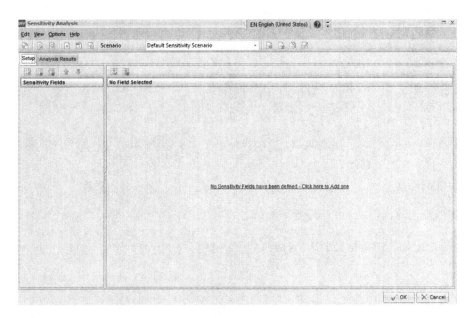

Figure 8-3. Initial Sensitivity Analysis screen

These characteristics tend to push users toward running limited, scenario-type analyses. As mentioned, simple sensitivity tests one variable at a time to determine the impact on returns or values. You can do this with Developer, although it is invariably the same few factors that always impact the outcome of the appraisal—anything to do with value such as rents, yields, sale values, and so on (in other words, those factors that the appraiser needs to pay the greatest attention to.)

The chance of single variables changing in isolation is limited; variables inevitably will tend to move together and thus provide the opportunity to create scenarios. For example, in an economic downturn, project duration tends to increase because the developer finds it harder to find tenants or sell units. At the same time, rental values tend to fall because of reduced demand. As rents fall, so do capital values. This happens not only because of the reduced income, but also because yields increase as investors seek higher initial returns to compensate for increased risk and lower future rental growth. On the upside, construction costs tend to fall in these conditions as contractors compete more strongly for what little work is available (although, of course, this only applies to construction work for which contracts have not yet been awarded).

The nature of the development environment thus suits scenarios. However, Developer is slightly limited by allowing only the three variables to be compared at any one time.

The variables I have chosen to test are construction costs, rental value, and yield (cap rate)—the three most important "physical" factors in most developments.

The first step in running the analysis is to select the sensitivity field. This gives the user the choice of components within that field to be tested.

Once the user has chosen the sensitivity field, another screen appears (Figure 8-4), where the element to be tested is selected for inclusion within the sensitivity analysis. Here we have only one element—a single building—but if you have multiple buildings, you have the option to test the viability against a single element. It would be normal practice to select every element for analysis.

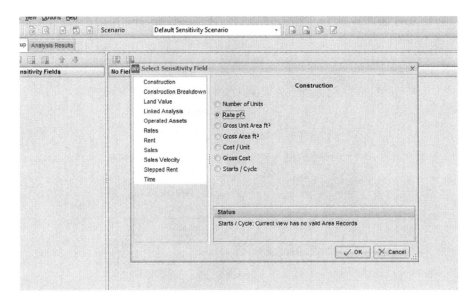

Figure 8-4. Here I've selected Construction from the list of options and chosen the element (cost per square foot) to be tested in the sensitivity analysis

In Figure 8-5, I have chosen the step type (fixed or percentage change in values), the step intervals, and whether the analysis is to be unidirectional (the sensitivity to upward or downward changes only), or whether it is to be up and down analysis.

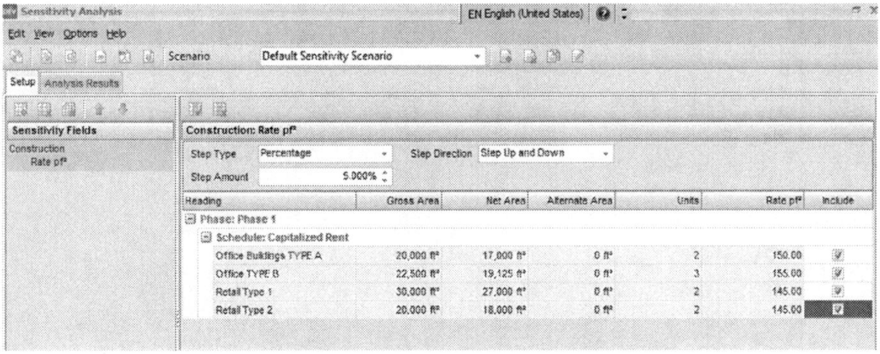

Figure 8-5. Setting the Construction sensitivity parameters

I will now add two sensitivity fields by clicking on the Add Field button (Figure 8-6).

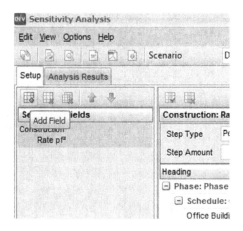

Figure 8-6. Adding a new sensitivity field

I have set similar sensitivity assumptions for Rent (Figures 8-7 and 8-8) and Cap Rate (Figures 8-9 and 8-10).

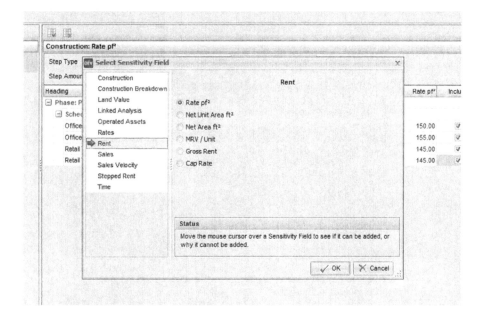

Figure 8-7. Rent sensitivity and options

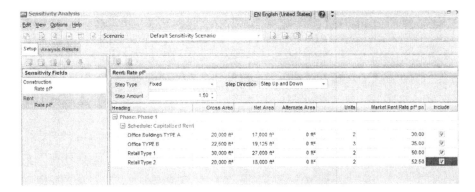

Figure 8-8. Rent sensitivity setup

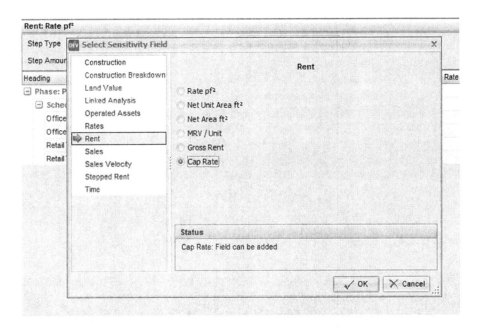

Figure 8-9. Cap Rate (yield) sensitivity chosen

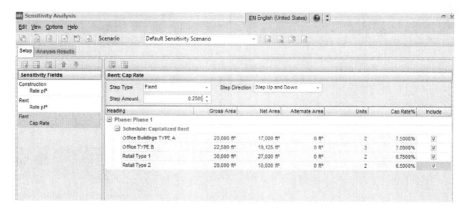

Figure 8-10. Cap Rate sensitivity setup

Once the user has chosen the sensitivity fields and defined the variable values, the sensitivity analysis can be run, either by clicking on the Analysis Results tab (Figure 8-11) or by using the drop-down menu

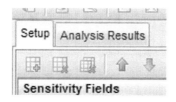

Figure 8-11. Sensitivity Analysis Results are accessed by clicking on the sub-tab behind the setup screen

The results of the sensitivity analysis are expressed in tabular form (Figure 8-12). When we include a third (or fourth—time) variable, we can explore its sensitivity impact using the slider function at the bottom of the table (Figure 8-13). All tables can be printed and reported.

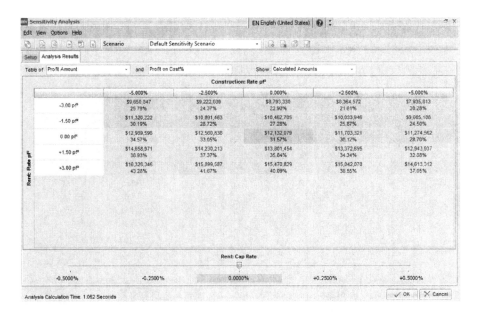

Figure 8-12. Sensitivity analysis outcome with Rent and Construction costs varied with yield static

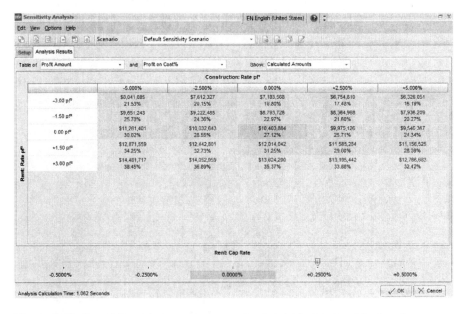

Figure 8-13. Sensitivity analysis outcome—varying the yield using the slider function

The sensitivity results can be exported into reports or printed directly in Word or a PDF:

Table of Profit Amount and Profit on Cost%

Rent: Cap Rate — Construction: Rate pf

Rent: Rate pf	-5.000%	-2.500%	0.000%	+2.500%	+5.000%
-3.00 pf	$13,254,274	$12,825,515	$12,396,757	$11,967,998	$11,539,240
	35.30%	33.78%	32.28%	30.82%	29.39%
-1.50 pf	$15,056,058	$14,627,299	$14,198,541	$13,769,782	$13,341,023
	40.01%	38.44%	36.89%	35.38%	33.91%
0.00 pf	$16,857,841	$16,429,083	$16,000,324	$15,571,566	$15,142,807
	44.70%	43.08%	41.48%	39.93%	38.41%
+1.50 pf	$18,659,625	$18,230,867	$17,802,108	$17,373,350	$16,944,591
	49.37%	47.69%	46.06%	44.45%	42.89%
+3.00 pf	$20,461,409	$20,032,650	$19,603,892	$19,175,133	$18,746,375
	54.02%	52.29%	50.61%	48.96%	47.35%

Rent: Cap Rate — Construction: Rate pf

Rent: Rate pf	-5.000%	-2.500%	0.000%	+2.500%	+5.000%
-3.00 pf	$11,383,675	$10,954,917	$10,526,158	$10,097,400	$9,668,641
	30.38%	28.90%	27.46%	26.05%	24.67%
-1.50 pf	$13,116,749	$12,687,990	$12,259,231	$11,830,473	$11,401,714
	34.92%	33.40%	31.91%	30.46%	29.03%
0.00 pf	$14,849,822	$14,421,063	$13,992,305	$13,563,546	$13,134,788
	39.45%	37.88%	36.35%	34.85%	33.38%
+1.50 pf	$16,582,895	$16,154,136	$15,725,378	$15,296,619	$14,867,861
	43.96%	42.35%	40.76%	39.22%	37.70%
+3.00 pf	$18,315,968	$17,887,209	$17,458,451	$17,029,692	$16,600,934
	48.45%	46.79%	45.16%	43.57%	42.01%

Rent: Cap Rate — Construction: Rate pf

Rent: Rate pf	-5.000%	-2.500%	0.000%	+2.500%	+5.000%
-3.00 pf	$9,650,847	$9,222,089	$8,793,330	$8,364,572	$7,935,813
	25.79%	24.37%	22.98%	21.61%	20.28%
-1.50 pf	$11,320,222	$10,891,463	$10,462,705	$10,033,946	$9,605,188
	30.19%	28.72%	27.28%	25.87%	24.50%
0.00 pf	$12,989,596	$12,560,838	$12,132,079	$11,703,321	$11,274,562
	34.57%	33.05%	31.57%	30.12%	28.70%
+1.50 pf	$14,658,971	$14,230,213	$13,801,454	$13,372,695	$12,943,937
	38.93%	37.37%	35.84%	34.34%	32.88%
+3.00 pf	$16,328,346	$15,899,587	$15,470,829	$15,042,070	$14,613,312
	43.28%	41.67%	40.09%	38.55%	37.05%

Rent: Cap Rate — Construction: Rate pf

Rent: Rate pf	-5.000%	-2.500%	0.000%	+2.500%	+5.000%
-3.00 pf	$8,041,085	$7,612,327	$7,183,568	$6,754,810	$6,326,051
	21.53%	20.15%	18.80%	17.48%	16.19%
-1.50 pf	$9,651,243	$9,222,485	$8,793,726	$8,364,968	$7,936,209
	25.78%	24.36%	22.97%	21.60%	20.27%
0.00 pf	$11,261,401	$10,832,643	$10,403,884	$9,975,126	$9,546,367
	30.02%	28.55%	27.12%	25.71%	24.34%
+1.50 pf	$12,871,559	$12,442,801	$12,014,042	$11,585,284	$11,156,525
	34.25%	32.73%	31.25%	29.80%	28.39%
+3.00 pf	$14,481,717	$14,052,959	$13,624,200	$13,195,442	$12,766,683
	38.45%	36.89%	35.37%	33.88%	32.42%

Rent: Cap Rate — Construction: Rate pf

Rent: Rate pf	-5.000%	-2.500%	0.000%	+2.500%	+5.000%
-3.00 pf	$6,541,709	$6,112,951	$5,684,192	$5,255,434	$4,826,675
	17.54%	16.20%	14.90%	13.62%	12.37%
-1.50 pf	$8,096,675	$7,667,916	$7,239,158	$6,810,399	$6,381,641
	21.66%	20.28%	18.93%	17.62%	16.33%
0.00 pf	$9,651,640	$9,222,882	$8,794,123	$8,365,365	$7,936,606
	25.77%	24.35%	22.96%	21.60%	20.26%
+1.50 pf	$11,206,606	$10,777,847	$10,349,089	$9,920,330	$9,491,572
	29.86%	28.40%	26.96%	25.56%	24.19%
+3.00 pf	$12,761,572	$12,332,813	$11,904,054	$11,475,296	$11,046,537
	33.94%	32.43%	30.95%	29.51%	28.10%

Summary

In conclusion, the sensitivity function in Argus Developer is relatively comprehensive and easy to use. It also links well with reporting. The scope of the analysis is, however, limited by the number of variables that can be tested together. This allows the user to explore limited scenarios. The user can look at these in series, changing the scenario fields and running the analysis each time for each variable.

The user is not able to run an "all-variables" sensitivity scenario, which is restrictive. In reality, in a development, more than three variables will change at a time, having a significant effect on the outcome. There is also no provision within the program to ascribe values to the risk of the variables actually changing.

An example of this is the cap rate. Our best assessment of the cap rate was 7 percent when we did the initial feasibility study. In the sensitivity analysis, we might explore the impact of the cap rate improving to 6.75 percent or 6.5 percent or deteriorating to 7.25 percent or 7.5 percent, but we have done nothing to assess how likely any of the movements are. Is there a one-in-ten chance of the yield deteriorating to 7.5 percent? Or is it one-in-five? If it is the former, our profit assessment is reasonably secure. If it is the latter, the project is rather more risky. To be really informative, a sensitivity analysis should include some assessment of risk and, within the system at least, Developer does not have this.

The answer is, of course, to do this risk explicit analysis outside of Developer and, for this purpose, the program's outputs, particularly from the Sensitivity Analysis module, are extensive and clear enough to be employed. It is a shame, however, that Developer does not, as yet, have the facility to do this analysis within the program. It is one of its few weak areas.

Wrap-up

Using Argus Developer in the Real World

Oddly enough, I am going to start this chapter by addressing some of the main criticisms of the software, ones that I came across when I was writing an earlier book on real estate development in the late 1990s, later when I was working for the company as one of its trainers, and, more recently while I have been working independently as a consultant. These comments are so common that I feel they need addressing.

I am going to explore three main criticisms. The first is that Argus Developer is too easy to use, enabling inexperienced appraisers to construct feasibility studies that *look* good, but may not be great in practice. The second criticism is that Developer hides too much, making some users suspicious about the outcome. The final area of critical comments concerns the main alternative to Developer and the other off-the-shelf solutions such as Estate Master or Microsoft Excel. Practitioners ask themselves why they should pay the not-inconsiderable license costs for Developer when they can use their skills and knowledge in creating their own Excel models.

It is this latter area that I will spend the most time on. However, readers may see a common thread here; some people consider Argus Developer almost as an affront to the professional, that using it is for amateurs, and that using it is a bit like cheating!

I'll respond to those beliefs by comparing Developer to two supe stars from the sports world: Björn Borg and John McEnroe. The two athletes were artists on the tennis courts in the 1970s and 80s, using their small-headed wooden rackets to duel. Many tennis fans mourn the passing of that time. But now consider this: If they were playing today, would they be using modern, big-headed, composite equipment? Of course, they would. The game has changed and evolved, and the new equipment has created a new breed of power players. Nonetheless, there is still room for a skilled artist such as Roger Federer.

Development is much the same way. The game, like tennis, is fundamentally still the same and is played by the same rules, but the technology for playing it has changed. Just as you would look foolish if you turned up at Flushing Meadow, Wimbledon, or Roland Garros with an old-style wooden racket, not using the technology now available to the appraiser seems very shortsighted.

It's not what you use—it is how you use it that is important.

And that leads nicely to the first criticism.

"Argus Developer is too easy to use: Inexperienced appraisers and developers can produce feasibility studies that look good but are actually garbage." This is a criticism that I have heard frequently, particularly from the older, grizzled veterans of many real estate cycles. To a certain extent, it is valid; Developer is easy to use, and it even prompts the users to consider things in the feasibility study that they may not have thought about. The outputs are very professional; superficially, at least, it is difficult to tell if a neophyte or a professional with 40 years' development experience has put together a Developer file.

However, just because something is easy to use does not mean that the true value of experience and knowledge is lost. The veteran, experienced practitioner will always get more out of the software; the program is a skill extender and enhancer, not a skill replacer. If you drilled down into the feasibility study produced by the neophyte, you would almost certainly find inconsistent and unsound assumptions. One would hope that that the neophyte's superior or financier would spot these. However, the fact that Developer is easy to use is not a valid criticism. The more difficult something is to use, the more difficult it is to spot errors. In fact, the ease and transparency of the software makes hiding errors very hard.

Which leads to the second frequent criticism.

"Argus Developer is too much of a black box. I can't see what it's doing." This is, again, something that I have heard frequently about Developer, and it is a criticism that has always surprised me. If you know how to use Developer, it should be obvious to you that the program either does show exactly what it is doing or there is a way—by looking at the specific distribution or examining the cash flow, for example—to check what the impact of an assumption made has on the project.

Certainly, this has not always been the case with project feasibility software. In the mid-1990s, I taught real estate development in a graduate program in the UK and reviewed a range of the competing software products for consideration for instructional use. One of my prime concerns was whether the systems were reliable. One of the primary tests I used to determine reliability was to run example appraisals on the systems against my own tried and trusted Excel models. I have to say that many of the models *were* inconsistent, and I often struggled to audit them to find out why they varied. The exception even then was Developer, and the reliability and transparency increased with later versions. Since then, Developer's rise to become the most widely used feasibility study software in the world has been built on this combination of reliability and power.

Which leads to the third criticism, relating to Excel.

"A really skilled appraiser would use Excel rather than Argus Developer." As the last section implied, I used to be a strong proponent of Excel spreadsheets for use in real estate, frequently using and creating them, employing them widely in both practice and in the classroom. I am now more wary of them, even though they are still the most widely used tool in the industry. Excel has been developed over a period of more than 25 years and most people are aware of the characteristics of the program: its flexibility and utility. It is an immensely powerful tool that can be applied to virtually any situation. It is employed in every field from financial analysis on Wall Street to engineering airliners, fighter planes, and spacecraft.

It is natural, then, that Excel be applied to real estate development tasks. It looks like the ideal tool for the job and, indeed, many practitioners pride themselves on their Excel abilities and the sophistication of the models they use.

There are, however, issues with using Excel that the practitioner should be aware of.

For reasons of accuracy, there has been a general pressure in the development industry to move from the simple accumulative models to cash flow approaches. However, there are problems with cash flow feasibility studies that have caused some in the industry to resist their use. The first principal complaint about such models is that they are time-consuming to produce from scratch, particularly compared with residual models. Once a template model has been developed, however, this time can be reduced. Nonetheless, there are inherent risks of error when existing models are adapted to meet the needs of different feasibility studies.

The second major complaint is the level of detail required in the assumptions that go into the construction of the cash flow template. Again, there are elements of truth in this; the models are far more complex and transparent, yet many of the assumptions required can reasonably be made from past experience with similar projects and are not that far removed from the sweeping, broad-brush ones made in the residual models.

The final major complaint is one that is valid: The increased complexity of the cash flow models means that there is more risk of errors creeping in. These are not so much errors of assumption but more simple mistakes in calculation or cell reference. Spreadsheet cash flow models have to be very carefully audited and, often, there is insufficient time to do this. This is undeniable and is the reason many people advocate using proprietary models, where these types of errors can be virtually eliminated.

A Deeper Look into Excel as an Appraisal Tool

There is, however, more than one type of spreadsheet model used in development appraisal practice. These spreadsheets still mainly use Excel, although some use the Open Office or Libre Office applications. Essentially, experience has shown that models fall into four broad types:

1. Automated, "active" accumulative, back-of-the-envelope models

2. Simple, self-created calculation sheets lacking time-specific dialog references

3. More sophisticated, self-created sheets with time-specific dialog references

4. Professionally created, complex sheets

These models' usability and propensity to be vulnerable to errors vary. It is, therefore, important to look at the outline characteristics of each.

The first type is spreadsheets, albeit simple ones in that the calculation is done behind the cell. As these reproduce much of the weaknesses of the accumulative models, there seems little attraction in using them. The residual layout has distinct advantages in presenting results; indeed most proprietary systems such as Argus Developer use them as an output, but in terms of calculation they are sub-optimal.

The second type is typical of the majority of self-created sheets, where the user, probably self-taught on Excel, has produced an often unique or tailored spreadsheet to conduct a particular project.

The third type is similar to the second. However, it is designed for use in a wide number of projects. Such applications overlap somewhat with the fourth type—professionally constructed models that use Excel as the calculation engine behind a prettier front end. The difference is probably arbitrary, but my experience is that this classification is just about right.

Although the previous section was intended as a review of the broad categories of spreadsheets used in development feasibility studies, I have already started to identify areas where these models are sub-optimal in terms of vulnerability to mechanical or construction errors (as opposed to forecasting errors that are an inherent risk in all appraisal models). A starting point is to identify the most likely types and sources of mechanical or construction errors in spreadsheets. It is difficult to be definitive about this and cite real-world examples, as few developers are willing to advertise or admit to their mistakes. However, these sources of errors have been observed in practice, and I have experienced them personally:

1. **Errors due to time pressure.** Many workplaces are high-pressure environments with appraisers having to do complex work within a short timescale.

2. **Failure to properly audit the spreadsheet.** Auditing can eliminate errors from a spreadsheet, but every creation of a spreadsheet item or change to a spreadsheet model requires an audit trail to be followed. That costs the developer time. Standardized models, such as can be found in Argus Developer, do not need the same audit and, as a result, save the developer considerable time in checking the mechanics of the calculations.

3. **Incorrect modification of an existing spreadsheet model** (and a presumed failure to audit). This is a common set of circumstances. Development projects are not static; there are always many changes from the initial appraisal, where many assumptions have to be made, to the final appraisal done immediately prior to work on site.

4. **Application of an existing model to new development projects.** It is natural when considerable time and effort have been invested in the creation of a spreadsheet model to spread the cost (and save time) by applying and adapting the model for different projects. This opens up not only the possibility of modification errors, as in the third item just mentioned, but also in the perpetuation of errors from earlier projects because the assumption will have been made that the applied model has been audited and is error-free on the earlier projects.

Type 1, the simple back-of-the-envelope models, and Type 2, project-specific, manually linked models, are particularly vulnerable to all of these sources of errors. This is quite serious, as these are the models probably most commonly used in development appraisal practice.

■ **Tip** Never underestimate the effect time pressures have on creating credible and usable appraisal spreadsheets. When it comes to fixing minor bugs or building audit trails, it is often far too easy to "get to it later." Later never comes, but the omission can lead to serious financial problems down the road.

The models will probably have been audited for errors in their initial use but, as noted, modification over the project life is inevitable. Also, almost inevitably, once a model has been created, used, and become familiar to a project team, it will almost certainly be applied to other projects. Smaller developers, who do not have the luxury of extensive staffing, often use these spreadsheets. Furthermore, it is likely that it is these organizations will be under the greatest time pressure and will have few resources available to properly audit and re-audit for errors when changes are made.

Type 3 models are more sophisticated and are usually designed for a range of projects rather than constructed for one in particular. They should, therefore, be more reliable. They are not immune to error, however, and their relative sophistication can lull the user into a false sense of security by believing that they are foolproof. In fact, their relative complexity is also an area of vulnerability; changes made are more difficult to do properly, and the downstream effects of the alterations are often more difficult to appreciate. Development projects are so varied—different phasing, special cost distributions, and so on—that it is very difficult, if not impossible, to design a spreadsheet template that will meet all variations. Ideally, the original model creator should make any changes and perform auditing. However, the practicalities of working on development projects means that this cannot be assured.

Type 4 models should be more reliable because they have been professionally produced and tested and designed for a range of projects, Yet again, this does not make them issue-free.

For one thing, they are complex and opaque. A user may make a data entry error but not realize that he or she has erred. Another issue arises out of the fact that these models have a special purpose in their design. This means that they are often limited in modeling other factors, elements that are probably very important to the developer.

Fundamentally, too, for all the protection placed on the input screens, the model is still based on Excel. People with sufficient knowledge of Excel can turn this protection off and modify the underlying formulas—and this applies to most, if not all, of these sophisticated Excel models. Although this can produce the required tailoring to suit the requirements of a specific project, the complex opacity of these models makes them equally vulnerable to errors.

A final point in this argument is to consider the increasing investment in time and money in these models. The advantages of the simple, project-specific models are that they are relatively cheap and flexible, if very vulnerable to errors. This situation can be improved by investing in a professionally produced system, but this still creates a sub-optimal result. Yet the cost of producing them almost certainly outstrips the cost of purchasing licenses of tried and tested, consistent and reliable, yet flexible proprietary systems.

Is development feasibility a very different animal from the more predictable world of standing investments, and, indeed, different from all of the environments mentioned in the introduction to this section—designing aircraft, modeling sophisticated financial instruments, and so on?

Absolutely.

The key differences are volatility, risk, time pressure, and heterogeneity. Although the mathematics and calculations in a development appraisal *are* relatively simple, because of the geared nature of the development calculation (in other words, you are calculating the margin of return), the results are extremely volatile, as we have seen from the section on sensitivity. Only minor changes in assumptions make huge changes in the output of the appraisal. A slight mistake can have a major impact.

However, what about the transparency of Excel? Surely you can just audit your models to find the errors? Well, in theory, yes, but in practice, two factors conspire to prevent that. The first is that most initial appraisals are done under a degree of time pressure; there often is simply not the time to run a comprehensive audit. The second comes down to a characteristic of humans—the inability to see our own mistakes. It is a fact that most Excel models are self-created by the people carrying out the appraisal. Anyone who writes anything knows that it is essential to get a second pair of eyes; this second viewer will instantly spot glaring mistakes the creator has missed. Most appraisers do not have this luxury.

Surely, it might be argued, as models are developed over time, these mistakes will be picked up and removed. This would certainly be the case with appraising standing investments, where many components will be consistent and repeated. It is *not* true of developments. Each development tends to be very different, even if it is only in the duration of the project. Whatever, every Excel model will inevitably have to be changed from project to project. As soon as you have made changes, you have the potential for error—and the effect of every error is magnified because of the volatility of appraisal yet you don't have time to track down that error.

This is why I am such a strong advocate of tried, tested, and reliable proprietary packages such as Developer. They are designed for the job, and they have uniformity and consistency, meaning that you are actually prompted to put in all of the components you need (another potential source of error). They even have the ability to import and export to Excel if you need additional flexibility or special calculations.

Excel is a fabulous tool with immense power. However, the special nature of development means that in using self-created models, you are playing with a ticking time bomb that will one day blow up in your face with potentially devastating financial consequences.

▓ **Tip**   Trust your feasibility studies to programs like Argus Developer over Excel or other custom-designed spreadsheet analyses. Even when done really well, they probably harbor a flaw or two that could end up doing serious damage to your project.

Beyond the Feasibility Study

I hope that you are satisfied that the case for Developer has been established. What about after the feasibility study? How does Developer fit into the development and post-development phases of the real estate life cycle?

In terms of the actual development phase, the cash flow that Developer produces naturally will form one of the most important development management tools for the developer mapping actual expenditures and revenues against those projected in the feasibility study. This can be done in a number of ways.

One way is to export the cash flow into Excel, something that the program allows from the backstage view on the ribbon bar. The drawback of this is that the software only allows a paste of figures into Excel. The formulas and calculation do not come into the spreadsheet (Developer is not an Excel application).

Older versions of Developer (up to Version 2) used to have an "actuals" extension, allowing the creation of a hybrid cash flow with a set of active lines inserted under each one created in the feasibility study. This allowed the user to enter actual expenditure as the project proceeds. This was removed in 2006 as the company launched its Budget software, a very sophisticated project-monitoring tool. Developer has the facility to incorporate cost codes within the system (Figures 9-1 to 9-3) and then to be exported into Budget (Figures 9-4 to 9-6). A full review of Budget is beyond the scope of this book. However, the system contains a very sophisticated forecasting and cost revision system and allows the user to pair its invoicing system with Budget.

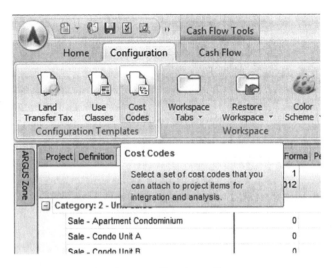

Figure 9-1. Incorporating cost codes into a Developer file

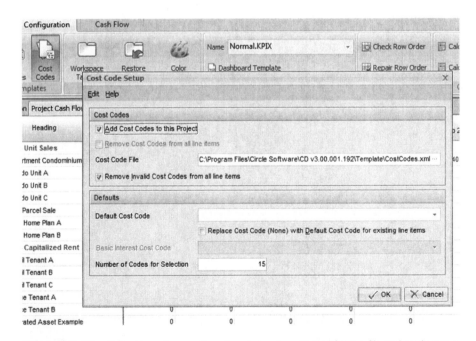

Figure 9-2. The dialog box where cost code sets can be selected from a file and made active

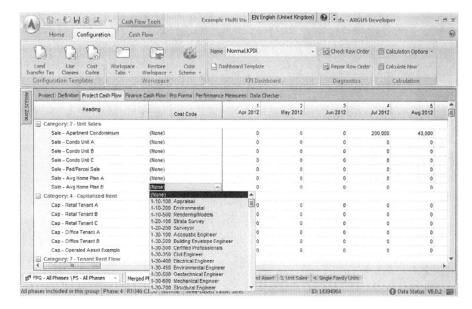

Figure 9-3. Incorporating cost codes into a Developer file—coding the individual cash flow lines

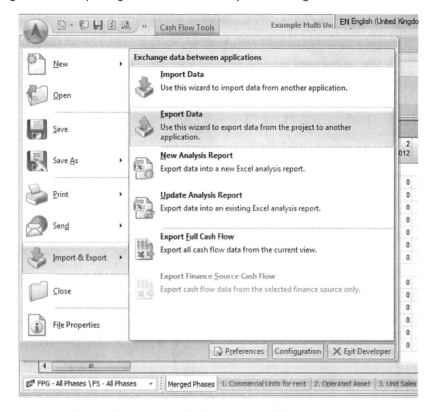

Figure 9-4. Preparing to export to Budget or another application

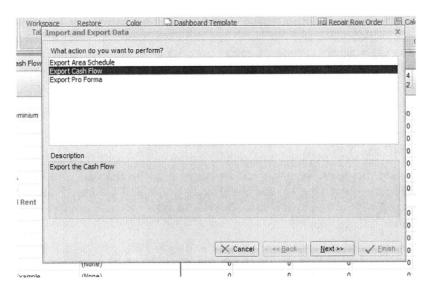

Figure 9-5. Selecting cash flow to export

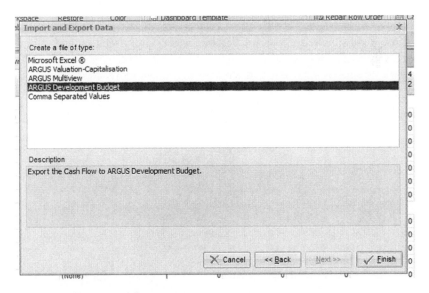

Figure 9-6. Selecting export to Budget

For the post-development period, Argus as a company produces a number of appraisal/valuation and investment management systems including Argus DCF for the US market/US-type appraisals and Argus Valuation Capitalization for the UK market/UK-type valuations. The latter system allows the importation of partial Developer cash flows, allowing development within the lifetime of a real estate investment to be modeled.

Summary

Hopefully, this book has given you an insight into the practical uses of Argus Developer—something beyond the training room and the user guide that is packaged with the software that shows you how to use it to appraise real projects.

Naturally, there are limitations as to how deeply I can go into the details; as I have stated many times in this book, development itself is infinitely variable in its nature, scope, characteristics, and financing and, therefore, an absolutely comprehensive book is impossible. However, I hope I have both done the software justice and helped you understand it in hopes of getting the most out of the system.

Developer is the most widely used real estate development modeling software for a reason; it is powerful, flexible, and comprehensive, and it has had nearly a quarter of a century of evolution. After using it myself for over 20 years, I continue to use it and am still impressed by its capabilities.

I think you will be, too.

I

Index

W, X, Y, Z

Get the eBook for only $10!

Now you can take the weightless companion with you anywhere, anytime. Your purchase of this book entitles you to 3 electronic versions for only $10.

This Apress title will prove so indispensible that you'll want to carry it with you everywhere, which is why we are offering the eBook in 3 formats for only $10 if you have already purchased the print book.

Convenient and fully searchable, the PDF version enables you to easily find and copy code—or perform examples by quickly toggling between instructions and applications. The MOBI format is ideal for your Kindle, while the ePUB can be utilized on a variety of mobile devices.

Go to www.apress.com/promo/tendollars to purchase your companion eBook.

Other Apress Business Titles You Will Find Useful

CFO Techniques
Guzik
978-1-4302-3756-3

How to Get Government Contracts
Smotrova-Taylor
978-1-4302-4497-4

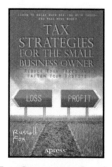

Tax Strategies for the Small Business Owner
Fox
978-1-4302-4842-2

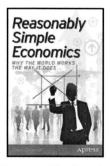

Reasonably Simple Economics
Osborne
978-1-4302-5941-1

Improving Profit
Cleland
978-1-4302-6307-4

Design Thinking for Entrepreneurs and Small Businesses
Ingle
978-1-4302-6181-0

Getting a Business Loan
Kiisel
978-1-4302-4998-6

Due Diligence and the Business Transaction
Berkman
978-1-4302-5086-9

Data Modeling of Financial Derivatives
Mamayev
978-1-4302-6589-4

Available at www.apress.com